THE WORST COUNTRY IN THE WORLD

The true story of an Australian pioneer family

Patsy Trench

Revised version 2018

Originally published 2012

Updated May 2018

Prefab Publications, London

For maps and family trees please go to:
https://marymatchampitt.wordpress.com/family-trees/

I do not scruple to pronounce that in the whole world there is not a worse country than what we have yet seen of this…'

Major Robert Ross, Lieutenant Governor of New South Wales (second in command to the governor), November 1788, ten months after the arrival of the First Fleet.

Contents

Prologue

1800: The loaf of bread

IT IS A BLEAK February day in the village of Fiddleford in Dorset. The clouds hang low and threatening and a light rain is beginning to fall.

Down a rutted lane strides a middle-aged woman. Her dress trails in the mud and her feet clad in unsuitable shoes splash through the puddles, yet on she goes, regardless. She looks like a woman with a mission and this could be a scene from a Jane Austen novel. Around the corner could be a Colonel Brandon or a Mr Darcy, waiting to ask for the hand of one of her daughters, to which she might reply – *Yes, oh yes!* – a little too eagerly perhaps.

At the end of the lane is Fiddleford Mill: a hive of people, noise and industry. The great wheel turns slowly, majestically. But the woman skirts the building and makes for the footbridge over the weir. A man, the miller himself perhaps, turns to greet her as she passes but she appears not to see him.

Halfway across the bridge she stops abruptly and turns to gaze into the weir. Looking over her shoulder into the swirling, bubbling water we can just make out – can we? – there among the circles and eddies and figures of eight, the image of a man's face, bobbing and twisting, fragmenting and then coming together. She reaches out a hand towards the image and it gazes blandly back at her, dancing, smiling, unreachable.

She makes to say something, then hesitates. How ridiculous to think the imaginary image of a dead man can help her now.

'Mrs Pitt? This is for you.'

A young girl has appeared beside her on the bridge, slightly out of breath, clutching something wrapped in cloth. The miller's youngest daughter – Maisie, Stacy...

'Pa told me to bring it,' says the girl, thrusting the bundle into the woman's arms. 'He said you had need of it.'

It's a loaf of bread, still warm. And the miller said she had need of it. He thinks she came here to beg.

'I baked it myself, just an hour ago.'

'Thank you – er – Maisie, but...'

'Martha.'

'Martha. Thank you but I couldn't possibly.'

She tries to give the bundle back. It's like a baby nobody wants. The young girl hangs back, stands there for a moment uncertainly and then turns and runs back the way she came.

Charity.

The woman makes to throw the bundle into the water, but hesitates. It's bread after all, freshly baked, and with prices as they are now...

She clutches the bundle to her for warmth and reassurance.

Introduction

Sydney, September 2009

WE ARE HALF AN HOUR away from our destination of Sydney Airport on what has been – insofar as any twenty-four hour flight from London can be – a relatively painless experience, when the pilot announces that due to local turbulence he is unable to land and we will be held in a holding pattern. The forecast isn't great, he tells us, so we may well be diverted to Melbourne, which is bad news for the jaded traveller. A while later he comes back on to say he's going to 'give it a go' at landing and if it doesn't work, he'll just turn the plane around and try again which, he assures us, is totally regular procedure.

I can't help noticing that in the intervening half hour the sky outside the windows, on both sides of the plane, has turned deep orange. That's not the clear, sharp orange of a Sydney sunrise but something resembling tomato soup. It's impossible to see anything at all – no buildings, no land, no water – which means we are either flying into an inferno or this is the worst case of pollution in living memory. In the event the pilot lands the plane perfectly smoothly first go and gets a round of applause, just like you see in the movies.

What the pilot has chosen not to tell us is that the 'turbulence' is a dust storm, the worst Sydney has experienced since World War II. By the time I leave the terminal the deep red has turned into an opaque off-white and the wind has got up, covering everything, my eyeballs included, in a thick coating of what presumably is topsoil from western New South Wales. It is an appropriate welcome to what my brother (who lives here) calls the 'land of extreme weather' and a reminder of one of the many ways in which this country, to which I have been travelling frequently over the past few years from my home in England, is so Very Different.

I'm here this time to attend a family reunion. Family reunions are big in Australia, and ours will be attended by 120 people, most of whom have never met before, and all of whom owe their existence to a woman called Mary Pitt.

Family history came late to me, and slowly. It began with my elderly aunt Barbara, the family genealogist, initially as a topic of polite conversation when I visited her in her retirement home in North Sydney. Barbara spent her retirement years researching our forebears, and I listened respectfully but with no particular interest to the story of her months spent poring over documents in libraries and history centres in Dorset and Sydney; and the story that emerged, of the woman who emigrated to Australia from Dorset, meant very little until I started to look into the history of colonial Australia itself and realised the significance of her arrival date: 1801.

The First Fleet arrived in New South Wales in 1788, which means that when Mary Pitt arrived the colony that later came to be known as Australia was barely thirteen years old. Whatever other motives the old country had for colonising the new, the original purpose of New South Wales was as a penal colony: to house the wrongdoers there was no room for back in England. What then prompted my great great great great grandmother, a widow aged 53, to uproot herself and her five children from village life in Dorset and travel across the world to live in a prison? There had to be a story there, and I had to tell it.

So I gave up my job, rented out my flat in London and over the course of the following four years I visited Australia as often as I could. I researched and read, travelled, looked and listened, and the more I discovered the more extraordinary was the story that unravelled.

But how best to tell it? How to bring Mary and her family

alive? To convey something of what she and her family went through?

The result is a hybrid: part family history, part memoir, part novel. The skeleton of the story – the facts, dates, movements and marriages – is as true as I could make it; as is the background, the ground the skeleton walked on, so to speak. But I have put flesh on the bones, invented personalities for real people, circumstances behind the facts, all in the cause of turning my family saga into what I hope is an entertaining read. The dramatised scenes are from my imagination but the outcome of them is fact: Mary and her family did emigrate to New South Wales in 1801 for instance but no one quite knows why. So I have offered my own reasons, based on what we do know of her, and of her cousin George Matcham. I have tried to make it clear within the text what is true and what is speculation, but for those family members eager for the detailed truth I have included an appendix, which spells out exactly where I've departed from acknowledged fact.

Direct quotes are in *italics*.

The rest of the dialogue is invented.

This is also a story about two other generations of women, both of whom, like Mary, were at some point in their lives migrants: my mother, who reversed the wheel and left her native Australia to settle in England, where I was born; and myself, who turned the wheel back again and emigrated to Australia in my twenties, where I spent three years before returning to live in England again, and who for the past decade or so has been flitting between the two countries like an indecisive migrating butterfly, no longer sure which of the two places, if either, she can call home. So it is also a story about belonging.

PART ONE

The old country

Chapter 1

Lord Nelson's brother in law

MY VERSION OF Mary's story begins with her first cousin, George Matcham.

In 1777, when young George was around twenty-four years old, his father died and left his entire fortune to his only surviving son. Like his father George worked for the East India Company, and when the province of Baroche, where he was resident, ceded to the Mahrattas in 1783 he decided to retire, aged then thirty, and make his way back to England. He travelled overland, riding on horseback through extraordinary places and attracting the attention of extraordinary people such as Emperor Joseph II of Austria, Mozart's patron. In 1785 he arrived in England and the following year he settled in Enfield, near Bath, to be with his mother.

A few years earlier he had written to a friend saying,

'If the bulk of our fortune shall come home safe, I mean to buy an estate jointly with my mother. I shall then marry and have three principal sources of amusement: my wife, farming and hunting.'

It was to fulfil the first of these 'amusements' that in the winter of 1786 George went to Bath to find a wife. His friends had lined him up with a wealthy heiress called Miss Dorothea Scrivener. She was living in Bath at the time and it is romantic to imagine them meeting in the ballroom at the Upper Assembly Rooms one December evening at the height of the season.

The ballroom, one hundred feet long, was packed.

'Which one is Miss Scrivener?' George enquired of his friends.

'She is seated at the top end of the room, by the fireplace. In the green. With the feathers.'

'And who is the young lady sitting next to her?'

'With the curly hair?'

'And the prettiest face you ever saw.'

'That I believe is her cousin, Catherine Nelson, visiting from Norfolk. Sister to Horatio.'

'Horatio Nelson. Should I know him?'

'Captain Horatio Nelson of the Boreas. Currently languishing in the Caribbean Sea, so the story goes.'

'Kindly introduce us.'

~

Thus it was that George Matcham, aged then thirty-three, tall, handsome, worldly and rich, met the sweet-natured, vivacious, nineteen-year-old Catherine, known as Kitty, or Kate, on her first ever visit away from her home in Norfolk, where she had lived all her life with her family and, most recently, alone with her father the Reverend Edmund Nelson; by whom, two months later on 26 February 1787, they were married.

~

I first met George through the pages of a book called *The Nelsons of Burnham Thorpe*, written by his great granddaughter Mary Eyre Matcham. And reader, I fell in love at first glance with this remarkable man, not just because he was tall, handsome and incredibly wealthy, but because of his kindness, his resourcefulness, his astonishingly progressive views, and not least for what he did for my ancestress and by association, for me.

I learned that Horatio and Kitty's mother had died when Kitty was a baby, and she had been brought up by her father, the Reverend: a kind, self deprecating man with eccentricities, such as his refusal to wear glasses even when his sight was failing, or to let any part of his body touch the back of the chair he was sitting on. I read that having married into the Nelson family George quickly became an indispensable and much-loved member of it, acting as the rector's confidant and unofficial business consultant, particularly concerning the affairs of Horatio's brothers, who were constantly in financial difficulties. I learned how Horatio and George became firm friends, to the extent that following the Battle of Cape St Vincent in 1797 – where Nelson, against all the odds, managed to defeat the Spanish by using his initiative against the orders of his superiors – George wrote him the following letter:

> *'I should be wanting in Common humanity, my Dear Sir, if I did not warn you of the danger of returning to England . . . from all that I can learn, every description of Persons, Especially the young Women, have a serious intention to eat you up alive (and God knows the Barbarians). Your Physical Corporeal Substance will not go much farther than a Sprat, but I suppose they mean to intoxicate themselves with the Spirit. Others, more moderate, will always keep you alive in their Mind's eye; among which Number you will class yrs very Sincerely G. Matcham.'*

What Nelson's reaction was to being called a 'Sprat' is not on record.

I spent days at the Maritime Museum at Greenwich poring over photocopies of the original handwritten letters written over the years by Nelson to George, both before and after he lost his writing arm. I read biographies of Nelson and genned up on his naval exploits. I got, in a phrase, quite carried away. I had to remind myself that while Nelson's name played a vital part in what happened to Mary and her children, the story ultimately is not about him. It's not even about George Matcham, even though I believe he was the ultimate mover and shaker without whom, etc. But that is the nature of family research – it's downright impossible not to find oneself wandering down fascinating if partly irrelevant paths on one's endless search for What Happened to Mary.

~

So here we are, on this chill day in February 1800, and I am seeing George pull up outside May Cottage, where his cousin Mary lives with her five children. The daughters – Susanna, Lucy, Jemima and Hester – watch him through the upstairs window, and as he makes his way to the front door they clatter one after the other down the narrow staircase, in time to see him bumping his head on the door frame, as he always does, at which they giggle girlishly, as they always do.

To the four Pitt girls cousin George is an exotic creature blown in from a distant land: a place of balls and assemblies peopled by dukes, lords and countesses. George's family came from Fiddleford but he himself has spent most of his life overseas, and now he is settled in Bath, in order that his children – girls as well as boys – should receive a good education.

'So, what news of Fiddleford?' he asks, now comfortably seated in the little parlour, his cousins lined up opposite him. 'Did anyone get married while my back was turned?' This is directed mostly at Susanna, the eldest, who blushes, smiles, and gazes at her lap. 'Surely you have some news for me, Susanna? Who is he, a baronet from Blandford or a parson from Poole?'

'Neither sir,' Susanna replies.

'Neither? Not yet. So, what is your plan? Your expectation?'

'I have considered, sir,' says Susanna. 'And I consider it preferable to live without expectation.'

'That sounds rather gloomy. Do you mean you've abandoned all hope?'

'I am doing my best, sir.' She smiles, slightly.

'Ah. I see.'

He turns to daughter number two.

'And Lucy?'

'In Fiddleford?' Lucy shrugs.

'We are poor, cousin George,' says Jemima, who has yet to learn circumspection. 'Hester no longer goes to school – mama cannot afford it – and no man in the world will look at a girl without a dowry.'

George nods thoughtfully.

'And Thomas is working all hours for Lord Rivers. Otherwise we would lose our home too.'

'How is Lord Victory?' pipes Hester. At thirteen, and the youngest, she has a different set of priorities.

'Lord Victory is well, thank you Hester. Apart that is from losing first an eye and then an arm in the course of His Majesty's Service he has also gained a knighthood and a baronhood, and most recently a dukehood.'

'A "dukehood?"'

'He is now Rear Admiral Horatio Nelson, Duke of Bronte.'

'What's Bronte?'

'It's a place in Sicily, in the Mediterranean. The King of Naples awarded him the duchy for saving his skin.'

'He's a hero now, isn't he cousin George? Everyone knows about him defeating the French and the Spanish and saving this country from invasion. And to think we are related to him! To a hero and a Lord Admiral, and now a duke!' Hester's eyes shine with excitement.

'To say nothing of his private life,' mutters Jemima.

There is a short silence.

'And what precisely have you been hearing about his private life?' George smiles gently.

'Something about . . .' Jemima hesitates, 'a Lady Hamilton. About Nelson and ...' she stops.

'And?'

'Living in the Mediterranean with Lady Hamilton and her husband, in a . . . in a . . . trio . . .'

'"*Tria juncta in uno*"?' George cocks an eyebrow.

'That's it,' says Jemima uncertainly. 'So,' she flushes slightly, 'is it true?'

George does not immediately reply.

'Come, cousin, we're family!'

'What I would say, in confidence,' says George, 'within these four family walls, is – how shall I put this? Lord Victory is a hero throughout the kingdom but for one place, which is at home.'

'What do you mean?'

'I mean that at home, by unhappy contrast, he receives nothing but complaining and reproach, which is why he feels compelled to turn from the spot.'

'"Turn from the spot"! I like it! So what' – Jemima has the bit between her teeth now – 'do you think of her? Of Lady Emma? In confidence of course.'

'Jemima, that is enough of this conversation,' says Susanna, quietly. And turning to her cousin she asks, by way of a change of subject, 'To what do we owe the pleasure of this visit?'

'To see you of course.' He gives them each a warm smile. They are in their own individual ways the sweetest women, he thinks to himself. None of them is a startling beauty, except perhaps Lucy, whose quaintly studied languor and haughty manner fail to mask her natural vivacity. Susanna, with her golden hair and her sweet gentleness, and Jemima with her energy and sharp intelligence would surely make fine wives for some men, somewhere. They deserve a better hand than they've been dealt, thinks George, and all that could be about to change. 'And to have a word with your mother.'

'She has gone to the village and should be back any minute,' says Lucy.

'Have a word about what?' asks Hester. 'Can we know?'

'Not on this occasion. You will no doubt find out soon enough.'

At which point Mary Pitt enters, slightly out of breath because on walking down the lane she caught sight of her cousin's chaise outside her house, so broke into a semi trot for the last few paces.

'I am so sorry, Mr Matcham,' she puffs. She clutches at her chest for a moment. 'I hope . . . the girls . . .'

'Have been entertaining me? For sure they have. You need not have hurried.'

They bow to one another cordially, take their respective seats, and after a brief moment to allow herself to regain her composure Mary addresses her four daughters.

'I have something important to discuss with your cousin. So you may take yourselves off wherever you wish.'

'But mama!'

'By which I mean out of the house Lucy. I do not want eavesdroppers.'

'But it's cold!'

'Mrs Foster is expecting you and I have no doubt she has a warm fire and some sponge cake, which she is this very minute decorating with icing and a preserved cherry on top, all ready for you. Off you go. And wrap up warm.'

And so they do, and the two cousins are left alone in the front room of May Cottage.

Chapter 2

1800: A proposition

'YOUR DAUGHTERS ARE looking well.' Cousin George leans back in his chair and crosses one elegant leg over the other. 'Fine young women,' he confirms with a nod.

'Thank you. I'm glad you find them so.'

'They should be married however. Susanna and Lucy at least – how old are they now?'

What a different world he moves in, thinks Mary.

'And Hester should be at school.'

'Did you come all this way to scold me, Mr Matcham?'

George smiles. 'Not at all. I have come to offer help.'

'Thank you but I have no need of it.'

'It is the least I can do, to share some of my good luck with you, as a family obligation. There but for fortune...'

'I have no intention of being an obligation.'

'Our fathers were brothers after all.'

This is true of course. Mary's father was a weaver and his younger brother was a high ranking official with the East India Company. Such is the way of things.

'If you will not accept financial assistance,' George looks his cousin straight in the eye. 'I have another proposition to put to you.'

'Which is?'

'An opportunity. But it means leaving here, leaving everything and everyone you have ever known. Do you think you are up to it?'

'Go on.'

George tugs at his waistcoat. Robert had a similar habit, Mary remembers, on the rare occasion when he wore such a thing, as he did for his portrait, the one he had done after . . .

'Have you heard of New South Wales?'

'New South Wales?'

'More familiarly known as Botany Bay.'

Mary pales. 'The penal colony?'

'It was originally a convict settlement, it's true. But it is becoming infinitely more than that. It is a place for free settlers these days, a country of opportunity for those enterprising enough to try their luck there.'

'And you are suggesting . . .?'

'I am suggesting you become one of them. Now, while there are still the opportunities.'

There is a long silence. Mary gazes into space.

'The government is eager to encourage people to emigrate of their own free will,' George goes on. 'So by way of inducement they are offering free passages and free grants of land on arrival.'

Mary looks down at her hands. She used to have beautiful hands, long, slender and soft, softer even than cousin George's.

'So you are proposing . . .' She gazes at her hands a moment longer and then clasps them tightly together. 'You are proposing that we, that I, a widow of 52 years old, with five children . . . You are telling me we should leave this place, the only place the children have ever known, and travel to the far side of the world, never to see our homeland again?' She looks up again. Her cousin is smiling gently at her.

'That is precisely what I am proposing.'

'But the girls have hardly ever left the village.'

'And they are unlikely ever to do so, if things remain as they are.'

'But to live in a strange country, in a penal colony, among strange people, without a decent soul to talk to?''You will find many decent souls to talk to. You will make friends. And the girls will find husbands.'

'How can you be so sure?'

'Because our family connections will open doors to the most exclusive households and people will vie with one another to be your friend. Moreover,' George twinkles, 'according to the latest reports the male population outnumbers the female considerably.'

'But - convicts?' Mary is reduced to a hoarse whisper.

'No no, by no means. As I said, much of the population is now free. There are plenty of men of ambition and spirit who've gone there for the opportunities. There are fortunes to be made! It's a new world, who knows what possibilities it has to offer?'

'How do you know all this?'

'I have made it my business, my hobby if you like, to study the colonies. I have already sponsored a family of farmers and I intend sending my younger son there at some point. Better in my view to enjoy the abundance of a country life under a fine sky than hazard the precarious profession of a merchant in the city, don't you agree?' George chuckles. 'Just imagine . . .' He places the tips of his fingers together. 'Imagine Lord Rivers arriving at your doorstep with the news that you have been given one hundred acres of land, a hundred times the size of your little garden and orchard at May Cottage, yours in perpetuity, to do with as you wish. And meanwhile, while you till the soil, with the aid of servants provided for you gratis, you will . . .'

'Servants?'

'Convicts.'

'Ah.'

'While you farm your land, until it bears fruit, so to speak, you will be provided for, you and yours. You will want for nothing until you are ready to stand on your own feet.'

Mary says nothing.

'Think of this,' George leans forward. 'Consider Thomas's situation. Where is he now? Out in the fields somewhere, working for Lord Rivers. In return for which you are given a cottage and enough, just enough, to live on. You are not starving, but you are not thriving. Thomas is an intelligent man. Why should he work for someone else? Why should he not own his own land and have people to work it for him? Or are you going to tell me he is content to do as he is doing for the rest of his life?'

'No,' says Mary. 'He is not. In fact he was considering moving away, to the city, to find work.'

'As what? My dear cousin.'

'The city is where the future is. There is certainly nothing for us here. We used to get by, but now . . .'

'But now?'

'The plan was that Thomas would make his way in the city and then he'd send for us.'

'All five of you? And what then?'

Mary does not reply. It sounded like a good idea when they discussed it before.

'I could see no alternative,' she says quietly.

'Well, now there is one.'

'Thomas Rose and his family already went to New South Wales some years ago,' she speaks fast, as if expecting interruption, 'and they've had nothing but trouble. He writes letters back home that are nothing but grumbling and complaints, so Mrs Topp tells me.'

'That is because they sowed the crops at the wrong time of the year. And the land was intractable. This will not happen to you, we will make sure you are granted nothing but the best, either at Rose Hill or by the Hawkesbury River.'

'You talk as if you'd been there yourself.'

'Dear cousin I know it as if I lived there. In my idle moments,' George muses, 'I am riding in a carriage around the shores of Sydney Cove, watching the boats skim back and forth on the calm waters of the finest harbour you ever saw. The sun is warm upon my face and the air is sweet with the soft smell of frangipani and hibiscus.'

'Frangipani?'

'The most perfect flower you saw in your life. I could not attempt to describe it, you have to see it for itself.'

A moment passes.

'I cannot leave Robert.' Mary speaks at last, with finality.

'Robert?' George frowns.

'It would be tantamount to desertion. I cannot do it.'

'Desertion? My dear cousin it is Robert who . . .'

'And nothing that you or anyone else has to say will change my mind.'

~

For some time after her cousin left Mary sat where she was, unmoving.

Then snatching up her shawl she left the house, slamming the door behind her. Off she went, down the lane through the puddles in the direction of the mill and around the pond to the footbridge over the weir.

The face in the water bobbed and smiled up at her, mocking her.

Distressed circumstances.

He had failed her. He'd failed all of them. And she was concerned about deserting him.

'Mrs Pitt?'

She looked up, startled. The miller's daughter was smiling shyly at her. 'This is for you. Pa told me to bring it. I baked it myself, just an hour ago.'

The cloth-wrapped bundle was still warm, like a newborn baby.

'Thank you – er – Maisie, but . . .'

'Martha.'

'Martha.'

Mary watched as the girl ran back along the pathway to the mill.

For a moment she clutched the bundle to her for reassurance.

Then reaching over the side of the bridge she dropped it into the water.

'Goodbye, Robert,' she said.

She saw the fleeting look of surprise on her late husband's face as the loaf of bread plopped into it, splitting his image into a thousand pieces, and she watched as the fragments of face and bread bobbed and tumbled under the bridge and floated away across the millpond to the far side, where they hesitated a moment and then sank, leaving nothing but a small circle of bubbles.

Chapter 3

2008: Looking for Mary

IT IS AUGUST 2008 and I am on my way to Dorset with my English cousin Frances, looking for Mary. The tiny village of Fiddleford, near Sturminster Newton, is probably not much changed since Mary's time and May Cottage, the house she lived in first with her husband Robert and then, rent-free, with her children, is still there. According to photos it is a picture-postcard cottage with pink-washed walls and a thatched roof draped over it like a blanket.

The photos turn out to be the nearest we can get to the real thing. I was hoping to see the inside of the house but I've been warned by another cousin, Salli Chmura, who tried to do just that a year ago, not to pitch up at the front door unannounced because the current owners don't like surprises. So I wrote them a letter a little while back saying I was planning on coming down on the August bank holiday weekend and would greatly appreciate the opportunity of seeing inside the house my ancestors lived in. I eventually received the following reply:

'Dear Ms Trench

I am in receipt of your letter dated 12 August. I regret that it will not be convenient to meet you next weekend, or for you to look at the property. Yours sincerely DF.'

Fortunately the previous owner, a charming lady called Olive Hall, is more forthcoming. We meet for lunch at the Fiddleford Arms and she shows us photos of the inside of the house. It is Grade II listed so is possibly quite similar to how it was in 1800, apart from an extension added in the 1990s. Downstairs is one long living room with a fireplace at one end. In Mary's time it would have been two smallish rooms (Olive and her husband removed the inner wall). The ancient exposed oak beams are still there, some of them low enough to clock the lofty George Matcham on the head, and as Olive describes it the whole house was built 'at crazy angles', its walls sloping outwards, the doorframes leaning to one side and no right angles anywhere. At one end of the room a narrow staircase disappears up to where the two bedrooms are, and presumably were in 1800. The upstairs floor is 'saucer-shaped', which means the furniture had to be wedged in order to stop everything sliding into the centre of the room. The two small upstairs windows peer down from beneath their thatched brow at the three-quarter acre garden where Mary probably grew apples and plums – Fiddleford is famous for its plums – which she may well have exchanged for flour from the mill.

Fiddleford Mill is still there but no longer operating, a couple of minutes' walk down the lane from May Cottage. We retrace Mary's footsteps around it to the footbridge where in my imagination she stood and pondered her future in the whirlpool of the weir.

If you walk on past the millpond and across the fields to Sturminster Newton, as Mary and her family would have done every Sunday to attend church, you could be stepping back a couple of hundred years. The only modern differences are the signs, and the railway line, now disused. Once again I am trying to be Mary. I am looking for her essence, her ghost as she walked across the muddy field, skirting the puddles, lifting her skirt out of the mud. I'm searching for the life she was contemplating leaving for ever.

~

Who was Mary? Where was she born, who were her parents, what sort of family did she come from? Why is it my aunt Barbara, fastidious researcher that she was, was unable to find any record of her birth?

The answer possibly lies in a letter written by Mary's grandson GM Pitt in 1885, in Australia. He was responding to a query from another family genealogist, his cousin Matilda Warren Jenkins.

'Sydney, February 26th, 1885

'My dear Miss Jenkins

. . . According to all I know of my ancestors, and that is not much – The Pitt family, that is the Mother and Daughters and one son came to this Colony in the early part of the Century, in the good ship Canada, under the Command of Captain Jenkinson.

My Grandmother's Maiden name was Matcham. She originally came from Ireland. Her father died, and her Mother married again, and she and her husband went to America. Mary Matcham crossed over to England and she lived with two maiden aunts till death carried them away at 82 & 83. She fell in with my Grandfather at a town called Bath. She married him from there. Her Aunts left her some three different estates, not large ones; and her husband managed to get rid of them. They had a family of seven children, three were boys, and four were girls; the two elder were boys, William and George by name. They were well educated. They went to America, and both had the misfortune to be killed – not together, at different times. My Grandfather died young, and he left his widow not in good circumstances. She was of an high cast of character, and she sold what she had, and finished her life here. I believe she was a good Mother, and truly religious. I know very little of my family connections in England. My Grandmother's first cousin George Matcham, married Lord Nelson's sister Catherine . . .'

GM, who was my great great grandfather, was only one year old when his grandmother died. And Mary and Robert were married in the nearby village of Child Okeford, not Bath. Moreover in a letter written a few years previously to the same person GM referred to his grandfather Robert as William. He also said that on his death Robert *'left a sorrowing wife and four*

Daughters and one son', which suggests the eldest two boys were already in America when their father died in 1787. At fifteen and eight years old respectively this was oddly young to be sent away from home.

So to what extent either of GM's letters is accurate is anyone's guess, but it's all we have to go on. And without knowing where in Ireland she was born it is impossible to find a record of Mary's birth, so we have to take that on trust.

According to Barbara Lamble Mary's father was Thomas Matcham, eldest son of Thomas and Mary (née Ford), who came from a family of weavers and quite possibly went to Ireland for the work opportunities, as other weavers were known to do at that time. As for her mother, again all we have is what GM tells us. We have no idea (yet) what her name was or whether or not Mary had siblings.

In George Matcham's obituary it says he - and by definition his first cousin Mary also - was descended from

> *'Thomas Macham* [sic], *who purchased the manor of Up Wimborne and Oakly Wood . . . formerly belonging to the Abbey of Tewkesbury, at the dissolution of the monasteries in the reign of Henry VIII.'*

That sounds quite grand, but it was six generations and over 200 years earlier.

But what was Mary like? We know she was educated, and there are hints here and there that she was not the sort of woman to put up with second best.

'A gt deal of complaint from Pits wife of bad behaviour of the old Tapper woman in Fidford House', say the Sturminster Newton court records of October 1780. The old Tapper woman was probably a tenant in the cottage belonging to the mill, which Mary and Robert were then renting out. *'A clamor also at Pew in the Isle'* [sic], the records go on, which suggests she was demanding a better position in church.

This implies that Mary expected more than she often got. So did she feel she married beneath her? Did she consider her marriage to Robert had brought her down in the world?

Rather late in the day I end up in the local records office in Dorchester – the very place, in its previous incarnation, where aunt Barbara spent all those months researching. I'm not here just for dry research, or to discover anything she did not (if only). I am here because it is the only way to get my own personal grasp on Robert and Mary, and my very own tangible feeling of the 18th century Dorsetshire world in which they lived.

So here I am looking for Robert, and here he is in the parish records, baptised in St Mary's Church, Sturminster Newton on 9 October 1734, second child of William and Rose Pitt. His father had held an innkeeper's licence and may once have been a clothier. He was also bailiff of the local manor court in the 1730s, a position his elder son Thomas took over in the 1750s. A bailiff being not the person who turns up at your house unannounced and removes all your furniture but *'one of the lord's representatives beneath the rank of steward'*.

The marriage certificate is here too: Robert Pitt, Batchelor, married on the 27th day of December 1770 to Mary Matcham, Spinster of this parish. And then there are the indentures.

The indentures, or leases, that Robert signed are numerous, and the originals are all there in the Dorset History Centre. They are large documents, rolled up and tied neatly with ribbon and when stretched out across the (necessarily) huge tables nearly as wide as the span of both my outstretched arms. They are beautiful things, meticulously hand-written in copperplate, much of it in a language incomprehensible to the layperson, or this layperson anyway. Words such as 'messuage' (house and outbuildings), 'curtilage' (area attached to a dwelling, which my helpful Word processor insists on altering to 'cartilage') and, most confusingly, 'seised' (possessed of).

On the indentures Robert is listed as a yeoman and a shopkeeper, and even, in the Alehouse Recognizances, a labourer. A yeoman, according to Barbara Lamble, was not a gentleman and would not have been entitled to call himself

'Mr' on official documents or refer to his wife as 'Mrs'. A yeoman would not normally frequent a place like Bath, nor would he have his portrait painted, as Robert did.

At the same time the portrait, by artist unknown and dated around 1780, when Robert was 46, may not have been such a big deal. As Barbara suggested there were jobbing artists in those days who travelled the country painting portraits for anyone who cared to pay – much as you would find nowadays setting up their easels in tourist spots in London. The portrait that exists today is a copy drawn by a descendant, and while it is not exactly a masterpiece it is lucky for us that somebody took the trouble, as the original was lost when later members of the family, who were carrying it with them on their way to England in 1859, drowned on board the *Royal Charter*.

The most significant indenture Robert signed was for the lease of Fiddleford Mill in 1779. Robert himself was not a miller but many of his ancestors had been, including his uncle William Belbin, from whom he took over the lease of both the mill and the house he lived in, which was known then as 'Trout Alehouse'. Uncle William had obviously allowed the mill to deteriorate and the lease held a condition that Robert should *'put the said Mill and Premises in good and tenantable repair'* within two years.

On the same day, 22 September 1779, Robert signed another indenture with Lord Rivers, this time for premises in Child Okeford for £300. How he got to lay his hands on such a large sum of money is not known; and with a commitment already to restore the mill, which would have been enough in itself to keep a man occupied for years to come, he must have been feeling pretty energetic to commit himself to further financial outlay. Significantly in November of that same year he borrowed money from a John Harrison, gent.

Six years later, in 1785, Robert signed another indenture. Fiddleford Mill *'being now very ruinous and out of repair and the said Robert Pitt not being able to repair and keep up the same owing to his distressed circumstances . . .'* the lease was to be handed over to John Newman, miller, for the sum of £15.15s. The outstanding mortgage of £129.14.0, plus interest, was repaid by Robert to John Harrison.

'Distressed circumstances.' Two words the cause of so much speculation.

Two years later, aged 51, Robert was dead.

A picture is beginning to develop: of an easy spender, a man who happily took on heavy financial commitments yet failed to fulfil them. An optimist, even perhaps a hedonist, who frequented Bath and dressed up in frockcoat, waistcoat and wig to have his portrait painted; who did not follow in his father's and brother's footsteps by taking on the unpaid but prestigious position of bailiff or rent collector for the local lord (which may or may not indicate a lack of social responsibility); whose most significant influence seems to have been not his father but his maternal uncle, William Belbin, who surrendered to Robert not just the leases of May Cottage/Trout Alehouse and Fiddleford Mill but the estate of his sister Margaret Matcham, who had died childless; who married an educated and forceful woman from an old Dorset family and lived with her and their seven children in a cottage rented from George Pitt, Lord Rivers; who died at the relatively early age of 51, perhaps from the same cause that brought about his father's death at not quite 41, and the death of his father's father at a similarly young, though unspecified age. It is evident the male members of Robert's branch of the Pitt family were not long-lived.

Aunt Barbara compared Robert's signature on the original lease of the mill with the same six years later, when he let it go, and declared it showed him to be a broken man. I studied those same signatures and did not see a lot of difference, though since he died two years afterwards it is fair to assume he had health problems. Barbara wondered if Robert really was the 'feckless spendthrift' some of his possibly embittered descendants believed he was, or whether his wife urged him beyond his capabilities. 'I hope we shall discover the true story,' she said, but I am doubtful.

Does it matter? Yes. Because Mary matters, and hence the circumstances that drove her to do what she was contemplating doing. Mary's grandson GM claimed Robert 'managed to get rid of' her remaining properties, but what evidence he has of that he doesn't say. By 1800 Mary had been a widow for thirteen years and it's possible she got rid of her properties herself. What we can assume is that, for whatever reason, Mary was having to live on charity. I think of myself at that age and wonder, had my luck run out on me as hers did, how I would have felt living on the 21st century equivalent of poor relief.

~

There were other forces even further outside Mary's control. Until the early part of the 18th century cottage industries such as spinning, weaving, glove- or button-making kept many families alive in rural England, and Mary and her family may have been among them. But then along came the Industrial Revolution with new machines that could do the jobs much more cheaply and so the demand ended virtually overnight, rendering many families destitute. New taxes were constantly being introduced to pay for the war with France, and a block on the import of foodstuff such as wheat made the price of everyday things such as bread rise steeply.

King George III was on the throne, William Pitt the Younger (no proven relation) was Prime Minister, America had her independence, France had revolted and was at continuous war with England and threatening to invade at any time. The Enclosure Acts – which meant that common land on which the local community had traditionally held grazing rights was now enclosed by law and farmed by a single landowner – meant life in the latter part of the 18th century was particularly tough for the villager or small tenant farmer. Moreover according to the records Dorset at the time was one of the poorest counties in the country.

At the same time village life was all that Mary and her

family knew. The village was their universe, discrete, complete, virtually untouched by the outside world. Travel along turnpike roads was far too expensive for the ordinary person, but then why should anyone want to go anywhere? Everything a person needed was right here, in Fiddleford. So for Mary to have contemplated leaving the village forever was almost inconceivable.

~

In an article called 'Grit and Gentility' in the *Blue Mountains Life Magazine* Michael Burge draws a parallel between the Pitt family and the Bennets of Jane Austen's *Pride & Prejudice.* There is a moment in the story when Mrs Bennet fears her husband will be killed in a duel with Mr Wickham, leaving her and her five daughters destitute, as the entire Bennet estate is *'entailed in default of heirs male'* on a distant relation. Had this happened the Bennets might also have been forced to consider emigrating to New South Wales. It was not a good time to be a mother of daughters, without husband, money or property.

Chapter 4

February 1800: A decision

A WEEK HAS PASSED since George paid his visit and Mary made her pilgrimage to Fiddleford weir. In the meantime she has summoned her son Thomas to May Cottage for a private consultation on the family's future.

This is Thomas's first appearance in a story in which he will play a major role. At nineteen he is the only surviving son and has been ever since his elder brothers George and William disappeared to America some time ago, where they died.

As head of the household Thomas takes his position seriously. He works for Lord Rivers, the local squire who owns a good part of Fiddleford, in return for which Mary and her family are allowed to live in May Cottage rent free. He has travelled here today from nearby Dorchester, where he lives with Lord Rivers's steward, a Mr Salisbury.

Having consulted at length with his mother it is now Thomas's duty to address his sisters on the topic uppermost on everybody's mind: the future.

~

I have gathered the family together in the sitting room of May Cottage in the fading light of a February afternoon. I've lit the fire for them – gently, so as to conserve wood – and augmented what little light there is with a few candles placed here and there; enough, barely, to make out their shapes and features.

Susanna, the eldest at twenty-six, perches straight-backed on an upright chair, her hands folded neatly on her lap. Lucy is stretched out on the chaise longue; Jemima and Hester, the two youngest, sit side by side on the settee, linking hands. Thomas stands facing them all with his back to the hearth.

Mary sits deliberately in a darkened corner of the room. She has handed full responsibility to her eldest son and she watches as, with care and in some detail, he describes the plan proposed by their cousin George Matcham. We do not need to hear Thomas's exact words because he is repeating, in essence if not quite with his persuasive confidence, his cousin's words to his mother.

What we do hear is the silence that follows; a silence so dense that the smallest noise, the ticking clock or the occasional creak of a floorboard, sounds deafening.

'So,' Lucy is the first to break it. She regards her brother through half-closed eyes. 'We are going to live in a prison.'

'It is no longer just a prison,' says Thomas.

'They still send convicts there, don't they?' says Jemima.

'Convicts?' Hester's eyes grow very wide. 'Why?'

'Because there is nowhere else for them to go. That's how the place started, as a settlement for prisoners, the ones they had no room for in the prisons. They packed them into sailing ships and sent them halfway across the world and forgot all about them.'

'Jem, there is no need.' says Thomas.

'Is that not true, Tom?'

'Where have you heard this?'

'It's common knowledge, isn't it?' Jemima looks at her siblings for support. 'I did hear . . .' She stops.

'What did you hear, Jemima?' asks her mother.

'That it's an experiment, that isn't working.'

Jemima is right. New South Wales was then still an experiment and one so far showing every sign of failure.

Hester starts to whimper.

'The climate is impossible – suffocatingly hot in the summer. And the people are starving, that's what I heard.'

'Then you heard wrong.'

'Not necessarily, Tom.' says Mary, 'It may have been true in the beginning, Jemima, but things are looking very different now, so I am led to believe. Go on, Tom.'

'It is a new country,' Thomas continues. 'Nobody even knows the dimensions of it yet. Think of it, think of being among the first to set up home in a new continent, on virgin land . . .'

Jemima snorts. Thomas pauses for a moment before continuing.

'On virgin land, that nobody has ever lived on or cultivated before.'

'What do you mean, nobody ever lived on before? Are you saying that up until – what was it – twelve years ago the place was empty?'

'Of course not. There is a native population of some kind.' Thomas glances at his mother. They never really discussed this aspect of it. 'But they are perfectly friendly evidently and they do not own the land, not in the sense in which we understand the word.'

'There have been skirmishes. So I've heard.'

'To continue,' says Thomas with meaning, 'the government is offering free passage and free land as incentives to encourage settlers to go there.'

'Why do they need to be bribed to go there, if it is such a wonderful place?'

'Jemima, will you let me finish?'

'Thomas you are only telling us part of the story.'

'I'm not telling you any of the story! You are not allowing me to!'

There is a pause. Jemima looks at her lap.

'As I was saying, the government will give us free land on arrival, convicts to work it and everything provided for a year or two until we find our feet. In addition, thanks to Mr Matcham's connection with Lord Nelson we will be given a letter of recommendation from the admiral to Governor King, which will ensure us the best possible reception and the first choice of land. From then on it's up to us to make of our lives what we will and what we can.'

There is a long pause.

If our children are, to some extent, what we make them, Mary should be able to see essences of herself and her late husband in her own. In Jemima, with her spirit, her sharp intelligence and her inability to keep her mouth shut, Mary might well recognise herself. Lucy's studied affectation and longing for adventure would be more Robert's. Hester's love of the home comes from her mother, and Susanna's calmness, wisdom and self deprecation are perhaps a mixture of both parents, perhaps entirely her own.

The responsibility for the family's future however rests mostly with Thomas, and if they depend on him now, which they do to a large extent, they will depend on him far more so in the new country. What skills the girls have here in 19th century Dorset may well be useless elsewhere. And while Thomas has some experience of working the land – which he has been doing for four or five years now – it has always been on behalf of somebody else. Owning and farming his own property is both an opportunity and a risk, and if he should fail...

'Exactly what are our prospects here, mother?' asks Susanna.

'We could survive,' says Mary, 'as we have done. We could carry on much as we are. But the truth is . . .'

'We will not find husbands.'

'Not without dowries.'

'What's a dowry?' asks Hester.

'It's a bribe,' says Jemima. 'A way of selling off the daughters.'

'And will no one marry us without a dowry?'

'It happens in novels,' says Lucy. 'There's always a knight in shining armour waiting to take on the beautiful but penniless daughter of the poor widow left destitute by her profligate but dead husband.'

'Life is not a novel,' says Thomas. 'And you are not *Evelina*.'

'I don't understand.' Hester clutches her sister's hand. 'I don't understand why we have to do this.'

'Because we are poor, Hes. You cannot go to school, we cannot get husbands. And it's all because your father, our father . . .'

'No!' Mary speaks again from her corner. 'I will not have you saying one word against your father. You know nothing. You were far too young. Both of you.'

'I don't remember my father,' says Hester in a rather small voice.

Hester, now thirteen, was one year old when her father died and her elder sister Jemima was only four. Whatever opinion they have of their father would have been largely the product of village gossip, as Mary is all too aware.

'So, mama, where exactly shall we live?' asks Lucy.

'Wherever we are granted land.'

'Yes, but I mean - what in, precisely? In a house like this one? Or in some primitive wood hut?'

'We will live as we can Lucy, according to what prevails. Moreover, so I hear, among the population the men outnumber the women by at least five to one.'

'So.' Lucy stretches and yawns. 'Plenty of husbands for all of us.'

'And three quarters of them are convicts.'

'Be quiet, Jemima.'

'I don't suppose we have a choice anyway, do we, mama?'

'I do not wish to foist anything on anyone, Jemima, if you feel strongly.' Mary shifts slightly in her chair and her face moves into the light. 'Susanna and Lucy are of an age anyway to make their own decisions.'

Jemima turns to look at her eldest sister.

'It would be a shame,' Susanna says after a moment, 'in our maiden dotage, to look back on an opportunity missed.'

'At least it will be a distraction.' Lucy yawns, again, to emphasise her point.

'Please don't make us go,' says Hester quickly.

Jemima clutches her younger sister's hand. 'She's terrified,' she says, rather unnecessarily.

'So are we all.'

'What I want to know is what made you decide that it would be . . .'

'Jemima, you've made your point.'

'No, Thomas,' says Mary, gently. 'It's a fair question.'

She takes a breath.

'I took a walk to Fiddleford Mill the other day,' she says eventually. 'I wasn't going there particularly. I needed to think. It was after cousin George had been to visit and presented me with – his proposal.'

She pauses.

'I really did not know what to do. My first instinct was that I could not leave your father. Odd though that may sound. And I could not expect you, all of you, to uproot yourselves from the only home you have ever known to risk - because it is a risk, there is no way of avoiding the fact.' She pauses again. 'We were muddling along, weren't we, quite adequately?'

No one answers the rhetorical question.

'Then the youngest Newman child, I forget her name . . .'

'Martha,' says Hester.

'Yes, of course. Martha came running up to me to give me a loaf of bread. It was a gift from her father. He said I had a need of it.'

Mary looks into the middle distance. 'He must have seen me coming and thought he didn't want to face me with a word, neighbour to neighbour, so he sent his youngest child, with bread for the beggar in their midst.'

The girls watch her wide-eyed. A tear trickles down Hester's cheek.

'He thought – they must have thought – a loaf of bread . . .' She clears her throat. 'It was at that moment that I asked myself – is this is what our lives have come down to? Charity? Is that how our neighbours see us, as paupers begging for loaves of bread? Now that may not mean much to you, but . . .' She blinks away the tears that are starting to appear. 'And then it came to me. You deserve better. We all deserve better. And now, out of the blue, is an opportunity. As Jemima says there may be difficult times ahead, I'm sure there will be, we will need all our strength.'

She pulls a handkerchief from her pocket and blows her nose.

'We have discussed other alternatives, Thomas and I. For my part, I'm old, I don't have long in this world, but I owe it to you – not just to you but your children and your children's children – I owe it to all of you to give you a better life, or the chance of a better life. It is the best offer I can make you.' She blows her nose again.

There is silence. The clock ticks.

'Then of course,' says Jemima quietly, 'we must accept it.' She goes to kneel by her mother and hugs her closely. 'And may God have mercy on our souls.'

'He'd better.' Mary returns the embrace.

~

And so a decision is made. And in that moment and that decision, as the authors of my life and the hundreds or maybe thousands of Pitts, Faithfulls, Woods, Wilshires, Laycocks, Forrests, Jenkins, Smiths and countless others, Mary Pitt and her family embark on a radically new chapter of the family book.

Chapter 5

The worst country in the world

> *'I do not scruple to pronounce that in the whole world there is not a worse country than what we have yet seen of this. All that is contiguous to us is so very barren and forbidding that it may with truth be said that here nature is reversed; and if not so, she is nearly worn out, for almost all the seed we have put into the ground has rotted, and I have no doubt but will, like the wood of this vile country when burned or rotten, turn to sand ... I cannot, I think, give you a more convincing proof than that every person ... who came out with a design of remaining in the country are now most earnestly wishing to get away from it.'*
>
> (Major Robert Ross, Lt Governor of New South Wales, November 1788)

IN THE LATTER PART of the 18th century Britain lost one colony and gained another. When America declared her independence in 1783 she refused any longer to accept transported convicts, which left the recently rejected mother country in a fix with the all too familiar problem of overcrowded prisons.

At the suggestion of Sir Joseph Banks, who had sailed there in 1770 with Captain Cook, it was decided to ship some of the overflow to the far side of the world to a country known as New Holland, or New South Wales. Such was the urgency of the situation, presumably, there was no time for an advance party to reconnoitre the place before sending over seven hundred convicts to a continent only briefly visited eighteen years previously by Cook, Banks and others, and since then more or less forgotten.

It was a country with an unpredictable climate and uninvestigated soil. There were no houses, no infrastructure, no cultivated land; there was nothing there at all in fact but a wild landscape, the dimensions of which were completely unknown; and an untold number of indigenous people who, according to Cook and Banks, were friendly enough and appeared to have no concept of ownership or property, which meant the powers that be back in the Old Country considered the country *terra nullius* and up for grabs.

So the First Fleet sailed in 1787 and eight months later they planted the Union Jack, not in Botany Bay as was originally intended but on the shores of a harbour called Port Jackson (named by Cook after someone in the naval office) at a place they called Sydney Cove (named by Governor Phillip after the British Home Secretary). They had brought with them provisions to last them two years, but after that time had elapsed with no sight of a ship and no message or communication of any kind with the old country it was presumed the colony had been completely forgotten and the people left to starve to death.

It didn't starve, thanks mostly to the resourcefulness of Governor Phillip, and the arrival after two and a half years of the next convict ship, which was then succeeded by a steady stream of more convict ships, bearing convicts of both sexes, and officials – military and civilian – whose task it was to keep order.

The convicts were by modern standards minor offenders. There were no murderers or rapists or, by definition, anyone who had received an uncommuted death sentence. Most had been sentenced to seven or fourteen years for petty theft; or for life, which was the mandatory punishment for stealing anything worth 40 shillings or more. Virtually none of them had any experience of growing crops or building houses. Few of them thought it in their interests to work their socks off for an employer who wasn't paying them. There was no advancement in initiative. There were few rewards for hard work but plenty of punishment for slacking. So an air of stagnation prevailed.

Soon after his arrival Phillip had written home to say,

'If fifty farmers were sent out with their families they would do more in one year in rendering this colony independent of the mother country, as to provisions, than a thousand convicts.'

Two years later he was still pleading for *'a few honest settlers who have been bred to agriculture'*. But the government took very little notice. They had other more important things on their mind, such as fighting the French.

It wasn't until 1792 – the year Phillip retired and the New South Wales Corps took over governership of the colony – that the first free settlers set sail on the convict ship *Bellona*. The majority of the fourteen passengers were members of the Rose family from Blandford, just down the road from Fiddleford, and distantly related to the Pitt family (Thomas Rose was Robert Pitt's first cousin once removed). With Rose went his wife Jane and their four children, a niece called Elizabeth Fish and a servant called Elizabeth Watts.

The Rose family took up land in Strathfield and struggled to make it productive – hence the letters of complaint that Mary had mentioned to cousin George. They later moved to Wilberforce on the Hawkesbury River, where they fared rather better despite being flooded several times. The house Thomas built is still there, reputedly the oldest timber building in Australia.

There is no evidence of direct communication between the Roses and the Pitts, before or after either family emigrated. The only reference to a member of the Pitt family in the book *The Roses of the Bellona*, published by the Thomas and Jane Rose Society, is in a letter written on 10 March 1798 by Jane's parents, the Topps, in which she says 'Will Pitt is dead'; which may or may not have referred to Robert's younger brother. (Or it could even have referred to Robert and Mary's son William, who died in America.)

So the majority of the founding settlers of New South Wales not only came from Mary's home county of Dorset but were distantly related to her.

The *Bellona* did not blaze a trail however. Only a smattering of free settlers migrated to New South Wales in the succeeding years, so that in 1800 out of a colonial population of around 5,000 fewer than 40 of them were there of their own volition. This is not surprising when you consider what they were up against.

~

Bearing all this in mind, while acknowledging that Major Ross's opinion of the place was extreme, his view was generally the prevailing one. Most of the inhabitants were convicts and while the sort of crimes they were convicted of would nowadays have earned them at worst a suspended sentence or an anti-social behaviour order, the colony was principally a prison and the majority of its inhabitants were prisoners. Like most prisoners they did not want to be where they were – even though, unlike back home, this prison had no bars. Also unlike back home these prisoners were not hidden away from public view but were visible on the streets, in chain gangs, or working on government buildings or farms.

George Matcham on the other hand, without having set foot in the place, saw things very differently. At a time when most people thought of New South Wales, if they thought of it at all, as a den of iniquity inhabited by apathetic rejects propped up (or battened down) by rum, almost totally cut off from what was known as civilisation so that no amount of government inducements could persuade anyone to go there no matter how hard their lives were back home, George almost alone saw New South Wales as a land of genuine opportunity. Which with the great benefit of hindsight makes him a visionary.

Chapter 6

1801: The adventurers

'1 January, 1801
My dear Mr Matcham,

*Long ago *Mr King has been asked the question about your friends journey to Botany Bay. Mr K says they shall be sent free of Cost, and desires that their names ages and descriptions as to their professions shall be sent ...The fleet sail for that Colony in March. I leave Town for Portugal next week which is much sooner than I expected.*

My sister's letter is just received, but it is written so fine that neither myself or Father can even with glasses make out a word. Better eyes will be employ'd.

... Remember me kindly to her and Mrs Matcham and believe me Sir
Your Affectionate Nelson.'
(*Under-Secretary to the Home Department)

IT'S DIFFICULT TO DESCRIBE the thrill of seeing my ancestors referred to directly in a letter written by one of England's most famous heroes.

Admiral Nelson's letters, particularly those to his brother in law, are informal, affectionate and often playful, and invariably signed *'Nelson, Bronte'* (except in the example above).

Nelson had a lot on his mind in January 1801, particularly domestically. He was in London, unusually, staying in a house with Lord and Lady Hamilton while his wife Fanny rented a place nearby. Nelson not only declined to see Fanny, he refused her request that he cease his relationship with Lady Hamilton, at which point she arranged for a legal separation and husband and wife never lived together again. What Fanny did not know was that Nelson and Emma were awaiting the birth of their first, and only, child. Horatia arrived in late January and was immediately placed into the care of a Mrs Gibson in order not to arouse suspicion.

Notwithstanding all of this, when his brother in law George Matcham spoke to him about the colonies and about his interest in sponsoring people to migrate to New South Wales, Nelson found the time to set things up for Mary and her family.

~

That January Mary went shopping. She ordered, among other items, seven yards of printed cotton, several pairs of black cotton hose, some ribbon, some gloves and some scarlet knap. The following month, February, she ordered some washed dowlas, quantities of durant, baize, serge and yet more cotton, leghorn bonnets, shoes, silk thread, needles, pins, buttons, stays, and much much more. £2 14s was paid for the making of 'cloaths'.

The longer the ship was delayed the more Mary bought. In May, two months after they should have sailed, she added to the list handkerchiefs, more hose, more tape, soap, quills and writing paper. The completed list, drawn up by Joseph Bird, dated 16 May 1801 and presented to George Matcham for payment, came to £63 5s 2¼d.

Joseph Bird was a local man, an attorney and a valuer, and seems to have acted as George Matcham's agent and general factotum when it came to the business of the Botany Bay migrants. He compiled the shopping lists not just on Mary's behalf but on behalf of a Mrs Jenkins and her sons and a William Small and his family. On the register of potential migrants he described the Pitt family thus:

'Mrs Mary Pitt aged 51 [sic] *years not a strong but a weak constitution.*

Susannah Pitt her Daughter 27 years
Lucy Pitt do 23 years
Jemima Pitt do 17 years
Esther Pitt do 15 years
Thomas Pitt her Son 20 years
He now lives with Mr Salisbury at Dorchester – Steward to Lord Rivers – he has been wrote to in the Occasion.'

It appears that George Matcham footed the bill for everyone.

On 10 April a list of settlers travelling to New South Wales on the *Minorca, Canada* and *Nile* was sent to the transport commissioners by Under-Secretary King. Six days later King wrote again, requesting that aid be given to those of them who were *'in very indigent circumstances* [and] *unable to provide themselves with the necessary cloathing for the voyage . . . The number of families in this predicament may probably amount to about forty.'*

Presumably King was not including Mary and her family among these people, although the total number of settlers travelling on those three ships could not have amounted to much more than 40 all told. But it goes to show the parlous state so many of those early settlers were in that they could not even afford to clothe themselves.

~

Meanwhile March had come and gone and the family was still waiting for instructions. At May Cottage tempers were fraying.

'Lucy, you can't possibly take all that.'

'Why not?'

'How much space do you imagine we are going to have? Susanna?'

'I have no idea, Jemima. Enough for a family of mice I should expect.'

'You see?'

'And how are we to know, sister dearest, what we will find when we get there? If we are going to be living among savages, of both the native and the transported variety, our things may have to last us a very long time.'

'You're certainly not going to need these.' Jemima picked through her sister's muffs and shawls. 'We're going to a hot country, remember?'

'And what business is it of yours?' snapped Lucy.

There are two bedrooms at May Cottage, neither of them particularly big. Ideas of personal space in those days were very different to ours of course. It would not take much to transform those rooms into total chaos. The girls had been packing for weeks now, packing and unpacking, never totally sure when the ship was going to sail, if the ship was going to sail.

'Hester, stop snivelling!' Lucy turned on her youngest sister, who'd been sitting unnoticed – so she'd hoped – in the corner and crying softly.

Hester broke into a howl.

'Now look what you've done!'

'She's done nothing but snivel for the past two days!'

'I can't . . . I can't . . .' Hester panted, 'find any of . . .'

'What, Hes? What exactly can't you find?'

'My. . .' Hester whispered something into Jemima's ear.

'It's her doll I expect,' scorned Lucy. 'You'd think she was still a baby who can't go anywhere without her toys.'

'You are one to talk! You cannot go anywhere without your wretched hats!'

'Girls, please!' Susanna stepped away from the window, through which she had been gazing distractedly for several minutes. 'That is enough! We have a lot to do! How do you suppose it's going to be when we are alone in a strange country? To say nothing of the journey. Are you going to quarrel like this all the way?'

Susanna's younger sisters glared at her, united in hostility.

'Where is mama?' sniffed Hester.

~

Mary was sitting where she had been sitting all morning, in the middle of the orchard beneath a plum tree.

It was her favourite time of the year. The fruit trees were in blossom and she liked to sit and ponder on what kind of a crop they could expect in the autumn. It was said the better the blossom the better the crop, but she wasn't sure it wasn't the other way around. Every year she made a mental note to remind herself to check if the story was true, and every year she forgot. Now it was too late. She would not be there this autumn to see it.

She was thinking about New South Wales. Would they have an orchard there? Who could tell what grew there and what didn't? They said the ground was hard and unyielding, so it was a bit fanciful to imagine a garden like this one, or a garden of any kind, let alone an orchard.

How little she knew about the place! Were there any churches? Did the inhabitants practise anything resembling a Christian religion? And what of the manners, the dress, the etiquette, how should a woman behave? How would her daughters be received? Her daughters . . . She was aware of the dramas in the cottage behind her – the girls were on edge, it was to be expected, she was on edge too, doubly so since she was the cause, the instigator of it all.

Since that day back in February a year ago life had flowed along much as always. And now, while her daughters squabbled and panicked over their packing, for her part until they received notification to proceed to Portsmouth – which she had been expecting every day for the past month or longer – she could not quite bring herself to think about all the things she had yet to do.

She heard footsteps and a muffled sob behind her and turned to see her youngest daughter, her face blotchy with tears. She beckoned Hester to her and put her arms around her quivering body and held her very tight.

~

March passed with no further news. April came and went. Then on May 5 Mary received a letter from cousin George.

'The Rev Mr Nelson [Horatio's father] *has written a letter to Governor King* on your behalf. I now enclose it, with another of*

my own. Mr Nelson's letter will be of great consequence to you. Pray put a handsome wafer on it when you have read it. Write me how you and all the rest are. Have as much patience as possible till the voyage is over, and then your comforts will crowd upon you.

Your sincere friend, George Matcham.'

(*Philip Gidley King, then Governor of New South Wales; no known relation to the Under Secretary at the Home Department.)

Two days after this George finally heard from the Commissioner of the Navy, Admiral Samuel Gambier, with the long-awaited instructions. Arrangements were in place for his friends to

'. . . proceed to Portsmouth conformably to what I at first wrote you, and on their arrival there make application to Captain Patton, agent for transports in that place . . . Let me, therefore, know how I am in future to direct you, as you say you are going into Dorsetshire to marshall your adventurers.'

Joseph Bird's next commission was to arrange transport for both passengers and luggage, a task made that much more difficult by no one knowing precisely who was intending to go or when and where they were supposed to be going.

Thomas was sent for from Dorchester. Bags were finally packed and what they could not take with them they sold or gave away. Then one day towards the end of May George Matcham arrived outside May Cottage with his own carriage, and a wagon for the luggage, and all six members of the Pitt family, with their cousin and patron, quietly made their way to Portsmouth.

~

The port was bustling. The dockyards were thick with people: dock workers loading and offloading cargo, sailors, and a number of women, some of them smuggling gin and rum on board while the quartermaster on duty turned a blind eye. Spithead was a cluster of warships, battle-scarred from the war with France and in port for quick repairs. On the near side of the harbour, at anchor, three ships lay separate from the others.

While George went in search of help the little family group stood there on the dockside, staring around them. The very busyness of the place was so overwhelming that for a moment there was little room in any of their minds for anything but astonishment. For the Pitt family, who had rarely left the confines of their village, the sight of the sea and the activity was, for the moment, diverting.

They stood there for some time, not speaking, not looking at one another. Each of them knowing that this was the point beyond which there was no return; that up until this very moment, at four o'clock on a blustery afternoon in May, minds could still be changed, chattels could be loaded back into the wagon, they could still clamber on board George's carriage and go straight back to Fiddleford.

It was at that same moment that George approached, in company with a man in naval uniform.

'This is Captain Patton, agent for transports,' he said. 'He will look after your every need before you sail.'

'Thank you Mr Matcham.' Mary smiled at her cousin and took his hand. 'We are grateful to you for everything.'

'Dear cousin,' said George. He lifted Mary's hand to his lips and kissed it. He opened his mouth to speak, but instead:

'Please do not let us detain you further,' said Mary.

George hesitated a moment, and then he smiled, and bowing in turn to each of his cousins, he said, 'Let me know how things go'. And he was gone.

In the company of Captain Patton the little group remained on the quayside, lost in their private thoughts. Then Mary said: 'I am so sorry to keep you, Captain. Now tell us, what do you want us to do?'

Chapter 7

1801: Going . . .

THE SHIPS THAT CARRIED convicts to Botany Bay were mostly merchant vessels, not built to house prisoners. So makeshift prisons, or cages, had to be constructed on the lower decks, and such was the size of these transports there was often very little separation between the convicted felons and the other passengers.

Canada was a new ship that had not been to sea before. She was 403 tons, carried ten guns and a crew of thirty-five men. Her captain was William Wilkinson, who had travelled to New South Wales before in 1794. In addition to her human cargo she carried sugar, shoes, ham, cheese, hats, cutlery, toys, port wine, whips, rum, coffee, haberdashery, tobacco, perfumery, tea, soap, stationery, telescopes, mustard, linen, gin, corks, tar, rope and green tablecloths.

Whether or not Mary realised she was to be travelling across the world in the company of convicts her first impressions of her living accommodation were not good. The day after embarking she wrote to cousin George in what looks like a stream of rising panic:

'31 May. On board 'Canada', Portsmouth Docks.

Good sir, We came on board yesterday. My situation here is very bad and the shocking account of the wicked country I dread I have brought up my children with fear and care God knows my heart I would rather fall into the hand of a merciful Creator or to sufer any poverty by his grace to restrain me from falling into the hand of wicked people a Gentleman who came from there informs me the whole land is a corrupted wicked people and if please God my children should live I hope they will find a friend in the Governor according to your good intentions I cannot expect to live long I am in a little hole among all sorts of people I can scarce see to write God almighty be my guide and send me a place of rest and his blessing attend you and yours for ever is the earnest wish of your oblidged humble servant Mary Pitt.'

Who had been talking to her? Who was the mysterious Gentleman who put such dread into Mary's mind about the country she was about to travel to?

He turned out to be a man named Lieutenant Robert Braithwaite. He was, as he described himself in a letter to George written after the meeting, *'a stranger to Mrs Pitt but heard by accident she was going to New South Wales. I called on her at the request of a person to whom she was known.'*

Braithwaite, a naval man, had just returned from the colony, where he had been living for seven years. Whatever passed between him and Mary at this meeting he was evidently not a man of great sensitivity. Maybe he thought he was doing Mary a favour by telling her in the bluntest terms exactly what lay waiting for her in the country in which she had chosen to make her new life.

Poor Mary. Better surely to travel in ignorance than in dread, and her expectation of her impending demise almost looks like a death-wish.

~

Now I have to digress for a moment.

A while ago a wonderful thing happened: my Australian cousin Libby, on a tip-off, paid a visit to the Blue Mountains Historical Society, where in a copy of a book called *The Letters of Rachel Henning* she saw a footnote referring to documents about Mary Pitt that were held among papers belonging to the 'Atkinson family'. She emailed our circle of family members asking if anyone had knowledge of this, and heard from one of them that the 'Papers of the Atkinson Family' were to be found in the Mitchell Library in Sydney. She visited the library and there, in a cardboard box among an assorted bundle of other documents she discovered Mary Pitt's original letters, written on board *Canada* waiting to sail.

Mary Pitt's original letters.

Not copies, not transcripts. We had spent years looking for these letters and assumed they'd been lost. So until this discovery all we had had to go on – and by 'we' I include other family genealogists, including aunt Barbara – were transcripts, punctuated, partly censored and the spelling 'corrected' by some unknown, well-meaning, upright family member.

So now I was able to touch the paper Mary touched, and read the very words she wrote, with its total lack of punctuation and its occasionally eccentric spelling.

She wrote with a rounded hand; not with the elegant calligraphy of a professional such as Joseph Bird, but with an ease and an evenness that suggested an educated woman who was very used to writing.

Anyone who's ever undertaken research knows of the importance of primary sources. But I'd never fully appreciated before what a difference it makes to read a document in the original handwriting. Before Xerox machines or cameras there was no other way of copying anything except by hand, but it never occurred to me that a transcriber might think to 'improve' on an original letter and thereby to mask – consciously or otherwise – the writer's personality. In their original raw form the lack of punctuation gave the letters an urgency and excitement the transcribed versions lacked. I could almost hear Mary's breathlessness, feel her heart pounding, sense the uncontrolled panic as her hand screamed across the page.

On the other hand it's possible it was Mary's style not to use punctuation. There's a bit of it, though not much, in her second, calmer letter, written in response to cousin George after presumably having received reassurance from him.

'11 June 1801

Good sir I received your kind letter likewise two letters inclosed which I humbly thank you Sir, and Mr Nellson [sic: Nelson's father] *in condescending for our future interest with the Governour we are all well, and I believe the ship will sail soon we have on board a hundred and six convicts soldiers, and near forty passengers is here and expected so that we have just room to creep out of our little nests the Captain told me had parted his cabin his Lady is with him and intends going the voyage big with child* at first the ship's Crew were continually passing by to the stores and the surgeons room close by us which I complained of to Captain Patten* [sic} *as being a very unfit place for women since is some alterations I hope Mrs Matcham yourself and family are well my best respects to your good Mother a blessing I hope will attend you and yours for ever*

I am sir with grateful respect, Your obliged humble servant, MARY PITT'

(*The phrase *'big with child'* had been expunged in the transcribed versions, probably by Matilda Warren Jenkins, a descendant. The *'alterations'* presumably had to do with being given a better cabin in a better position, and again it shows Mary asserting her authority.)

Finally, on 21 June, the ship sailed from Spithead, by Portsmouth. The journey to New South Wales was to take Mary and family six months and none of them was ever to see the old country again.

Meanwhile in the same fleet, hidden deep in the depths of the ship *Nile,* was a convict called Margaret Catchpole, who was about to be transported for life for stealing a horse and then breaking out of gaol. She was to play an important role in the lives of several families in the colony, not least the Pitts.

Chapter 8

1801: . . . gone

IT TAKES ROUGHLY twenty-four hours to get from London to Sydney by air these days, with one stopover. I have done it more times than I should probably admit to; once with my fifteen-month-old son, once with my elderly mother, once with my teenage daughter and once with my English cousin Frances, but most often on my own.

I've done the journey in emotional turmoil, after the break-up of my marriage and on my way to what I thought was to be a new life. I've done it with hope and I've done it in desperation. It is not a comfortable way to spend an entire day but one thing it does do is offer plenty of time for contemplation. And if the discomfort gets too much then all one has to do is to think back a couple of hundred years.

In 1801 the journey from Portsmouth to Port Jackson took six months, stopping, in the case of *Canada*, only once, at Rio de Janeiro. It was tough-going and hazardous.

No convict ships had ever yet been wrecked or lost en route, which was a miracle in itself. But in addition to the usual hazards of a long sea voyage – which at this time included the strong possibility of being attacked, usually by the French, which is why the ships were armed – there was the problem of being cooped up together, passengers, crew and convicts, for months on end without respite.

There were 106 male convicts on board Canada. They greatly outnumbered the rest of the passengers and crew. Captain Wilkinson had to see that they all reached their destination safely and in good health. To this end he was under strict orders as to how the ship should be fumigated, the decks scraped, the berths cleaned and aired and the windsails trimmed. He also had to make sure none of the convicts escaped. There had been mutinies on other journeys. There had been floggings, death and madness. On the notorious Second Fleet a third of the convicts died during the voyage. On one ship (*Royal Admiral*, bearing one of Mary's future sons in law) the surgeon, the most vital member of the crew after the captain, died three weeks after leaving port. Passengers gave birth – Captain Wilkinson's own wife produced a son while they were at sea – and others died of natural causes. There was scurvy. There was typhoid, flux (dysentery), and 'Scotch fiddle', otherwise known as 'the itch'. There had been duels, drunkenness and insurrection and, under lax leadership, a complete breakdown of law and order, with ships' crews breaking into (female) convicts' quarters and getting up to goodness only knows what. Often the crew were worse behaved than the convicts. Some of the ships had been so badly provisioned some passengers, convicts of course, died of starvation.

The ships that sailed across the world two centuries ago look almost toy-like in comparison with the juggernauts you can see on the horizon off the coast of Sydney today. With its 200 passengers there was very little room to move about on *Canada*. The convicts were separated from the rest on the lower deck, but from contemporary accounts it's clear there was a good deal of intermingling, not all of it quite legitimate, and everyone appeared to know everyone else's business. If there was illness or madness among the convicts, crew or passengers, Mary would have known about it.

There were not just humans on board. Between decks could be heard the squawking and snuffling of dinner. Some people had brought along their own sheep or goats, which they slaughtered when needed. Passengers often found themselves tripping over a duck or a goose that had escaped its quarters.

Mary had brought the portrait of her husband along with her and was reluctant to let it out of her sight. Two things concerned her – that it would get wet or stolen; and so she enveloped it in several layers of canvas and tucked it away in the darkest corner of her tiny cabin. On occasion she would unwrap it and prop the picture up against the bed while she talked to him. At times she found his image, frozen at the age of 46, calming. At others it seemed his expression, the hauteur, the faint smile beneath the borrowed wig, was laughing at her. In any case she found his presence a comfort, if only in portrait form. It reminded her of the time before he lost his confidence and his health, when he knew he could conquer the world.

Despite her 'weak constitution' in my version of the story Mary spent much of her time out of her cabin. It was still a hole notwithstanding its improved position, and the longer she spent in it the harder it was not to brood over the dreadful stories Lieutenant Braithwaite had, rather thoughtlessly, regaled her with about the country she was travelling to.

For distraction she took herself whenever possible onto the upper deck. On a calm day, and there were not many of those, it was sheer pleasure to feel the breeze and the warmth of the sun on her face. The immensity of the sea jolted her out of her self-absorption.

She found the presence of the convicts on deck confronting. She had heard of prisoners being kept in irons throughout the whole journey to New South Wales, but Captain Wilkinson was of the mind that the conditions these poor creatures had to endure – cooped up in cages with no proper sanitation, no privacy, very little light and not enough air even to light a candle, often for days on end if the weather was bad – was punishment enough. To say nothing of what awaited them at the other end. He had instructions to allow the convicts on to the decks for fresh air and exercise twice a day, weather permitting.

They were a sorrowful sight, as they emerged from the lower depths, pale, shabby, blinking into the daylight. Once

Mary caught one of the men staring at her; she tried to smile back but the man's haunted expression didn't change and his stare did not falter. So this is what I will have to get used to, she told herself.

Other than Mary's experience crossing the sea from Ireland as a child it would have been the first time any of the Pitt family had been on board a boat of any kind, on a journey that is the furthest anyone can travel between one place and another on this planet. Sometimes the sea was so violent it smashed right across the deck, shattering anything that was in its way. More than once Mary thought the ship would split into pieces. On several occasions the water washed right into her cabin, drenching everything, clothes and bedding included. At such moments, when she caught herself coming close to despair, she only had to think of the man with the haunted face, and his companions, and she thanked God for the few blessings she was aware she still had.

She still had her five children with her, and it helped take her mind off her own predicament by observing them. Thomas, unused to idleness and at first restless and rather irritable, took it upon himself to befriend members of the crew. He could often be seen discussing with one or other of them the finer details of sails, and rigging. Lucy, her mother noticed, very often accompanied him.

Susanna, whose health had always been delicate, suffered so badly from seasickness she spent most of the time in the cabin. The two younger sisters spent much of their time walking the deck, looking for conversation with anyone who was willing to pass the time of day with them. Jemima in particular was eager to make herself useful, whether as amateur assistant to the ship's surgeon or nursemaid to the Captain's wife, before and after she had given birth to her baby son.

~

Midway through the journey the ship stopped at Rio de Janeiro. Mary stayed on board to look after Susanna, who was disinclined to disembark. Lucy meanwhile, chaperoned by

Thomas, wasted no time at all in jumping ashore and checking out the sights, which she described, in breathless detail, to her mother later on the first day.

'You have no idea how good it is to feel dry land beneath one's feet,' she breathed. 'And mama, the streets are stuffed with shops, with every essential imaginable – silks, satins, ribbons, it is altogether charming! And fresh fruit – oranges, berries, pineapples – cascading from baskets onto the street. There are churches and convents everywhere, all lit up, and a virgin on every corner!'

'I beg your pardon?'

'She's referring to the statues,' said Tom.

'The people are of all colours, and everyone so gay and friendly! Men smile and blow kisses quite brazenly! – it's as well that Thomas was with me or my head would be completely turned! Mama!' she turned to her mother with barely a pause for breath. 'I have to ask your permission to attend a ball tomorrow night.'

'Oh?'

'I have . . .' she glanced at her brother briefly, 'been invited.'

'By whom?'

'By some of the ship's company.'

Lucy turned to her brother again, this time in appeal.

'It's perfectly in order mother,' said Thomas. 'I will be with her to keep an eye.'

'But Lucy, what shall you wear?'

'I will wear my lilac muslin, enhanced by some very pretty ribbon which I happen to have purchased this very morning.' At which Lucy produced a small package of said ribbon, which was delicately unwrapped, and at which all four girls peered and crowed and exclaimed, with greater or lesser degrees of delight.

Mary couldn't help but smile. She could not remember the last time any of the girls attended a ball, or had reason to dress for a special occasion. Who would have imagined it? It had even jolted Lucy out of her ridiculous languor. Nothing but good must come of it, thought Mary, with something approaching satisfaction.

The ball was held at the house of the His Excellency the Viceroy of the Brazils, and even Lucy's brother could not fail to notice that she was the belle of it. She was in great demand and danced almost every dance with a different partner. But there was one man who paid her more attention than anyone else and who, in the brief intervals between dances took pains to engage her in conversation; to which, Thomas observed, Lucy showed no objection whatsoever. He was third mate on *Canada* and his name, as Thomas knew well, was John Wood.

From Rio de Janeiro the ship sailed south, around the Cape of Good Hope without stopping, and on. At times the sea was so fierce passengers and convicts were confined to their cabins for days at a time. On one occasion following a violent thunderstorm the ship sprung a leak, and while she was assured it was above the water line Mary couldn't help but wonder as she listened to the water rushing in how they could remain afloat. On calmer days she sat on the deck and watched porpoises, and occasionally a school of whales, leaping simultaneously and unexpectedly from the sea with a cry that was quite unearthly.

For the most part the biggest problem was boredom. The sun shone, it did not shine. The wind blew or it did not. Weeks went by with no sight of land – nothing to look at but the endlessly rolling sea. For Lucy, who between the hours of eight and noon each day could invariably be found standing on the deck 'on watch' alongside the third mate, the sight of the sea was surprisingly absorbing.

And so the ship sailed on with its cargo of dreams and dreads, and on 14 December 1801, six months almost to the day since she left Portsmouth, *Canada* and her sister ships *Nile* and *Minorca* arrived at Port Jackson and docked at Sydney Cove. Despite storms, leaks, childbirth and illness not one passenger had been lost.

And there was another thing for Mary to ponder on: her

second daughter had received a proposal of marriage. So one of the primary purposes for her great journey had been partly fulfilled, and before they'd even touched dry land.

PART TWO

The new British

Chapter 9

The authors of our existence

'All women become like their mothers. That is their tragedy. No man does. That's his.'
(Oscar Wilde, *The Importance of Being Ernest*)

ONE OF THE SURPRISING things about the BBC TV series '*Who do you think you are?*' is how little the subjects of the programmes appear to know about their past, and how amazed and moved they are by what they discover about people whose existence they were hitherto completely unaware of. I realise of course the ignorance is probably exaggerated in order to make good television, but it's interesting to see how every one of them seems to gain substance from their antecedents, even if those antecedents were rogues. If you've ever delved into your family history, however cursorily, you'll recognise what I mean when I say We Are Not Alone. Like it or not, every one of us is a link in a chain that goes back to the beginning of human time.

The implication in the title of the BBC programme is that no matter how hard we may try to do otherwise we end up like our parents. But I prefer to think of our ancestors as I have George Matcham describe them – 'The authors of our existence' – because it allows us that much autonomy, or free will, to write our own stories and muck them up in our own unique way.

For example I am completely unlike my mother, in my view at least. People used to say I look like her and even I can see some physical resemblance. But in every other way we are utterly different: different priorities, different values, different likes and dislikes, different outlooks on everything from the bringing up of children to how we see or would like to see the world around us. My mother was brilliantly sociable and apparently liked by everyone when she was young; but she was not particularly brainy and had no interest in intellectual matters. I am not particularly sociable or as comfortable in social situations and while I'm far from being an intellectual I do enjoy acquiring knowledge (if only I could retain it). The only real thing we ever had in common was our love of the theatre. Oh, and the sunshine.

If anyone took the trouble to go through the records however they would find distinct likenesses.

My mother was twenty-three years old when she left Australia and went to live in England in order to pursue her career. I was twenty-three years old when I left England and went to live in Australia, partly in order to pursue my career.

We were both actresses when we were young but gave up when we had children.

She got married when she was almost thirty-one and had her first child (a boy) at thirty-three. Her only other child, a daughter (me), was born three years later. I was just thirty-two when I married and thirty-three when I had my first child (a boy). My only other child, a daughter, was born two years later.

And so on.

But all that proves nothing. They are just statistics. If you are looking for what sort of people your ancestors really were, what made them tick, how they spoke and related to other people and the world around them – that is another matter altogether.

In the case of Mary Pitt for instance you would never have thought that anyone contemplating migrating across the world to another country, let alone embarking on a six-month sea voyage, would have been described as having 'a weak constitution'. Of course that was one man's perception, and

Mary might have been feeling under the weather that particular day. But it goes to show how easy it is for the family biographer to make assumptions, and why it is that the truth is so much more complex and unexpected than the stuff we make up.

Family history is not like any other form of history. On the one hand it can offer unique glimpses into the social conditions of a particular time; on the other it isn't a subject that's likely to be of any interest to anyone outside the family. To announce to the world in general that you are 'writing the family history' is a quick way of clearing the room.

Family history like all forms of history relies on primary sources, but unlike other forms it tends to be undertaken by amateurs, some of whom have more or less respect for the checking of facts. A story repeated is not necessarily a true story, and it doesn't take long to realise how quickly a misreport in a newspaper for instance can gain credibility through repetition. And while there is no excuse for relying on newspaper reports for the 'truth' there is reason for listening to family lore.

My aunt spent years noting down every single mention of Robert and Mary Pitt in the Dorset Records Office, but when I asked her for instance how she knew our ancestors stayed with Governor King and his wife on their arrival in Sydney, she looked at me rather vaguely and said, 'I don't know dear, I expect it's family lore'. That's to say it was something that had filtered down through so many generations even aunt Barbara didn't think to question it. This does not negate the importance of family lore; just because it's not in the record books doesn't mean it didn't happen.

And there's another thing: people tend to be exceptionally loyal to their own branch of the family and may turn a blind eye to anything bad said about them. A generation ago our family genealogists were particularly anxious to find our aristocratic connections to the Earl of Chatham (Prime Minister William Pitt the Elder), and/or to William Morton-Pitt, MP.

This same generation on the other hand denied the existence of convicts among our ancestors, as did most people in those days. Our generation tends to go in the opposite direction and brag about our convict ancestry. Which all goes to show that family history is subject to personal bias, generational prejudice, prevailing fashion and selective interpretation, and is all the more fascinating because of it.

According to historian Babette Smith in her book *Australia's Birthstain* there is no other country in the world *'where family historians are more important than in Australia.* [They are working] . . . *at the cutting edge of historical research.'*

What she is saying is that by digging into their own convict heritage family historians in Australia are unearthing not just facts about their own ancestors but about the country's origins as a penal colony; facts that have been suppressed for generations, to the point where she calls it censorship. For instance at the Bicentenary in 1988 celebrating the arrival of the First Fleet the only person said to have mentioned Australia's convict background was the Prince of Wales.

To this generation that seems extraordinary. Australians now flaunt their convict heritage, for good reason. To know that your ancestors have pulled themselves up in the world on their own merits without the advantage of background or money is something to be rightly proud of. In the old world meanwhile, where class was thought to be ordained by God and therefore irrefutable, a person reduced by circumstances to committing crimes stood little or no chance of climbing up in the world. Australia offered opportunities and the people grabbed them.

Members of my family married into the convict community, which is an interesting story in itself but does not form part of this book. Our original forebears however were settlers, not convicts. They were by comparison privileged people, albeit driven by hardship. They were given land by an authority who in today's thinking had no right to give it, in a country that had been 'stolen' from its indigenous people. I should feel guilt, rather than pride, at what my ancestors achieved. Then again it was their extraordinary hard work, their enterprise in impossible conditions, that made them what they were, and what I am now. I should feel pride rather than guilt. It is complex, and contradictory. Knowing how to face up to its past is a continuing Australian conundrum, and in that respect I am a true Aussie.

Whatever one may think of the country as it is today, for me it is a thrill to know that my ancestors played if not a starring role nonetheless a very real part in the shaping of it.

~

But is the BBC right in implying the more you know of your antecedents the more you will understand about yourself? Do I stand a better chance of fitting into Mary's shoes than someone who does not share her DNA? How far back do we have to go to understand why our mothers were who they were, and consequently, why we are who we are?

It was partly to find the answer to those questions that I set out to write this book. The rest, the ancient linking chain, I discovered unexpectedly along the way. I find it reassuring to think of myself not just as an individual but as a link in that chain, fettered for good or ill to those ancestors watching over us, knowing we share so much DNA, that we can rejoice in their successes but not be held accountable – as was the case until recently – for their mistakes; hoping they are looking out for us, and hoping in return we will not disappoint them.

Chapter 10

Reinvention

'SHE WAS A DAREDEVIL,' said my aunt Barbara. 'Absolutely fearless in the surf. Good at more or less everything. She'd spend hours on the beach and go as black as a native.'

Excuse me, but is this my mother we are talking about?

'She didn't bother with school much. She had the record for the most knitting under the desk. She was sociable, it was more or less what was done in those days. She was pretty in a way that wasn't dolly. You know, she had the retroussé nose, and a nice big wide mouth, which I think is essential. She was good at tennis, and all the boys liked her. I thought she was perfect.'

This is aunt Barbara quoted verbatim.

There's a certain amount of sisterly envy here. Barbara always thought of herself as the plain one, not particularly good at anything and shy with boys, in all ways the exact opposite of her sociable, pretty elder sister. But the woman my aunt was describing, this sporty daredevil, who spent her youth in Sydney frolicking in the surf, partying, laughing, playing tennis and subversively knitting, bears as much relation to the mother I knew as a wombat to a King Charles spaniel. Apart from the knitting, I do remember that.

The woman I knew was 'more English than the English', as the saying goes: cut glass accent, not the slightest trace of Oz in her. I knew about the Australian link, obviously, in fact I was rather proud of it, except for those endless convict jokes, but you would never have guessed in a million years that this sophisticated, impeccably turned out, butter-wouldn't-melt-in-the-mouth Englishwoman had ever gone near the surf, let alone frolicked in it.

I wonder on occasion what my ancestor Mary Pitt would have said had she known that four generations down the line her descendants were starting to return to the old country she had gone to so much trouble to put behind her. Of my grandmother's seven siblings three left Australia permanently: two settled in America and one in England. And of her three daughters, the eldest of whom was my mother, only one of them, aunt Barbara, stayed put in Australia.

My mother left Australia first on a world tour with her parents in 1927, when she was twenty. Two years later she returned to England and enrolled at RADA (the Royal Academy of Dramatic Art), where she successfully eradicated every trace of her Australian accent.

In this she was replicating, though she would not have been aware of it, what her three times great grandmother had done over a hundred years before: travelling across the world to a country she did not know, where she knew no one and where, unintentionally or otherwise, she went through a process of total personal reinvention.

In both cases it was a pretty brave thing to do. In both cases these women were jettisoning the familiar to seek better opportunities in strange parts. Some 40 years after my mother I did the same – emigrated from my home in England to live in Australia, for much the same reasons, although in my case my brother had done it before me, so I was not totally alone.

I have no idea where my mother's acting bug came from. Both her sisters had brief acting careers in Australia: the youngest, Lorraine, co-starred in a film called *Strike Me Lucky* with a man named 'Mo', aka Roy Rene, well known in Australia as a music hall comedian. A few years later Lorraine also went to England to pursue her career there but gave it up when a producer offered the part she had been promised to his girlfriend. Barbara spent a few years performing in the 1920s Sydney version of fringe theatre before travelling to England to study at RADA, but she also gave up after a while and returned to Sydney and to another life. Their mother, my grandmother, had been a talented pianist apparently and was once offered the opportunity to travel to Europe to be taught by an Austrian maestro, which her parents would not allow her to do. In those days, in that sort of family environment, a young woman was not expected to follow a career. My mother's generation was different.

On leaving drama school mum changed her name from Nancy Smith to Nancy O'Neil. It was what actors, or specifically actresses, used to do in those days, give themselves stage names, usually alliterative: think Diana Dors, Marilyn Monroe, Greer Garson, Helen Hayes and countless others. Nancy O'Neil's first job, so far as I can make out, was performing twice-nightly in weekly rep at Salisbury, after which she toured in a play called *The Breadwinner* by W Somerset Maugham, playing the part Peggy Ashcroft played in the London production. She then became seriously ill with an ulcer and her mother insisted on travelling to London and fetching her back to Australia. She spent a year in Sydney recuperating in the surf, playing tennis, riding and going flying with her chum Charles Kingsford Smith, 'the well-known Australian record-breaker', after whom Sydney Airport is named. With her doctor father's permission she appeared in a play in Melbourne called *Doctor Pygmalion* by Australian playwright Harrison Owen and starring Margaret Rawlings. (The play premiered in London in 1932 and I am assuming it reached Australia later that year.) However the pull of the surf, or of her family, were not enough and as soon as she felt fit enough mum returned to England, where she spent the rest of her working life.

She made a good career as an actress. In 1933, the year after she returned to England, she was understudying in a play in the West End called *The Rats of Norway*, again by W Somerset Maugham and starring Laurence Olivier – his West End debut – when she was given a letter of introduction to the director

Walter Forde, who was looking for someone to play the young lead in a film called *Jack Ahoy,* starring Jack Hulbert. Despite telling her right away she was too small to play the part he went on to cast her. Meanwhile she acquired a part in a West End play called *Man Proposes,* where in the words of a devoted admirer called Cameron Gordon – a doctor, who followed mum from Australia to England but who according to aunt Barbara was regarded by her as no more than a 'chum', unfortunately for him – she was *'perfect as the young thing . . . and she had "a hand" at every exit'.*

According to none other than John Betjeman, *Jack Ahoy '. . . is the best British comedy I have yet seen on the screen. It is never dull, because it is ruthlessly cut . . . Nancy O'Neil, on the screen for the first time, looks like an admiral's daughter and acts like one. There is a quiet reserve about her, an air of sophistication and lack of it, both at the same time, that suggests a gala night at Southsea'.*

It was a pretty silly film, or so it looks to modern eyes. But it was an unhappy experience for my mother. In a letter written by Dr Gordon to Nan's mother Mimi on 6 December 1933 he said: *' . . . through the whole film he* [the director Walter Forde] *has not directed Nan in any way, just let her go ahead without correction or advice . . . about mid length of the film (according to Nan) this attitude changed to one of definite dislike, which she interpreted as a failure on her part or alternatively she had offended them in some way.'*

The 'them' refers I assume to Walter Forde and his wife.

It seems odd, having cast this newcomer in a starring role, for the director and his wife to then ignore her and even turn on her. Yet it echoes my own early experiences of working in weekly rep, with no experience whatsoever (perhaps that was the problem) and having to learn my trade the hard way: by being blasted by my fellow (highly experienced) actors for upstaging or blocking them – unwittingly of course – and being ignored so completely by the director that I had to deliberately do something outrageous for him to even notice my presence.

Then again, the inexperienced and unconfident actor is prone to paranoia.

Despite her bad experience *Jack Ahoy* launched mum's film career. For the next few years she went on to perform in several West End plays and make over twenty films, many of them 'quota quickies', working with the likes of Jack Buchanan, Max Miller, Michael Powell and Seymour Hicks.

The quota quickie was the film that got made, usually on a tiny budget and in very little time, to fulfil the quota laid down by the Cinematograph Films Act of 1927. In the mid-1920s the British film industry was virtually moribund, thanks to the influx of motion pictures from America, so the Act decreed that a given percentage of films, rising from seven and a half to twenty percent in ten years, should be British-produced. It gave birth to a number of poor quality films, but it succeeded in that it revived the British film industry to a large extent, and it gave opportunities to inexperienced directors and technicians to learn their craft, Michael Powell among them.

I also became involved in an attempt to raise the quota of local product when I lived in Australia in the late 1960s/early '70s. With the relatively small population and its commercially-minded owners Australian television was fighting a losing battle against the tsunami of programmes imported from both America and Britain, at a fraction of what it cost to make original material. I joined a campaign called, rather awkwardly, 'TV: Make it Australian!' We managed to raise the quota a tiny bit, but unlike the English experience the success didn't seem to have much lasting effect.

Nan was excellently type-cast as the impeccably-spoken, archetypically upper middle class 'sweet young thing'. (Not an easy role to play by the way, I know from my own experience.) She wore lovely frocks and looked gorgeous. She also got excellent reviews, although they mostly referred to her sweet nature, or her liveliness, or her good looks, rather than to her extraordinary acting talent. The exception was the writer Aimée Stuart, who wanted her for a part in the play she had co-written and who said of her, *'she has a rare quality of emotional restraint and of depth behind that restraint.'*

Mum would have been pleased with that.

All this I gleaned not from my mother herself but from newspaper cuttings. By the time she had children she'd more or less given up her acting career, by choice or otherwise, so I knew nothing of her background until one day, left alone in the house and snooping, as kids are wont to do, I came upon two scrapbooks of photos and cuttings, caringly compiled by her youngest sister Lorraine. I had no idea mum had been such a celebrity. I had no idea she was once so beautiful. I never knew her in her acting days so the pretty, sweet young woman with the sparkling eyes smiling out at me from the pages was completely unfamiliar.

I have to admit that almost everything I know about my mother's acting career was gleaned from these scrapbooks. This is due partly to my stroppy teenage indifference and partly to my mother's 'emotional restraint': what I'd call her over-developed resistance to talking about herself. It showed a terrible lack of breeding, was the prevailing view in those days, to mention the word 'I' in conversation. The same applied to the topic of one's children, about which the less said the better. Boastful behaviour belonged exclusively to the common people.

So the discovery of the scrapbooks came as quite a shock. I was both surprised and slightly jealous. I wanted to be as famous as my mother, famouser. Looking at her, and reading about her, I began to understand why she had found motherhood such a drag, after all that fame and all that fuss.

In the pages of the scrapbook I came upon yet another surprise. In interviews she was described as 'reserved' and even more oddly, 'shy'. This is not how I thought of her and certainly not how her sister Barbara described her. Shy people are not normally such determined socialisers, surely. The mother I knew didn't know what shyness was; she found mine – which in retrospect was bordering on the certifiable –

incomprehensible. She tried to cure it by force-feeding me cocktail parties, and couldn't understand why it just made me that much more determined to become an actress so I'd have something else to do in the evenings.

Like many in her profession she did all she could to dissuade me from my chosen path. She knew how tough it was, how heartbreaking. But I didn't want to hear it and I didn't want to hear her talking about her career either, which is a shame because it is only with hindsight that, professionally at least, I realise we did have things in common: the director who did not direct her, her constant fears of being a 'flop', her belief she was no good (and, perhaps unwisely, her readiness to admit it in print), her yearning to be cast as something other than the sweet young thing, to be taken seriously as a 'proper actress'.

My mother rarely talked about her Australian background and childhood and she never seemed to show much interest in the place, except when it came to cricket. She went back to Australia twice in her later years, once as part of a world cruise she took with my father after he retired, and once to attend my brother's wedding in 1987. (Admittedly it was a good deal less accessible then: in the 1930s it took six weeks to sail there and thirteen days to fly. Unless of course you were Charles Kingsford Smith, who broke the world record by doing it in ten and a half.)

Ironically, the newspapers made much of mum's Australian origins. *'Another Australian storms the London stage!'* shouted the headlines. Some of the cuttings in the scrapbook came from Australian newspapers; most were undated, and when I was trying to work out what year she worked at Salisbury for instance I found on the back of one of them a story about the completion of Sydney Harbour Bridge, which usefully placed it in 1931.

Everything my mother did and said was in some way a performance. She had remodelled herself: new voice, new manner, new behaviour. She was an Englishwoman now, through and through. In a family history sense you could say she had turned back the clock. She had become Mary Pitt, the woman who in order to regain the gentility she considered she was entitled to was forced to migrate to a foreign country. By migrating in reverse my mother transformed herself from a parochial (though well-bred) Aussie beach bum into a genteel Englishwoman. Or that's how I saw it.

She had been packed off to boarding school in Australia at eight years old, the only one of the three sisters to be sent away at that age. The reason, according to my aunt, was because 'she was a handful'. She was only there for a few years and she didn't like it apparently.

I was also packed off to boarding school when I was eight, and my brother at seven. Unlike my mother it was not because we were a handful, and unlike her we stayed at boarding school throughout our school lives. Mum was fond of telling us, rather too often, that she 'couldn't wait to get rid of us', which sounds harsh in these child-centric days, but it was the sort of thing certain people said in those days. It meant we came home at holiday time to a couple of strangers, which probably more than anything else accounted for the lack of intimacy and closeness between mum and me when we were older. I used to resent her for what she did to us. But since I had children of my own I could only feel sorry that she missed out on the extraordinary, exhausting, infuriating yet astonishingly rewarding business of witnessing small people grow up.

Suffice to say I'd have died rather than see my kids go to boarding school. My mother could not understand this at all. But then I could not understand why she did to us what she'd disliked her own parents doing to her. After she died I came upon letters written by her from school to her parents telling them how lonely she felt and how she missed them. Boarding school, it was felt, was supposed to bring you independence. In actuality it brought misery, loneliness and estrangement.

As a child I grew up with 'rules'. They were not written

rules – it would have been easier if they had been, at least then I may not have made so many mistakes; I remember to this day the look of horror on my mother's face when I responded to the greeting 'How do you do?' with 'Very well thank you' – but of course that was the whole point: they were rules to be absorbed, by osmosis, not taught. If they'd been written down then any old common-or-garden Tom, Dick or Harry could have got their dirty hands on them and learned them by rote and, heaven forfend, tried to pass themselves off as proper people.

There is a song in *My Fair Lady* – which I am unable to quote directly for copyright reasons – in which Professor Higgins, in the words of Alan Jay Lerner, exclaims that the moment an Englishman opens his mouth to speak he is damned. Well he could have met my mother. No matter how posh the accent or impeccable the clothes or manners of the utterer, certain patterns of speech proved beyond doubt that a person was common. Words such as 'pardon, toilet, settee, couch, lounge, phone, serviette' were tantamount to profanities. And of course the correct, the only response to 'How do you do?' was 'How do you do?' in return. Made no sense maybe, but that was the rule. My father, born of ancient English and Irish stock, well-to-do but not wealthy, didn't seem to pay much attention to a person's background; he didn't have to.

I always assumed my mother's snobbery came from a sense of 'cultural cringe': that her reinvention of herself as the archetypal upper class Englishwoman was an attempt to eradicate her colonial Australian roots. But when I began talking to my Australian aunt I discovered – despite the fact the two sisters had had very little contact with one another throughout their lives – remarkable similarities in outlook and viewpoint, and precisely what a person should or shouldn't say. When I compared notes with my Australian cousin Libby, who'd been brought up in Australia and with whom I'd had no contact until we were both in our fifties, we found we had a surprising amount in common. Both our mothers were highly conscious of class and background. Both had pretty extreme right-wing opinions, and their views on race were, let's say, of the time, and best not repeated here. Both were incapable of giving or receiving compliments and had difficulty showing much warmth or emotion.

So I came to the shocking conclusion that mum's snobbery did not originate in England at all: she and her sisters had been brought up that way. Their attitudes were dinky-die Australian. Coming from the most aggressively egalitarian country in the world I found this almost incomprehensible. It wasn't until I began looking into my family history that I began to understand.

PART THREE

The new Australians

Chapter 11

1801: Arrival

PRIVATELY, MARY HAD NOT expected to survive the voyage. So it was with some surprise that she woke one December morning to find the ship no longer rocking beneath her. The next thing was the sound of a cannon firing, and there was shouting, and her first thoughts were that they were under siege. But then there was Susanna . . .

'Come quickly, mama!'

'Why, what's happening?'

. . . grabbing her hand and pulling her out of her cabin and onto the deck, and right there, towering over them, she saw the sheer face of a cliff, and on top of it a flag was flying, and just beyond it the ship made a sharp turn left and she came upon the most beautiful sight in the world.

As *Canada* sailed through the heads into Sydney Harbour Mary saw a stretch of water teeming with small boats: sailboats, rowing boats and rough canoes with dark-skinned people in them. She saw people on them waving and shouting and realised it was just for them, that this was their welcoming committee. After six months on the open sea it was enough to make a person weep. As the ship sailed with its escort the six miles up the harbour to Port Jackson she saw on either side wooded hills sloping down to the water's edge, fingers of water reaching far inland, sand-flecked bays and beaches punctuated by rocky headlands. And all of it empty, untouched, primitively perfect.

By contrast the port itself was heaving. This was Sydney

Town, December 1801, population circa two thousand, and every single one of them, or so it seemed, had turned out to greet the newcomers. The arrival of new ships was a momentous occasion – they brought food, clothing, furniture, fabrics, luxuries from the old country. They brought people too, convicts for inspection as potential labourers. And perhaps most exciting of all they brought news: letters from family and friends, news of the King, of Nelson's victories, of the continuing war with France – all of it needless to say already six months old. (It's said by the time the news had arrived in the colony of King George III's mystery ailment – known then as madness but since diagnosed as porphyria – he had already recovered.)

As *Canada* anchored at the Cove a small boat came to meet her and from it stepped two men, one in naval uniform. This was the inspection by a surgeon and a naval officer to check for contagious disease. Once that was done a short man with a ruddy face stepped on board and spoke first to the captain, and then to the convicts, and lastly to the passengers.

'Philip Gidley King, at your service.' He bowed to Mary and tipped his hat.

'Governor King, it is a pleasure.'

'How was your journey? Any complaints?'

It was a question he asked of everyone, convicts and crew included. He made it his business to find out how well they had been treated, whether they had received their due rations and if there were any grievances that should be looked into. With *Canada* and her sister ships *Nile* and *Minorca* the governor found no grounds for complaints at all. They and their passengers were, he was to announce later, in the best condition he had ever seen and the convicts ready to start work right away.

The following day the Pitt family were still on board.

'Why can we not go ashore mama?' asked Hester.

'We have to wait until we are instructed. Besides, it isn't safe.'

'What do you mean it's not safe?'

'It's a penal colony Hes, remember?' said Jemima. 'Filled with robbers and murderers and thieves and scallywags and the most desperate and wretchedest people in the world.'

'Enough, Jemima,' said Mary.

'It looks all right to me,' said Hester. 'It seems quiet enough.'

'At a distance, maybe.'

At a distance the thirteen-year-old settlement did look quiet, peaceful even, like something out of a picture book. Not quite real, but pretty in a ramshackle sort of a way, with its criss-cross pattern of single-storey thatched huts, like dolls' houses, zigzagging up the hillsides in irregular patterns, each set in its own plot of land with its own little piece of kitchen garden. The camp – it was more camp than town – was divided by a small river colloquially known as the Tank Stream. On the western side of it the huts were made of bark, or slab, or here and there canvas, and Mary surmised, correctly, this was where the convicts lived. Dominating everything and outstaring one another were the two brick-built, two-storey buildings that symbolised the power struggle that had gripped the colony from the beginning: Government House and the military barracks.

What Mary and her family could not see were the gallows, hidden away among the trees of Hyde Park, the convict chain-gangs, the drunks lurking in the mean and doubtful streets where no innocent person could walk in safety, the grog shops, the litter and the prevailing atmosphere of degeneracy and decay.

'So what happens now?' asked Hester. 'Are we to wait on board for the rest of our lives?'

'We're going to Parramatta,' said her mother.

'Where?'

'It's up the river fifteen miles. It's where the Governor lives.'

'And are we staying with the Governor?'

'We are. We will be the guests of Mr and Mrs King. So we

have to be patient a while longer. Parramatta is a pleasant place by all accounts, and perfectly safe for women.'

~

It is said that on their arrival Mary and her family went to stay with Governor King and his wife at Government House in Parramatta. I have searched for evidence of this and not found any (the Kings did not keep a visitors' book) but I am allowing it to be true because it makes a good story; and it's nice to think Mary and her family were allowed a short period of relative luxury before they set off on their tough new life in the bush.

The Governor of New South Wales was the British monarch's representative in the colony and it was a rare and special honour to be invited to stay with him. None of the other settlers on any of the three ships in the fleet appeared to share this privilege. Government House as it was in those days was not strictly speaking big enough to accommodate six guests, but then people were used to cramming into small spaces in those days, the Pitts not least among them.

If the story is true the clue once again would have been the family connection with Viscount Vice-Admiral Horatio Nelson. No other naval hero had ever been so honoured and for Governor King, who was a naval man, no other name could carry more weight and esteem.

Parramatta is a small town 24 kilometres up the Parramatta River from Sydney. Nowadays it's a business centre, all glass and concrete and virtually a suburb, but in Mary's time it was a second capital, safer, cleaner and altogether more salubrious than Sydney Town. Government House was the governor's 'country residence' and was built by Governor Hunter in 1799. The house is still there, enlarged since the time of Governor King and his lady wife Anna Josepha, who were about to become Mary and her family's hosts.

It was built on top of a slope with views looking down over the river. It was what is now referred to as Georgian in style, though its design probably owes more to Indian colonial architecture than anything to be seen in the old country. A wide, two-storey building, elegant, spare, and so concerned with symmetry some of the windows are fake, it contained six large rooms, three up and three down, connected, rather oddly, by an outdoor staircase at the back. The kitchen and the storeroom were housed in separate outbuildings behind the main house.

In 1801 the house was barely two years old and like other grand houses in the colony it was furnished in the English style. The front door was made of local wood, cleverly masked behind a veneer of English oak. Everything had been designed to make a person feel 'at home', even if home was several thousand miles away.

From her room on the upper floor of Government House Mary could look down over the garden to the river. It would have been a lovely sight were it not for the convict huts flanking the main pathway. Mary watched the men as they went about their business in the governor's garden. She found the sight unsettling. To her eyes it seemed they were little more than slaves.

I have her broaching the subject one morning with the amiable Mrs King.

'I understand your concerns,' the good lady responded. 'I thought much the same when I first arrived. But this is no ordinary prison – there are no bars, or compounds, so strictly speaking a convict is free to run away into the bush, which they occasionally do, to very ill result.' She frowned. 'But if you compare this with the sort of life they would have back at home, languishing in prison cells and hulks – what good is that? Here they can work for their ticket-of-leave, and then if they continue to work hard and keep out of trouble in due course they can achieve their pardon, and then all manner of opportunities are there for them!'

That was all very true, thought Mary, but it did not make the sight any less disquieting. At home felons were neatly packed away out of the public eye, you could live your life without giving them a moment's thought. Here they were right there in front of you, every day, on the streets, living among but not with you. Being forced to witness their public humiliation was something Mary thought she would never get used to.

'This country . . .' Mrs King continued, and then paused for a moment to glance out of the window. 'This country is a melting pot of the good and the unspeakable With the right leadership it could become the most glorious place on earth. But . . .' She paused again and shook her head.

Anna Josepha King was tiny, just four foot nine inches tall, a child's frame containing a woman's mind, and a woman's energy. Mary found the governor's wife most engaging. She was intrigued by the younger woman, by her intelligence and her lively interest in everything around her.

'Here, an individual can do only so much,' said Mrs King. 'But again one individual can achieve great things – my husband for instance, is a great man, a very great man, but sometimes even he despairs. There are factions, you understand Mrs Pitt – you know something of the history of this place?'

Mary nodded a little vaguely. 'Factions?'

'Yes. My husband has been in the colony since the very beginning, you know, so he has seen it all. Once, many years ago, he had such fervour, such energy. Now . . . We fight an upward battle, Mrs Pitt. But I don't mean to sound discouraging. You have done a brave thing by coming here. The country is in need of people like you.'

Mary Pitt smiled tremulously. She wasn't sure about the word 'brave'.

'And anyway,' Mrs King sighed, and then laughed merrily, in her curious but endearing way. 'We are the pioneers you see, Mrs Pitt. We can only trust in God to guide us in the right direction.'

Mary concurred.

'But enough of that. Tell me about your children.'

And so the two women got to talk of easier things. And

Mary learned that the governor and his wife had three children, two of whom were currently in England being educated along with *'Mr King's former two boys'*, whose names were Norfolk and Sydney (no prizes for guessing why), his children from a previous liaison with a convict. Needless to say they were part of the governor's former life, before Anna Josepha arrived on the scene, but such was her nature that she brought them up as if they were hers and insisted they receive as good an education as her own children.

~

In time Mary would have written to her cousin George. She would have described, in her punctuation-free way, the house they were staying in and its impressive garden, designed by Mrs King. She would have praised the intelligence and amiability of her hostess, and told him something of that good lady's good works with the orphans found running unregulated in the streets.

'She has founded an institution to take care of them which is colloquially called "Mrs King's Orphanage" in Sydney where the waifs are taken in fed educated and trained. It occupies her every waking hour and she visits daily. She is a resourceful woman and puts me to shame.'

Of her host she had little to say as yet because when he did pay one of his rare visits to the house he was to be seen only in glimpses, racing between one meeting and another. Sometimes his raised voice could be heard remonstrating with one of the many red-faced men who'd been kept waiting in the hallway, sometimes all day, for the opportunity to speak to him.

'He is an exceedingly busy man,' wrote Mary. 'And his health is not what it was, so Mrs King assures me, due to the stresses of trying to turn this "den of iniquity" as he calls it into the paradise he believes it could be. At the moment his priority is to reduce the consumption of what is termed "grog" which he claims is the scourge of the colony. Although he is it should be fair to say not averse to the odd drop himself and suffers gout as a result.

'It appears he is both kind and hot-tempered impatient and concerned but above all he is totally dedicated to the job in hand. He struggles with the British government back home and he struggles with the military in the name of the notorious New South Wales Corps with whom he is at permanent odds.

'There is one man in particular by the name of John Macarthur who was once with the Corps and now farms sheep and whose sole intent it seems is to overthrow each successive governor in turn. As a result of various misdemeanours Mr King has had him deported back to England in disgrace where he will surely be court martialled and probably hanged meanwhile his wife stays at home looking after the sheep which he insists will be the future of the colony.'

A few days after arriving the Pitt family experienced that most eccentric of occasions: the antipodean Christmas.

Christmas in Australia is by and large the European Christmas, with tinsel, trees with mock snow, reindeer and of course Father Christmas in full regalia – not much fun in 30 degrees. When I lived there in my younger days we did the full thing, ate hot turkey with trimmings in the middle of the day followed by Christmas pudding. It was one of the many British traditions that traditionalists held on to (and still do, though to a much lesser extent – nowadays it's more likely to be seafood and sparkling wine).

Mary described the event to her cousin thus:

'We have been hearing all along of food shortages and of the almost complete absence of beef or beefsteak. The day itself began with profuse apologies from Mr and Mrs King and then we were presented with a table groaning with roast chicken vegetables potatoes pumpkin and plum pudding. Lord Nelson's food you could say. And all this in the middle of the hottest day imaginable.

'After dinner Mr King sat us all down and regaled us with his dissertation on New South Wales which included his difficulties with the government back home and his views on the native people.

'We have yet to catch sight of one of them though I gather they are around and about living mostly nomadic among the trees. Mr King says his orders and his inclination is to strive to live peaceably with the people who he claims are "the real Proprietors of the Soil" and should be treated in no way different from a European. However his best efforts have all too often been rewarded by what he calls their "ungrateful conduct" and unpredictable behaviour.

'Finally dear Mr Matcham I have to give you news of the impending marriage of my daughter Lucy to John Wood who was third mate on board 'Canada'. The ceremony will take place here in Parramatta in a few days' time.'

~

Whether a seaman, third mate, was quite what Mary had in mind for her second daughter we'll never know.

What is recorded is that on 11 January 1802 under special licence granted by His Excellency Governor King, Lucy Wood, aged twenty-four, married John Wood, aged around twenty-seven, at St John's Church in Parramatta, which was then a little wooden hut that doubled as a carpenter's workshop. The ceremony was conducted by the Reverend Samuel Marsden and the witnesses were Thomas and Jemima Pitt.

Chapter 12

1801: The legend of Margaret Catchpole

WHILE MARY PITT and her family were standing on the deck of *Canada* waiting to make the journey to Parramatta the convict Margaret Catchpole was languishing in the bowels of *Nile* awaiting her fate.

According to one account this is what a female convict could expect on arriving at New South Wales:

> *'It has been a common Custom . . . that shortly after a Ship has anchored in the cove with female Convicts; Settlers, Soldiers, and Prisoners, have been permitted to go on Board; and make their respective Selections amongst them: and to induce these poor unfortunate women, some by threats and some by Promises, to accompany them to their Habitations & to become their mistresses . . . sometimes at the turfing out of former wives or mistresses to make way for them; and they in turn will be replaced and turfed out often with small children, to starve or fend for themselves.'*

It is hard to believe the authorities would have allowed what was effectively a pimping session to take place quite so brazenly. At the same time convict assignment in the new colony did seem to be much of a lottery.

For some reason the records for convicts on board *Nile* and *Canada* did not travel with them, so there was no official information on the prisoners' crimes or sentences or how long they had already served. Margaret's sentence, handed down at Bury Assizes in 1800, was for life.

~

I first met Margaret Catchpole many years ago. It was in my scriptwriting days in England and my aunt on my father's side, who lived in Suffolk, gave me a book called *The History of Margaret Catchpole* by the Reverend Richard Cobbold. It told the tale of a simple, hard-working Suffolk girl, a local heroine, who led a blameless life and whose courage and quick-thinking on different occasions saved the lives of a farmer's wife, and of several of her neighbours' and employer's children; but who was led astray by her passion for a smuggler called Will Laud and ended up being condemned for death twice, first for stealing a horse and then for breaking out of gaol, and wound up transported to Botany Bay. My aunt thought it would make a fine television series and I agreed with her. I spent the best part of a year writing Margaret's story, but the series never did get made, so I packed her away and forgot about her.

Then in the course of family research she cropped up again. And I realised this extraordinary woman not only travelled to New South Wales in the same fleet as my own family, she worked for them at various times in various guises: as midwife, nurse, companion and general helper. It was yet another exciting link in the family chain, and so I got to make Margaret Catchpole's acquaintance once again.

I quickly discovered the gap between the Reverend Cobbold's version of Margaret's life and the truth. While he had her working at the female factory and meeting and eventually marrying a man she once worked with back in England, who on being rejected by her had migrated to Botany Bay and became a wealthy businessman, the truth, while slightly more prosaic, was no less remarkable.

In her inimitable way, Margaret had somehow managed to impress Captain Sumpter of the *Nile* – possibly by helping deliver the baby of a passenger and free settler, Elizabeth Rouse. So on arrival at Port Jackson he recommended her as household cook to John Palmer, the colony's commissary, and his American wife Susan.

The commissary was in charge of the government stores. It was an immensely important and influential position and it was well rewarded. In the early 1800s the Palmers were building a substantial dwelling near Sydney Cove called Woolloomooloo House, which commanded what would now be million dollar views of the harbour.

'I am pretty well off at present . . .' wrote Margaret to Mrs Cobbold in January 1802.

It was Mrs Cobbold, mother of the Reverend Cobbold and Margaret's ex-employer, who originally taught Margaret to read and write, and who preserved the letters Margaret wrote back to her, and to her uncle and aunt, from New South Wales. It was those letters that provide a rare record of the early colony seen through the eyes of a convict. The first was written soon after her arrival, when Mary Pitt and her family were still, allegedly, staying at Government House with Governor and Mrs King.

New South Wales was, said Margaret, surprisingly like England, and parts of it reminded her of the Cobbold home in Suffolk. The gardens were full of geraniums seven or eight foot high and the birds were beautiful. She wrote of the convicts who'd had their heads shaved and were sent up the Coal River and forced to carry coal from day to night; of Norfolk Island, where prisoners were sent with steel collars around their necks; of the natives, who to her consternation walked around stark naked carrying spears, so she didn't know where to look. Like Mary she described the place as *'a wicked country'*, which she didn't like, *'no nor never shall.'*

Interestingly, she appears to have a certain amount of freedom. She could walk about - *'if I go but any distance here is going through woods for miles'* - so long as she was in the right place to attend the occasional muster. If she wanted to venture further afield, to the Hawkesbury River or to Parramatta, she could do so as long as she had a pass.

Margaret became a legend – though not in her own lifetime, fortunately for her – thanks partly to the Reverend's book.

Having married her off to a childhood sweetheart he had her ending her days living on the Hawkesbury in domestic bliss, surrounded by her children. She was dramatised on stage, screen and radio. Some years later a distant relative of the Pitt family, G B Barton, wrote his own version of her story, called *The True Story of Margaret Catchpole,* in an attempt to put the facts straight. As recently as 2010 her name was projected onto the walls of historic buildings in Macquarie Street as part of the bi-centenary celebrations of the arrival of Governor Macquarie.

There was something about Margaret that endeared her to the people she termed her 'betters'. Mrs Cobbold, whose children's lives she had saved and whose husband's horse she had stolen, remained a lifelong friend, correspondent and confidant. Mrs Palmer likewise. As she wrote to her uncle and aunt in May 1803,

> *'. . . i am well Beloved By all that know me and that is a Comfort . . . i all ways Goo into Better Compeney than myself – that is a monkest free peopell whear they mak as much of me as if I was a Ladey – Because I am the Commiseres Cook.'*

At one point, some years after Margaret died and thanks mostly to the Reverend's book, the newspapers were full of her. A party of literary gentleman made a pilgrimage to Richmond to visit what was reported to be her grave, only to find it was someone else's. She was seen riding around in a carriage in Sydney. There was no such person. She had been mistaken for another convict called Mary Reibey (Reibey threatened to sue the Reverend when this word got out). Oddest of all, there were two Margaret Catchpoles. This particular rumour came about from a remark in a letter written by GM Pitt, explaining the cause and time of her death.

But we are not there yet.

Chapter 13

1802: Settlement

WITH CHRISTMAS FESTIVITIES and his sister's wedding out of the way there would have been nothing to delay Thomas Pitt setting out for the Hawkesbury River, leaving the rest of the family behind at Government House. With him I am sending two convict servants and, quite probably, other new settlers such as William Small, Charles Webb, William Bowman and Richard Rouse.

In 1801 the 6000 European inhabitants of New South Wales were settled mostly in three places: Sydney Town, Parramatta and the Hawkesbury River. Very little of the country beyond those boundaries had been explored to any extent and no one had yet found a way through the barrier to the west of Sydney called the Blue Mountains.

The Hawkesbury River – aboriginal name Deerubbin – begins its journey of just under 300 miles as a series of streams rising a few miles inland from the Pacific Ocean, 50 miles south of Sydney. The streams travel west to converge and become the Nepean River and from there the river flows north, growing in size and momentum as it picks up other waterways on the way, then turns east and changes its name before gouging through perpendicular cliffs on its route back to the Pacific Ocean, emerging at Broken Bay, 50 miles north of Sydney. In the early days of settlement two sets of explorers set off from Sydney and Parramatta in different directions at exactly the same time – one group travelling southwest, the other northwest – and discovered two rivers hundreds of miles apart, which they called respectively the Nepean and the Hawkesbury, before realising some time later they were one and the same.

On a calm sunny day the Hawkesbury is the most beautiful river imaginable and nowadays you can travel upriver by boat with the postman, delivering mail and food to the little settlements crouched along its banks and only accessible by water. Or you can drive along the cliff tops several hundred feet above it and if the mood takes you drop down to picnic on a patch of grass by its banks, or catch one of many ferries across to the northern side, because there are not many bridges across the Hawkesbury.

But when the clouds come and rain threatens the river turns dark and deeply circumspect. 27,000 square miles of countryside spills its water into the Hawkesbury-Nepean so when it rains, and it can rain in New South Wales, the river becomes a monster.

It was near the banks of this river that, on 31 March 1802, Mary Pitt, William Bowman, Charles Webb, Richard Rouse, William Small, William Burgess, John Dight and Thomas Spencer were granted one hundred acres each of prime land at a place colloquially known as Green Hills, 'in the district of Mulgrave Place'. Most of these were 'second line' grants, meaning they were set back from the riverbank. The original thirty-acre plots on the river had been granted previously, mostly to emancipists.

It has been said, by Barbara Lamble among others, that there was a delay in issuing Mary's grant due to a missing signature on official papers from Nelson, which is why they had to wait for the admiral to return from Portugal to sign them. I have found no evidence of this. Governor King granted the same acreage in the same place on the same date, 31 March 1802, to a number of new settlers and there is no indication that Mary received special treatment at that stage.

Mary's grant was originally in Thomas's name apparently, altered later in the year to hers to allow him to receive his own

100 acres next door. As a female 'grantee' Mary was exceptional: very few women were given land in those days in their own right – her neighbour Jane McManus for instance had inherited hers from her late husband – and she was the only female in the Hawkesbury district to have come to the colony by choice.

Governor Phillip had first explored the Hawkesbury back in 1789 and found it the most fertile ground he had come across. After the relative barrenness of Sydney and the only slightly more fertile soil at Parramatta the land at the Hawkesbury at last offered the colony a real chance of survival. However Phillip also noticed debris caught high up in the trees some 30 or 40 feet above the normal height of the water. The river obviously flooded, badly, so he recommended that no one settle there until they were *'better acquainted with the country'*.

His successor, Lt-Governor Grose of the New South Wales Corps, was not so cautious however. In 1794 he proudly wrote,

> *'I have settled on the banks of the Hawkesbury twenty-two settlers, who seem very much pleased with their farms. They describe the soil as particularly rich . . .'*

And so it was, thanks partly to the constant flooding. The Hawkesbury took back with one hand what it gave with the other, and the early settlers paid a terrible price for their privileged position.

In 1800, less than two years before Mary and family arrived, the river flooded three times in four months, taking with it houses, livestock, crops, and on occasion, people. Each time it not only ruined the livelihoods of the local farmers it threatened the survival of New South Wales as a whole. The floods of 1800 wiped out half the grain produced in the colony and put it back onto starvation rations.

~

Mary's grant was not officially logged until 31 March 1802, though the records show that the Pitt family was on government stores from 26 December 1801. The location of the grant may have been recommended by Governor King, or it is possible Thomas was allowed to choose it. Whatever, I am imagining him setting off with his companions and covering the 50-odd miles from Parramatta by the as yet barely made-up road, keeping a close lookout for bushrangers.

The countryside around the Hawkesbury had never been cultivated before. The Aboriginal people did not farm in the sense in which we know it; they took what they wanted from their surroundings and moved on. The land at Mulgrave Place was covered with a blanket of trees so thick you could barely see the ground, let alone pitch a tent on it. So it had to be cleared before anything resembling a house could be built, or a crop grown.

Thomas had two convicts to help him but they only had the most primitive tools for the job. They not only had to hack the trees down – leaving stumps of course, as there were no means for removing those – they had to dispose of them, probably by burning. It's unlikely any of them had built a house before, or hacked down a tree. The task that faced them was overwhelming.

In due course Thomas would have written to his mother:

'February 1802, Mulgrave Place.

Dear mother,

The land is heavily wooded. Parts of it are on high ground and the remainder slopes steeply down towards the river, though the boundary stops some way short of it. First a space must be cleared in order to build some form of habitation for us all. At the moment I am living under canvas, but soon we will dig posts and begin constructing a house big enough for us all to live in in some comfort. I am confident this can be achieved in the next few weeks.

Already we are turning what turf we can by hoe and planting wheat. It is hard work, but rewarding to see progress. I have taken to strolling down the hill at daybreak to gaze through the trees at the reflection of the light on the water, and as I do so I think of you and imagine how your heart will swell at the sight.

In the morning before dawn we hear the cackle of the kookaburra, and as the light breaks all manner of birdsong bursts forth, some melodious, most of it quite raucous and none as gentle or tuneful as the birds at home.

I trust you are keeping well mother. Please remember me to the girls, and to Mr and Mrs King. Be a bit more patient, and in less time than you know it, as cousin George promised, "Your comforts will crowd upon you" indeed.

Your devoted son, Thomas.'

~

Of course this was not the full story. Already Thomas had been there a month and between them the three men had barely scratched the surface of his mother's tree-clad acres. The wood was harder than any he'd ever come across, and the only tools they had were saws, picks and primitive axes. There were no animals to pull a plough so everything had to be done by hand, from the lopping of trees to the hoeing of the ground to prepare it for planting. He worked from sun up to sun down with his convict workers, and they had to be constantly needled in order to do anything at all. As for taking the time to stroll down the hill and gaze at the river, there was barely time to eat, let alone contemplate. At night Thomas would lie awake in his tent, exhausted, listening to the alien sounds of crickets, frogs and bats and the distant howling of dingoes, pondering the enormity of what lay ahead.

From nothing, from less than nothing, he had to build a family home for five people to live in, miles from anywhere, on alien soil teeming with who-knows-what manner of unfamiliar creatures, snakes and insects he didn't know the names of and didn't understand, amid foreign trees in a foreign climate where the sun beat down on him like a hammer, sapping every ounce of energy he had; where every movement among the trees could be a native about to stick a spear through his back.

What he also had not told his mother, and never would, were the grim stories he'd picked up on the local grapevine. The previous year the Hawkesbury farmers had sent a petition to Governor King asking for extra time to settle their debts on account of the hardship they were suffering as a result of *'successive floods within the last two years, which have almost ruined them.'*

And then there were the natives.

There had been problems between settlers and Aborigines at the Hawkesbury from the start, and in 1795 a detachment of the New South Wales Corps had been sent there to keep order. In September 1799, just over two years before Thomas's arrival, two Aboriginal boys had been murdered on the Hawkesbury by a group of white settlers and their bodies dumped in a ditch, their hands tied behind their backs. The boys, aged seventeen and thirteen, had been known to the settlers and their bodies were witnessed by, among others, Lieutenant Robert Braithwaite, Mary's unexpected visitor on *Canada*. (Hopefully he did not burden Mary with this story.)

The murders, it transpired, were in revenge for the recent killings by Aborigines of two white settlers on a hunting trip, which in turn was in revenge for one of the hunters living with an Aboriginal woman. There was no evidence the two boys were involved in the crime but they had been foolish enough, so went the official report, to turn up at a settler's house with a musket belonging to one of the dead men. That in the settlers' view was enough to make them legitimate targets.

The boys' murderers were quickly identified, rounded up and tried. The court unanimously found them guilty but could not agree on the sentence and so, to Governor Hunter's consternation, the guilty men were set free pending a decision from England on their fate. Hunter was horrified. It was not the first time he had brought a case to court in order to prevent what he called *'this horrid practice of wantonly destroying the natives'*. Having to refer the business back to England only made things worse; in this case it took two and a half years to receive the 'official' verdict, which was to free the men on conditional pardon. So effectively they got away with it completely.

Governors from Phillip onwards had been given specific instruction by King George to befriend the indigenous people and encourage the settlers to *'live in amity and kindness with them'*; and if any of his subjects wantonly destroyed them or interfered in an indigenous person's business they were to be punished accordingly.

Try telling that to a jittery settler.

The defendants at the trial claimed that they had been given official permission by the Commanding Officer at the Hawkesbury, Lieutenant Thomas Hobby, to shoot any Aborigines on sight. Hobby denied this but said there was a rumour going around, told to him by Lieutenant Braithwaite, that a large number of Aborigines were threatening to come down from the Blue Mountains to massacre some white people, particularly soldiers, in revenge for the killing of an Aboriginal woman and her child *'by a soldier called Cooper'*.

And so it went on. Despite the governors' best efforts there was very little trust and virtually no understanding between settlers and Aborigines, on the Hawkesbury or elsewhere. If one side created a disturbance – burned a settler's crops for instance, or raped an Aboriginal man's wife or murdered a settler or an Aborigine – the other side considered it perfectly acceptable to avenge themselves on the first Aborigine, or the first settler, they came across, regardless of whether or not they were involved in the original crime. When questioned, the settlers swore they only attacked the Aborigines when provoked. Had the Aborigines been asked the same question (they weren't) they may well have pointed out that since the land belonged to them in the first place any crops grown on it, by whoever, were theirs to burn, or to steal, as the mood took them. And that the overall provocation created by a bunch of foreigners moving into their country, growing crops on their land and taking the fish from their rivers far exceeded anything any Aboriginal person had ever done to any settler.

~

Meanwhile back in Parramatta Mary and her family were

getting restless. Government House was splendid, but they did not want to overstay their welcome. One afternoon in March Thomas received a letter saying they were arriving in seven days, 'whether you are ready for us or not'.

Ready? Of course he wasn't ready – how could he be, what could one man with two not very willing helpers be expected to achieve in such a short time? They'd be lucky to see walls and a roof over their heads, any kind of roof. As for the floor...

And so I picture Mary, Susanna, Jemima and Hester – and probably Lucy also, whose new husband was in Sydney at the time looking for work – climbing into a wagon one day in late March 1802 and being driven with their few possessions along the track that was not yet a road from Parramatta to the Hawkesbury River.

Chapter 14

1802: Foundations

JAMES HORSE STOOD WATCHING as the wagon appeared at the end of the rough track and rumbled slowly towards him. His boss, Thomas Pitt, stood next to him, shifting nervously from one foot to the other. They had been there for the best part of an hour.

At last the wagon pulled up and James watched as Mr Pitt went forward to greet his family. A grey-haired woman with a glowing face and a broad smile stepped carefully down from the carriage and bent to kiss her son on the cheek. Behind her appeared a tall, blonde, pale-looking woman, smoothing her skirt as she gingerly placed both feet on the ground. Next came a woman of similar height but with a darker complexion, gazing about her in a languid fashion. After her scrambled a smaller, younger, anxious-looking girl with freckles, and finally, with a flourish and a merry little leap, the last of the daughters – not unlike her sisters but without the anxiety.

'So here we are!' cried Jemima, stretching out her arms and taking a deep breath. 'Thomas!' She turned to her startled brother and clasped him to her. 'How wonderful to see you! You look terrible!'

'Thank you Jem and welcome,' said Horse's boss, smiling over his sister's shoulder. 'Welcome everyone – Susanna, Hester, Lucy. Welcome mother, to your new property.'

'Thank you Thomas,' said the grey haired woman. She had a soft voice, with the slightest country burr. She turned and gazed around her. 'So this is my home.'

'Mother, you have to realise . . .' The boss was gabbling slightly. Horse had never seen him like this before. 'Let me explain. It's primitive. And it isn't ready. I – we've done what we can, we've worked all the hours there are, day and nights too, but it's not what you're expecting. It's . . .'

'Tom!'

'What?'

'Shut up,' said the girl called Jem.

'Show me my new home,' said his mother.

The grey-haired woman tucked her arm into her son's and the little party, picking up its skirts and stepping delicately, made its way through the trees to the little hut on the hill overlooking the wooded slope that led down to the river. Horse found the sight both faintly ridiculous and strangely moving: these women with their fresh frocks and their stately manners picking their way nervously through the brush to inspect their new home, which was frankly no more than a bark hut – the walls part wattle, part strips of bark, with bark for a roof and bare mud for a floor. He watched as they stepped tentatively over the non-existent threshold of the structure he had unwillingly toiled over. He heard their chatter and the odd burst of laughter and wondered that anyone could get so excited about something made out of nothing more than sticks and the skins of trees.

They emerged again a short time later, still bravely smiling. The boss was prattling on about nothing very much, nervously batting away non-existent flies. And then a surprisingly moving thing: his mother placed a finger on her son's lips and said softly, 'Thomas, I would be happy with a strip of canvas. This is my home.'

'Yes,' he said.

'My first, remember?'

'Yes, mother.'

Her first home? Well there was a thing. Horse had conjured a picture in his mind of some great manor with an ornamental lake somewhere in the British countryside, and she the lady of it. So what in God's name made her come to this godforsaken place?

'And who is this?' The dark-haired one called Jem was staring at him. The boss was momentarily speechless. Goddammit he's gone and forgotten my name, thought Horse.

'This is . . .'

'James Horse,' he said. 'Government man.'

'You're Irish!' The girl's eyes lit up. 'Where from?'

'Longford.'

'And you work for the government?'

'He's a convict,' the boss explained. 'It's the local term for convict.'

'A convict!' Jem's eyebrows twitched. 'So, what did you do? What terrible crime did you commit that got you sent out here?'

'I made the oath.'

'You swore? Is that a transportable offence?'

Even Horse had to smile at this. 'No, miss. I gave the oath. The Defenders' oath.'

'The what?'

'Jem, that's enough for now,' said Thomas. And he put his arm through his sister's and wheeled her away.

Mary went to stand in front of her house. Her heart had relocated itself in the region of her delicate and totally inappropriate lace-up boots.

She'd expected her new home to be primitive, but this was beyond anything she could have imagined.

It was a mess. What ground had been cleared was strewn with stumps and broken branches, and the trees in front of the house were so thick you could barely see through them to the river she'd been assured was beyond.

As for the house itself: the floor was mud, impacted mud, not soft and wet like back home but mud nonetheless. It was one room divided roughly into two by a strip of ragged-looking hessian hung from the roof. At one end there was a primitive fireplace made out of randomly collected rocks, with a hole in the roof where the chimney should be. There was no privacy at all. The whole thing looked as flimsy as a pack of cards – one puff of wind and it looked as if it would collapse into pieces. It had none of the solidity, the permanence of May Cottage. It was a pretend place, like something out of a weird fairy tale.

Thomas had done his best, she knew that, she had no right to be disappointed. But as she stood there gazing over her land, the first piece of land that was ever truly hers, all 100 acres of it – a hundred times the size of her place back home – it was all she could do not to weep.

Yet it was hers, all hers. Everything had to start somewhere. She drew herself up straight and took a deep breath of the clear, autumnal, Hawkesbury air.

'I shall call his place Pitt Farm,' she pronounced, to no one in particular, and to everyone.

Chapter 15

1802: Government men

THOMAS'S CONVICT WORKERS shared 'quarters' some distance away from the boss and his family. It was not much more than a piece of bark strung between two trees and strips of canvas laid on the ground to remind the lizards, snakes and other creeping things that there was some difference between the wretched creatures who crawled the earth and the wretched ones who walked on it, even if it was only a layer of cloth.

In all the time they'd been there the two men had barely spoken more than a dozen words to one another. James Horse had been transported for life from Ireland for (presumably) swearing an anti-British oath; and Thomas Christmas, convicted at the Old Bailey for stealing a sheep and transported for life from London, was an Englishman.

Separately they observed their boss's family going about the business of making a home for themselves. It was both an amusing and an occasionally touching thing to watch those delicate ladies with their pale skins trying to make sense of their surroundings. Their preoccupation with their personal appearance, their insistence on washing themselves every time a speck of dirt appeared on a cheek, their reluctance to replace their skimpy unsuitable bonnets with tougher, wide-brimmed hats. But through it all they had to admire their spirit, their determination, their energy.

The mother and the tall fair-haired girl, the one they took to be the eldest, kept themselves to themselves and spent their time sowing seeds and gardening. The youngest meanwhile, the little one with the freckles, not much older than twelve or thirteen years old by the look of her, spent most of her time in close encounters with the wild life. She could frequently be spotted on her hands and knees, tracing the movement of some creature through the undergrowth, stalking a grasshopper with a finger or gazing for minutes on end at a spider's web. And those spiders were something to be reckoned with – ten times the size of anything back at home and probably ten times as venomous – who knew what was venomous and what wasn't? One time she came running up to Christmas to tell him she'd seen an alligator down near the waterhole, and something that looked like a squirrel only not a squirrel, and then she checked herself, looked flustered, and scampered away, as if she realised she shouldn't really be talking to him at all.

The older sister, Jemima, had no such qualms. As often as not she was the one handing out the orders – do this, fetch that, bring me this – as if she was in charge of things. But she worked hard herself too, a good deal harder than they did, truth be known.

Horse had perfected, or hoped he had, the technique for appearing to work without putting much effort in. You could look as if you were hacking away at a tree and, with a bit of exaggeration, you could stagger a bit and stand there hanging your head with sheer exhaustion, wiping away the non-existent sweat from your brow, and so on, especially if you knew you were being watched.

'You're taking a very long time over that tree, Horse,' said Jemima one day.

Horse stood upright and clutched his back, breathing heavily.

'I heard you were flogged seventy-two times on board Britannia for taking the Defenders' oath.'

She was watching for his reaction.

'And where did you hear that?'

'Never mind. Is it true?'

'Maybe.'

'And what is it, exactly, the Defenders' oath?'

Horse gave her a sideways look. She stood with one hand shielding her eyes against the sun, the other on her hip, smiling at him in what may or may not have been a faintly mocking manner.

'You really want to know?' he asked eventually.

'I can hazard a guess. It's to do with republicanism, obviously, and a hatred of all things British.'

'You tell me then.'

You swear "to overthrow the kings and restore the true religion that was lost in the reformation". Or words to that effect.'

'You've been doing some homework.' He squinted back at her through narrowed eyes. She spooked him.

'And look where it got you.'

Horse did not reply.

'I also heard,' continued Jemima, 'you had a rough trip over.'

'You could say.'

'Why was that?'

Horse leaned his axe on the ground, sighed and stretched.

'I could tell you, if you really want to know,' he said. 'But I'd need to park my backside first.'

'By all means.' Jemima took the initiative and sat down on a tree stump. She waited, back straight, hands folded neatly on her lap, for all the world like a lady about to embark upon social intercourse in a Chelsea drawing room.

Horse found himself a stump a short distance from her.

'So?' she said.

'The journey took us six months, from Cork to Port Phillip,' Horse began. Then he paused, for a moment lost in thought.

'Yes?'

'We were kept in irons throughout the journey. Irons are heavy metal cuffs bound around the feet.'

'I know what irons are.' said Jemima. 'The convicts on 'Canada' had them, but they didn't have to wear them all the time.'

'The slightest movement and the cuff rubs the skin so after a day or so the skin is so chafed it's starting to bleed and any further movement and it's like a bank of razors scraping across your ankles. After a few more days the blisters are starting to harden and callous, and then a few more days after that the calluses are beginning to fester.'

Jemima kept her gaze fixed on him.

'The captain kept us in irons throughout the journey,' he continued. 'When we were allowed on deck, which wasn't often, he had us chained to the sides of the ship in case anyone decided to jump overboard and swim across the ocean to the nearest continent. And if any man was caught tampering with the irons he was given six dozen lashes. That's for a first offence.'

'On 'Canada' they let the convicts on deck at every opportunity,' Jemima offered. 'And they weren't in irons.'

'That's because she was an English ship carrying English convicts.'

Jemima's stare didn't waver.

'The captain got it into his head there was mutiny planned. James Brannon was given 300 lashes on one day and 500 the next. It took him six weeks to die. Patrick Garnley was given 400 lashes and died the next morning, not from the lashings, from the thirst. Patrick Garodby the same, and Connor. When Brannon was flogged the third time the Captain decided the cat wasn't cutting into the flesh deeply enough...'

'The cat?'

'Cat o' nine tails. So he got some horseskin and knotted it, so it could do the job properly. They beat the women too.'

'There were women on board as well?'

'They had their heads shaved and the troublesome ones put in neck-yokes. Then the captain took it upon himself to personally cut off Jenny Blake's hair and beat her with a cane, and all because she tried to kill herself.' Horse laughed, without humour. 'Six of us were killed by the captain for the sheer brutal hell of it and not a soul stood in his way. Not the surgeon, not any of them.'

There was silence.

'Shortly after we left port the water started coming in and it went on coming in the whole of the journey. So some of the men had no bed to sleep in and had to spend the nights sitting. Ten men died and one woman. Not from sickness but from cruelty and deliberate neglect. There'd have been a good deal more of them if we'd been British.'

'What do you mean?' asked Jemima.

Horse gave her a hard look. 'When we got to Port Jackson, word got out and the Governor tried to have the captain and surgeon tried for cruelty. But the British government didn't want a bar of it. No surprises there. So yes, it was a rough trip, you could say.'

There was a pause. Horse looked into the distance.

'Would you call yourself a political prisoner, Horse?' Jemima asked.

'Every convict in the colony is a political prisoner,' Horse replied, after a moment. 'If a government forces its people to have to choose between starving to death and stealing in order to stay alive, the government is the guilty party. Every convict in this land is a political convict.'

'I'm not sure I agree with that,' said the young woman rather primly. 'A felony is a felony after all.'

He shrugged.

'You can ask me about me if you want,' Jemima went on.

'That's all right,' Horse replied. 'I'm not that interested, tell the truth.'

He regretted it the moment he said it. Not because he was afraid of insulting the boss's sister but because it would have given him a little longer to go on sitting on that tree stump.

'Very well,' she said, getting to her feet. She stood looking down at him. 'Now that you're here, Horse, are you going to put your grievances behind you?'

'Isn't that a damned if I do, damned if I don't sort of a

question?' said Horse, with a slight smile.

'I'm sorry to hear your story,' said Jemima, smiling back. 'But I don't need to tell you there will be no tolerance here for any kind of – Irishness.'

'Irishness?'

'We're all in the same boat here, Horse. It's an opportunity to put political differences behind us, don't you agree?'

Horse did not reply.

'Time to get back to work,' she said, as she turned and went.

~

In 1802 there were over 1000 Irish convicts in New South Wales, roughly half of whom had been transported for political crimes. Of those political prisoners a good proportion were Defenders, and a good proportion of the Defenders had arrived on the *Britannia*.

Almost without exception Thomas Pitt's convict workers over the years were lifers. Convicts with life sentences were considered a good bet, likely to serve some years before receiving their pardon. Lifers were not murderers or serious criminals: they were most likely petty thieves who'd been transported, like Thomas Christmas, for stealing an item such as a sheep.

Thomas Christmas, aka Spicer, was tried at the Old Bailey on 17 September 1800.

'Joseph Thomas and Thomas Christmas were indicted for feloniously stealing, on the 7th of September, a wether-sheep, value 40s., the property of John Ireson.'

The sheep were being penned at Smithfield Market, ready to be sold the following day. The man who brought the case was Ireson's drover, Thomas Sculthorpe. In court, Sculthorpe said he saw Joseph Thomas and Thomas Christmas blatantly stealing one of Sculthorpe's 'pole-wethers' – whatever they are, he had three of them and they were specially marked – and placing it with their own. The following morning he took Ireson down to the pen where the pole-wether was and showed him the identifying marks that had been 'ruddled', or tampered with.

'. . . We know that a shepherd knows the face of every sheep as well as a man knows his wife's face; but you, as a drover, cannot know the faces of the sheep?' challenged the defending counsel.

'No,' replied Sculthorpe.

'But I suppose you are pretty well acquainted with the marks of sheep?'

'Yes.'

'. . . You did not tell the prisoners that they were doing wrong?'

'No.'

'If you had supposed the defendants were stealing it, you would have stopped them?'

'I knew they were doing wrong; I followed them, and saw the sheep safe.'

'Therefore, in point of fact, you had never lost the sheep at all, you always knew where to find it?'

'They might have taken it away.'

'. . . But, you know, you might have saved the sheep, and saved this prosecution, if you had told them they were doing wrong?'

'I followed them to see where they went.'

'Upon your oath, don't you know there is a reward for sheep-stealing?'

'I have heard of it.'

'So this sheep was never lost at all; and you came here to prosecute, in order to get a share of the reward?'

'It was drove away,' Sculthorpe persisted.

It is shocking to think a man like Sculthorpe could deliberately condemn two fellow drovers to death just in order to get his hands on a reward. Joseph Thomas and Thomas Christmas pleaded guilty and offered no defence. They were sentenced to death, commuted – in Christmas's case at least – to transportation to New South Wales for life. He was twenty-eight years old.

Chapter 16

2007: Bronte

It is 2007 and I am sitting in the Hawkesbury Library in Windsor, New South Wales, with my Australian cousin Libby. It's early days in our researches and among all the other books and papers piled up on the table in front of us is a folder with a cutting from a local newspaper about a woman who is restoring an old house called 'Bronte', in Agnes Banks on the Castlereagh Road a couple of miles west of nearby Richmond. We think the house must have some connection with our family, but when we ask the librarian if it is open to the public she tells us firmly 'no'; it is a private residence and we can't just roll up and expect to be invited in.

Fair enough. Still, it's an easy place to find as it's marked on the Gregory's street map of Sydney. And we're thinking what the hell, the worst thing that can happen is we'll be greeted by the wrong end of a shotgun and a lady yelling at us to get our filthy something selves off her land.

So we're on the Castlereagh Road and here it is, a sign by the road: 'Historic Bronte. Est 1809'. The gate is wide open and Libby drives through it and up the short driveway to the house. A very pregnant cow stares balefully at us over a fence, and a middle-aged woman in gumboots is standing outside the house gazing at the cow. No shotgun. We pull up. She switches her gaze from the cow to me as I open the car door and struggle to remember the name.

'Margaret Betts?'

'Yes.'

'Hello, you don't know us, we're descendants of Mary Pitt, Mary and Thomas Pitt, they used to live here back in 1802, we just thought we'd . . .'

'Okay.' She shows no surprise at all. 'You better come in.'

She leads us around the side of the house to the back door. We pass trees bursting with lemons and oranges, and a bush weighted down by what back home we call pomelo – a form of thick-skinned grapefruit. An old dog waddles across the courtyard to check us out, stretches, yawns, and waddles away again.

The lady of the house opens the mesh door and holds it for us as she kicks off her boots.

'I've no idea why they built it facing this way.' She gestures at the courtyard. 'Gets the full blast of the westerlies. What they should have done, they should have moved it around this way, facing north, then you'd get the shelter, yeah, and the outlook. But they didn't know what they were doing in those days, and they still don't. Come in.'

'You don't seem particularly surprised to see us,' I venture. We are inside her kitchen now and she is already filling the kettle.

'Not at all,' she says. 'I know who you are. You're not the first Pitts to come knocking on my door out of the blue looking for your ancestors. They've been coming here for years, from all over the world. I've got a dossier on you. I know all about your family. America, England, all over the place they come from. And everyone brings their own bit of information – I've got a file somewhere. I know more about the Pitt family than I do about my own. Sugar? And I told myself as I saw you stepping out of the car looking sheepish – here comes another lot, I told myself. No offence. Sit down. Milk?'

Phew.

So here we are, sitting around the kitchen table with cups of tea and Margaret Betts, short, ruddy-faced, a mass of grey hair, smiling broadly and looking at us expectantly.

She pushes up her sleeves.

'So, what can I do for you?'

It's a good question. I haven't really prepared myself, I am a bit overwhelmed to tell the truth to find myself so quickly and easily on the very same piece of land my ancestors first lived on and farmed in 1802 (the date on the sign on the road is wrong).

According to the piece in the local paper we know that Margaret Betts is going to some lengths and expense to restore the exterior of the house to its original 19th century glory. It is pretty surprising to find in this country of 'knock-downs' that such an old house still exists. And it's even more of a thrill to find it retains the name of 'Bronte', given to it 200 years ago in honour of our not-quite-relative Admiral Nelson.

It is not the original house that Thomas built, however. It is, says Margaret, probably the third house to be built on this particular piece of land, dating from some time in the mid to late 1800s. 'After the big flood of 1867,' she says, 'on account of there's no sign the house itself was ever flooded.' (Since then an informed friend has visited the house and dated it at around the 1840s, which suggests the great flood didn't quite reach that high.)

'There's no cellar, which is unusual,' Margaret goes on. 'I inherited it from my family, my mother was still farming the place in her nineties – here's a picture of her aged 92 riding a quad bike – they bought it back in the '50s, and when she died, that's when I moved in. And I'm here for the duration no matter how hard they try to get rid of me.'

'Who's 'they'?'

'The council. They'd get more rates if it was divided up, but I'm not dividing up, not for anyone. Come and have a look around.'

She takes us through the house. It is a solid structure, and rather magnificent. The doors are cedar, as were the original floors apparently until the white ant got to them. The interior, as designed by Margaret, is more 1950s than 1840s, and the only obvious modern additions are the kitchen and the bathroom, the latter of which in true Aussie style is only accessible through an outside door leading off the veranda.

We follow Margaret along the hallway to the front of the house. There's a beautifully kept garden, and now we can see the house in its full glory.

It is an immensely pleasing sight. There is something about the proportions of this low, wide, single-storey building, with its tiled roof and a second corrugated iron roof sheltering the wide veranda with its delicate-looking cast iron supports, that give the house an air of confidence, balance and timelessness. The overall effect is simple but stunning, very colonial Australian.

The house is built on a rise, facing northeast, and on the northern side the land slopes steeply down to the Hawkesbury River flood plain. Cattle graze in the fields – or paddocks, as they are called here – below. We could almost be in England, or perhaps Wales. It is surprisingly green for a late Australian summer.

'You should have been here a couple of weeks ago,' says the lady of the house. 'Not a blade of grass to be seen. We've had a shocking summer. But all it takes is a shower or two and you'd think you were in paradise.'

And it's at that very moment that I realise why I am here.

I am standing where my four times great grandmother would have stood, gazing down over the lower paddocks to the Hawkesbury River – more visible now than it would have been 200 years ago because there are fewer trees; but otherwise it's the same view that Mary and her family looked out on every day.

This is why I came to Australia.

I am looking out at what appears to be the lushest of fertile countrysides and beginning to appreciate something that every true-blue Aussie knows from the moment he or she leaves the womb: the significance of water. I am beginning to realise how quickly and totally a shower of rain can transform the parched earth. I am imagining how time and again Mary and her family would have prayed for rain in a drought, and then gazed in horror as their prayers were answered with a vengeance and the river burst its banks and advanced at horrific and unbelievable speed towards the house.

Margaret walks us round the side of the house to a place slightly lower down on the edge of a paddock. 'We reckon this spot roundabout here is where the second house was built, whenever that was, where these old bricks are. And the first house, the house your Mary and Thomas first built we reckon was pretty much right there.'

She is pointing at a modern building beyond her boundary fence.

'Your neighbours built over it?'

'Yes. There was nobody to stop them. Nobody knew anything in those days and they still don't. Each house was built on slightly higher ground because of the floods. It still floods mind you, but not as badly it used to, not now they've built the Warragamba dam. They say 1867 was the worst, the river came right up over the rise as far as the road.'

'How much land do you have?'

'Seventy-five acres. The other twenty-five were sold off before my time.'

'So it's nearly intact?'

'Yes. Nearly the very same 100 acres your Thomas was granted way back in whenever it was. It's the only property around here that hasn't been subdivided into a dozen lots or more. Like your Mary's property next door.'

It gets more and more astonishing.

'I'd like to buy some of it back again, only they're asking one and a half million for a five acre plot that's only got a shed on it.' This is prime land indeed.

We have found the original piece of land granted to Thomas Pitt in September 1802. It could have been a multi-storey car park, or an office block or shopping mall. It could have been subdivided into tiny pieces, like all the other plots around it. It could have been the property of Mr and Mrs DS, who the following year will refuse to let us inside the house Mary lived in in Fiddleford.

But not only is it still farming land, very nearly the size and shape it was two hundred years ago, but the house on it, built for a later Pitt generation, is being restored single-handedly, with love, care and at a great deal of expense, by a redoubtable, resourceful, big-hearted, no-nonsense woman with a strong sense of family – our family, that is – and heritage.

She shows us some of the original tree stumps, and a pile of wood that may have once been an early slab hut. She points to the far side of the main road, which is thickly wooded, and you can see, assuming it was all like that once, what Thomas and his family had to contend with.

There's more: the whole farm having been laboriously cleared, not just by the earliest settlers but by more recent owners who grew vegetables and thought the trees sapped the goodness out of the soil, Margaret is now in the process of replacing the original trees, including casuarinas – which she has discovered naturally soak up pesticides – and others not native to the region such as hoop pines, bunyas and kurrajongs. All to the annoyance of her neighbours.

'They don't like that it attracts birds,' she says, with something approaching a scoff.

In addition to restoring the house and planting trees Margaret farms her 75 acres on her own, with some help from her son Brendan. She farms cattle which, she says, is so unprofitable at times she feels she is 'going out backwards'.

~

An hour or so later we're driving back down towards the road, the boot of the car laden with lemons, limes and pomelos. The pregnant cow that Margaret was looking at as we first arrived is still staring balefully at us over the fence. But she is no longer pregnant. At her feet, all but hidden in the grass and so new it isn't yet standing up, is her new-born calf. I can't help feeling it's an omen.

Chapter 17

Settlers or invaders?

YOU CANNOT RESEARCH your Australian family history without becoming engrossed in Australian colonial history, and you cannot research Australian colonial history without sooner or later coming upon the 'history wars'.

History is written by the victors, so it's said, and in Australia's case it also changes according to the government of the time. In my travels to and from that country over recent years I've witnessed some of its more poignant moments. I was there in 2000 for the great Reconciliation March across Sydney Harbour Bridge. I was there for the general election in 2007, when Labour's Kevin Rudd replaced the long-serving Liberal Prime Minister John Howard, and again the following year when Rudd made his famous apology to the 'stolen generation' of Aboriginal people: a symbolic gesture perhaps but one that meant a great deal to Australians in general, and signalled a possible new direction in the interpretation and understanding of Australian history.

Were the British, or Europeans as they are generally referred to, settlers or invaders? Should Australia be celebrating itself as one of the most successful countries in the world, which was John Howard's view, or apologising for its dark past – what came to be known as 'the black armband' version of history: the colonial guilt resulting not just from the taking of land from the indigenous population who had lived in the country successfully and unmolested for over 60,000 years, but the cruel and often barbaric treatment of those people by the settlers or invaders; some – but not all – of it done for well-meaning, if paternalistic reasons?

When the Europeans first hit on the idea of settling in Botany Bay it was their intention to buy the land from the indigenous people. But Sir Joseph Banks told them they didn't work that way, that since they were nomadic they would happily give up whatever land was required, which was why the country was declared by the British government to be *terra nullius*, or no-man's-land.

Almost all the more bizarre opinions and decisions about the colony were created by people living thousands of miles away from it. Yet the concept of *terra nullius* was frequently challenged by men on the spot. In *Australia: Origins to Eureka* Thomas Keneally quotes David Collins, judge advocate in the colony, writing in the 1790s:

> '*. . . strange as it may appear, they* [the Aborigines] *have also their real estates. Bennelong, both before he went to England, and since his return, often assured me that the island of Me-mel (called by us Goat Island), close by Sydney Cove, was his own property; that it was his father's, and that he should give it to Bygone, his particular friend and companion.*'

Nonetheless it was the first two or three generations of European migrants who drove the indigenous people back. It was people like Mary and Thomas Pitt who were responsible for divesting the original inhabitants of the land they had roamed freely on for thousands of years.

At the same time it was the first two or three generations of migrants who by sheer bloody-minded, backbreaking hard work turned what to the western eye was a hostile, uncultivated and undesirable country into one of the most coveted places on earth. Times were hard in 19th century Britain, but the kind of fight for survival that was part of the Aussie pioneer's daily life was something else entirely.

It didn't help matters that from the very beginning the colony was regarded with some derision back in the old country, again by people who'd never been there. It was the butt of jokes in the press and particularly in cartoons. When William Wentworth published a book entitled *A Statistical, Historical, and Political Description of the Colony of New South Wales* in the 1820s, calling for among other things self government in New South Wales, the powers that be back in Blighty hooted with laughter.

'At present,' said the Reverend Sydney Smith a few years later, *'we are afraid that a Botany Bay parliament would give rise to jokes.'*

Not much has changed in the 21st century. Australia rarely features in the British press, other than on the sports pages, with the exception of major disasters such as the Victorian bush fires of 2009, or the occasional stories about the big drought in New South Wales or the floods in Queensland (and more recently all over east Australia); or – because it made for spectacular pictures – the Sydney dust storm of September 2009. From time to time on an inside page you can find a human interest story, so-called, usually featuring a person from Queensland and a crocodile, a koala or a kangaroo, which helps perpetuate the myth of Australia as the land of whacky people and weird wildlife.

A while ago I heard the usually wise and witty Sandi Toksvig, following a piece of news concerning an Australian university on 'The News Quiz' on BBC Radio 4, comment: 'Ah, so they have universities in Australia, do they?' That annoyed me almost as much as a few years before, when I found myself sitting on a boat on a trip up the Swan River in Perth and being bombarded by an endless barrage of anti-pom jokes from the commentator; as in 'Wave at the folks on the towpath ladies and gents, and if they don't wave back it means they're a stuck-up pom.' All of which goes to show old stereotypes never die.

Chapter 18

1802: The house that Thomas built

THE FIRST HOUSE THAT Thomas and his convict helpers built would most likely have been in the ancient wattle and daub design, a system that goes back to early Anglo Saxon days. The frame was made of wooden posts set into the ground several feet apart, and between them were woven layers made from saplings, or whatever pliant wood could be found. Gaps would be left for a door and for windows and, that done, the outside would be coated with mud. The roof was made from bark stripped from the trees, which was hardly weatherproof, leaving a space for a chimney. The floor was the bare earth and the windows and door were hung with bark.

When it rained the mud, lacking mortar to hold it together, would have washed away and had to be replaced. The roof would have leaked and whatever fire they had built in the kitchen area would have been instantly extinguished. This was most likely the sort of house that Mary and the girls lived in during those first days.

The year before at the Hawkesbury had been humid but dry, so the ground was hard and planting crops was tough going, especially since the only tools they had were rough spades and hoes. Come June there was a chill in the air and frost on the ground at night. Of firewood there was no shortage.

By the middle of the year, according to the census, Mary Pitt was in possession of 130 acres – she and Thomas at some point acquired the extra thirty acres nearby – of which seven were cleared and planted with wheat and maize. They had two sheep, four goats and ten hogs, donated by Governor King. In addition to Mary there were four children and two servants 'on stores', and Mary was listed in the 1800/1802 muster as 18th in the 'Top Owners of Larger Stock of Hawkesbury'.

By that time the original wattle and bark hut would have been enlarged and transformed, the wattle mostly likely replaced with slabs and the bark roof with shingles. By then they'd have had a proper fireplace but probably, as yet, no glazed windows.

When compared with the little whitewashed cottage back home in Fiddleford with its thatched roof and tidy garden, it still wasn't much. But this house belonged to Mary Pitt, built by her own hands – and her son's and daughters' – so there was no real comparison. The patch of cleared ground surrounding the house was still stubbled with tree stumps, but in her mind's eye she planned her garden, an English garden of course, with roses and dahlias and a climbing clematis and, who knows, maybe the odd fruit tree. In no time at all it would feel just like home.

Meanwhile the girls did their best to turn the house into a home by lining the walls with whatever strips of canvas they could lay their hands on, and every day they collected wild grasses and flowers to place in improvised vases to brighten the dinner table. 'Dinner' was still mostly salted meat from the government stores, with small rations of flour, sugar and tea and perhaps the occasional piece of locally grown fruit or vegetable.

~

The original Hawkesbury settlers had acquired a bad name among the local powers that be. David Collins claimed they were *'oftener employed in carousing in the front of their houses'* than in putting in a hard day's work. They had also been criticised for putting in the wheat late, but the fact was that there was no such thing as an instruction book at the time to guide the already inexperienced farmers. Word of mouth would have told Thomas to plant later than Sydney (the advice still applies), but at the best of times farming anywhere in the colony was still a case of trial and error, and the need to grow food to feed themselves was more immediately important to the farmers than getting rid of the roots and stumps of trees.

The Pitt family was lucky: there were no floods that first year on the Hawkesbury. In September Thomas was granted 100 acres of land next door to Pitt Farm, which he named Nelson's Farm in honour of their sponsor. With the exception of Lucy, who was off the stores by the end of January 1802, the family lived on government stores for eighteen months, which meant that by the middle of 1803 onwards they were self-sufficient.

At dawn every day Mary lifted the flap of bark that covered the hole in the wall by her bed and watched the sun rise through the branches of what she now knew was a casuarina tree. It was a wonder for her to see the sun cross the sky the 'wrong' way, from east to west via the north. It was a marvel that the moon was so bright at night-time that even when it was half full you could see through the trees right down to the river as if it was daylight. It was a miracle to see the stars more brilliant than she'd ever known them. She could close her eyes and know precisely what time of day it was by the birdsong: from the hysterical laughter of the kookaburra before first light to the late afternoon cacophony of cockatoos, crows and magpies as they flew home to settle for the night in the trees; the sudden silence the moment the sun dropped behind the mountains, as if someone had flipped a switch. And then the late shift, the buzz of crickets and frogs, and the distant howl of dingoes. Later still as the dark settled over the countryside like a shroud, the chatter of the willie wagtails gossiping to one another throughout the night.

It was beginning to feel familiar. She was starting to understand the landscape, to know that the sudden appearance of the big black cockatoo with its six foot wing span heralded the arrival of rain. She recognised the crash of the possum jumping from the trees onto the roof of the house. She'd learned that the bigger the spider the less dangerous it was likely to be. She knew the red-bellied black snake was only harmful if you threatened it or accidentally trod on it. She realised the alligator that had so terrified her youngest was a monitor lizard. It was all becoming less strange.

There were even moments when she could forget to be homesick.

Chapter 19

1802: The true proprietors of the soil

LATE ONE SPRING MORNING one of the shadows Thomas had been constantly sensing in the surrounding bush manifested itself as a human being.

He'd seen the movement in the trees and he knew the stories – of how the natives were always there, always just out of sight, of how one day, any day, they might appear in front of you and stick a spear into you for no apparent reason.

I like to think that Thomas was an enlightened man. He'd listened to Governor King talking of the Aboriginal people as the *'true proprietors of the soil'* and he respected them for that. He was aware that he and others before him had laid claim to the country right under their noses without so much as a by your leave; but he also hoped, or assumed, the difference in cultures did not mean that black and white could not live together in *'amity and friendship'* and share the country between them, since there seemed to be plenty of it (who knew what lay beyond the Blue Mountains). I like to think he did not subscribe to the view held by some that since the Aborigine was blatantly ignoring the instructions so plainly set out in the Bible to *'replenish the earth and subdue it'* he had no rights to the land in the first place; and that in time he would naturally decrease in number and, with a bit of luck and according to God's will as interpreted by western man, die out altogether.

From the Aboriginal point of view the situation looked rather different. He had watched the arrival of these strangers with their bleached faces and their elaborate 'skin', which he soon realised was something that could be taken on and off at will, and which seemed to have multiple significance as a symbol of status, or gender, or even as a way of keeping warm, with a mixture of astonishment, amusement, fear and intense curiosity. He was tentative but not unfriendly, helping the strangers navigate the rivers and find their way around. He showed them the best places to fish and even, so it appeared, welcomed them with open arms. Which was why the white man – like a gatecrasher at a party – walked right in with a smile on his face and began to make himself at home. At which point the Aborigine, seeing that the strangers were here to stay, that they were building houses and sewing seeds in the ground where he had been used to hunting and picking yams; that they were taking the fish from the waters right under his nose and, most outrageous of all, they were preventing him from walking in places they seemed to consider theirs, became decidedly less friendly. But by this time it was too late. The gatecrashers had taken the party over. And that's when the trouble began.

After the skirmishes of the 1790s and the killing of the two Aboriginal boys, Governor King issued a strict order that the indigenous people were to be left alone, and that if the settlers found themselves or their property under threat they were to 'use the most humane means of resisting such attacks.' Since then a relative peace had reigned, or appeared to, especially around the Green Hills area where the farms were by now fairly established. The flip side of this was that having had their hunting grounds taken from them the Aborigines for the first time in their history found themselves dependent for their survival on the usurpers.

In the safety of the dining room at Government House, or even around the campfire at a neighbour's farm Thomas had pondered on how he would cope in a situation such as the one he was in now. He liked to think that if confronted by a native he would be calm, reasonable, enlightened and of course incredibly brave.

But that had been then, in the security of a quiet evening around a campfire. This was now. Here was an Aboriginal man, stark naked, approaching him slowly but deliberately across a patch of land Thomas had recently cleared, gesticulating and jabbering incoherently. He held a spear. He seemed to know what he wanted and what he was talking about, which put Thomas at a multiple disadvantage. The young Englishman stood facing the Aborigine with nothing but his intellectually enlightened ideas and a flimsy hoe; and behind him, somewhere, hopefully out of sight, were four unprotected women (Horse and Christmas being predictably nowhere to be seen). Two thoughts, neither of them very enlightened, came into Thomas's head simultaneously: what makes this jabbering idiot think I can understand a word he's saying? And how dare he walk across someone else's land uninvited?

When he was about ten feet away from Thomas the man stopped. He dug his spear into the ground and carried on jabbering. Thomas found himself saying, in a ridiculously petulant tone that would have embarrassed him had there been any other witnesses, 'Look here, I have no idea what you're talking about'. He tried to appear as if he was standing his ground but in truth he was still trying to make up his mind whether to fight or flee, and in the meantime he was doing neither.

'What is it you want?' he said. As he spoke he wished he'd tried to learn a bit of the local language. It would have given him some advantage.

The man continued gesticulating and when Thomas had calmed down enough he recognised what he was trying to convey. He was gesturing with his hand towards his mouth. Still Thomas hesitated, through bewilderment rather than incomprehension. He could not bring himself to accept what was obviously being asked for.

'You want food?' He repeated the man's gesture.

The man nodded.

As he turned to make his way back into the house it struck Thomas how bizarre it all was. There was he, newly arrived just weeks before from the opposite side of the world and struggling to make the ground yield up anything that might one day be edible, giving food to an Aboriginal man who had lived in this country for who knew how many years, surviving perfectly well on his wits and his knowledge of the land. It was already well known that, whereas the indigenous people had managed to exist in this country for thousands of years without planting anything, a white man hazarding his luck on his own in the bush – as many truanting convicts had tried to do – stood no chance. And yet here was a black man begging a white man for food. It made no sense.

He felt uncomfortable about handing over the piece of salt pork, which was the first thing he could lay his hands on and which, in truth, was well past its best. But the man seemed happy enough. He took the meat and gesticulated with it for a moment, then turned his back and walked away.

Once he was out of sight and Thomas's heart had stopped pounding, he felt strangely sad.

This was the first of many visits, sometimes from Jabbering Joe (so-called because he never stopped) and sometimes from others – friends, family, extended family. Soon Jemima and Hester began to look out for them and the moment they arrived they were raiding the kitchen and settling them down as if for a Sunday picnic. Thomas did not approve.

'Why not?'

'You'll only encourage them,' he said.

'I beg your pardon? They're not wild animals.'

'We have barely enough for ourselves as it is, Jem,' he went on. 'And what's more . . .' He hesitated. What exactly was he trying to say? That it was wrong? That it was not proper etiquette? That they were not like them?

The truth was – and it was something Thomas found difficult to articulate, even to his sisters – he felt it was fundamentally wrong that the proprietors of the soil should be depending on the white settler for his sustenance. In a sense yes, it was like feeding wild animals who could and should be surviving in the wild. It was unnatural, against nature.

And another thing: he was afraid of them. He didn't trust the Aboriginal people, yet he didn't trust himself to admit it. He didn't understand them. Like his fellow settlers, he could find no common ground with them. And so he took the easy route: he tried to pretend they were not there.

But Jemima and Hester would sit them down and try to swap languages, with a certain amount of success. They managed to understand enough to know that these people were from a nation called Darug; that there existed countless other nations within the country, each of which had its own language; that their name for the Hawkesbury Nepean river was Deerubbin; that there was something called the 'dreaming', which was as near as they seemed to come to a religion; that the land, which they appeared to wander through more or less at random, meant something mysterious and sacred to them; that it had boundaries, invisible presumably to the eye of the white man; and that they had lived here since the beginning of time.

But the communication only went so far.

'Tell us,' asked Jemima one day, using a mixture of sign language and pidgin Darug, 'why do you come to us to eat our food?'

There was baffled silence.

'Food,' Jemima repeated. 'Why do you ask us for food?' She did not use the word 'beg', but it was implied.

There was no answer to this. They appeared not to understand. Later on the girls may have realised it was not the question that puzzled them so much as the concept. They were not begging. The food was theirs in the first place. Just because someone else had gone to the trouble to produce it didn't make it any less so.

And then one day, just as they were beginning to become a fixture and even Tom was starting to get used to them being around, they went away and no one ever saw them again.

~

There were several attempts on the part of the authorities in New South Wales to 'civilise' the Aboriginal people over the years. Governor Phillip gave some of them land, a boat and a house. They abandoned all of them. Some years later Governor Macquarie, without irony, again granted some indigenous people particular pieces of land, which again they ignored.

There is a strong opinion now in Australia that says the problems that occur in that country – the droughts, the floods, the dust storms, the bush fires – are due not only to climate change but to the way the country has been handled by its imported keepers. There's a point of view that says that every 'exotic' (ie foreign) interloper, whether animal, tree or human, has had a detrimental effect on the environment. That the soil is too delicate to support animals such as cows, sheep and pigs; that imported trees take too much moisture from the ground and clog up the waterways; and even damming the rivers has caused problems by increasing the salt content in the water. As for bush fires – the indigenous people had been creating small but controllable fires for centuries to flush out the wildlife and regenerate the vegetation. It wasn't until the Europeans appeared that bush fires raged so uncontrollably and destructively over such vast swathes of the countryside.

Many years later, in 1839, under the auspices of Governor Gipps, a questionnaire was circulated by the Legislative Council to New South Wales pastoralists soliciting their experiences employing 'Native Blacks'. The response from two of them, William Ogilvie and George Wyndham, went like this:

> *Q Can you suggest any means by which they* ['Native Blacks'] *may become readily induced to engage in the above* [work]?
>
> *A Much could be made of them in every way, provided only they were caught young.*
>
> *Q Can you suggest any means by which they may be more induced to engage in the above?*

A By cutting off their great toes. They could not then climb the trees for opossums. Two hours so spent or in fishing will supply them with all they want for the day; why then should they vex themselves with the drudgery of labour? They are not fools.

Q Please state the amount of labour you have known any of them to accomplish, by the day, week or month; what do you consider their average service compared with Europeans; and in what manner may they be most readily induced to exert themselves?

A They are not labourers at all, and for the same reason that any other gentleman is not, viz that he can live without labour. So also can they, and as comfortably as they wish to live.

Q What do you consider their prevailing character?

A They realise the philosophy that Diogenes only dreamt of, yet are no Cynics, rather Gymnosophists. But surely the Council will not encourage a 'degraded class' among our pure population.

Unfortunately the comments were not taken seriously. On the front page of the document someone from the Council had written, *'As it conveys rather more insult to the Committee than information, I shall be authorised to exclude it from those selected for publication.'*

Chapter 20

1802: Shipwreck

IT HAD PROBABLY NOT been John Wood's intention to settle in New South Wales, or anywhere else for that matter. As an employee of the East India Company he would have lived his life at sea, most likely travelling between Britain and the east. But on marrying Lucy he resigned from the company and went freelance.

According to the official musters John was at the Hawkesbury in April 1802, in possession of a sword. But the following month he was back in Sydney looking for work, and his first assignment was as mate, deputy to the captain, on a trading brig called *Margaret* on an expedition to the south Pacific. Lucy, for whatever reason, decided to go with him.

The brig was jointly owned by her captain, John Buyers, and a man named John Turnbull. Turnbull, an Englishman, had travelled to New South Wales in order to spend some time sailing the Pacific and investigating trading opportunities. He subsequently wrote about his travels in a three-volume book called *A Voyage Round the World in 1800 – 1804*.

Margaret had a crew of around twenty-eight men, mostly convicts, and Lucy was probably the only woman on board. It would have been quite a desirable job for John, working for a pioneering adventurer like John Turnbull and spending months on the open seas, visiting the islands of the south Pacific and trading with the islanders. Why did Lucy choose to accompany him? Was it because she did not want to spend the first months or maybe years of her married life apart from her husband? Or was it in order to satisfy her appetite for adventure – an appetite that by the end of this particular voyage would have been well and truly satisfied. Or was it because she already knew she was pregnant?

Their journey began by sailing north from Port Jackson to Norfolk Island, where they collected John Turnbull. From there they sailed east to Tahiti and the Society Islands, their mission to buy pigs to import back to Sydney.

In Tahiti their arrival caused a buzz of excitement and a visit from several members of the Tahitian royal family including King Otoo, whose *'unusual stupidity* [of look and manners, according to John Turnbull] *was doubtless the effect of an immoderate use of the Ava'* – a local plant not unlike opium. Otoo showed a keen interest in the visitors' version of Ava, otherwise known as spiritous liquor, while his father and his estranged wife – the latter of whom became irritatingly giggly when drunk – were transfixed by the crew's weaponry, which they had to be kept carefully away from. The Tahitians loved music, though they only had four notes apparently, and were particularly impressed by the bagpipes, with which they said 'Taptain Toote' (Cook) had often entertained them. They even put on a dance show for the visitors. It all sounded like a lot of fun and it is not surprising the captain's greatest fear was that the crew, seduced by the 'indolence' of the islanders and already close to mutiny, would desert. Some of them did, with the aid of the king of the neighbouring island of Ulitea, though His Highness denied it.

The Tahitians were friendly enough, but their neighbours, the Uliteans, were something else. One night the natives of Ulitea cut *Margaret's* anchor cable and she was nearly grounded on a coral reef. The islanders then threatened to roast the crew alive, which concentrated their minds wonderfully. It took them the rest of the night and the whole of the following day before they found a way to escape, by which time there was no longer much talk of desertion. At the next island they visited they pretended *Margaret* was a warship and the crew paraded the decks in military uniform to discourage the locals from attempting to invade. Exciting times they were, and there was more to come.

At some point in the midst of all these thrills Lucy gave birth to a baby boy and named him George Pitt Wood. Little George was baptised by missionaries in Tahiti, so he may have been born at sea, or on Tahiti itself, who knows. It is possible that Lucy missed the bombardment off Ulitea, but it's equally possible that both she and her newborn son witnessed the whole thing.

By the end of the year Lucy was no longer the only woman on board. In the Society Islands they'd picked up an Englishman named Pulpit along with his fifteen-year-old Tahitian bride. Then the second mate threatened to desert unless he could take a Sandwich Island woman with him on board, and on John Wood's advice he was allowed to do so.

By March 1803 the ship was back in Tahiti. The hogs, the object of their original mission, had in their absence been purloined by the crew of another trading ship called *Nautilus*. So it was decided that John Turnbull would remain on the island with a couple of assistants while *Margaret,* along with Captain Buyers and the rest of the crew, including John, Lucy and baby George and a handful of Tahitians, headed for the islands east of Tahiti in search of the elusive hog. The ship with her twenty-odd passengers sailed in early April 1803 and the expedition was expected to take them three weeks.

Two months went by and there was no sign of *Margaret.*

~

Meanwhile back in Mulgrave Place Mary must have been wondering. It was now a year since Lucy and John had sailed from Port Jackson and she probably hadn't expected them to be gone so long. It must have crossed her mind at some point that she might never see her daughter again, not to mention the grandchild she may or may not have known about.

~

On 27 May 1803 a large sail was spotted in the sea off the coast of Tahiti. It had to belong to *Margaret,* Turnbull realised. He then heard a report that the *'fatal remains'* of the brig had been discovered about ten nautical miles north of the island, so he dispatched some islanders in canoes to investigate. They returned with the news that the remains were indeed of the *Margaret,* converted into a punt. On board were eighteen starving, exhausted and frozen passengers, among them John, Lucy and their infant son.

The story as told by Captain Buyers went like this:

Due to adverse winds it had taken *Margaret* and her passengers more than two weeks to sail from Tahiti east to their destination (believed to be the Palliser Islands). They arrived on 17 April and the Captain immediately began trading with the locals, quite satisfactorily to all account. Having wound up business for the day and with the intention of continuing the following morning, he and his crew were manoeuvring the ship in order to drop anchor overnight when, at 10.30pm, there was a terrible grinding noise and *Margaret* shuddered to a halt, grounded on a reef.

The crew fought for two hours to save her, cutting down the masts in a desperate attempt to get her moving again. Half an hour after midnight the order came to abandon ship. Lucy wrapped her tiny baby in a blanket and, with the others, clambered onto a nearby sandbank. The men loaded up a small boat with whatever stores they could reach, along with muskets and ammunition as protection against unfriendly islanders, and settled down to get what rest they could in what remained of the night.

The following morning they woke to find the boat and all its contents had been stolen by the Tahitians they had brought with them. So the crew set about constructing another boat out of planks from the ship. As they did so neighbouring islanders began gathering in large and increasingly threatening numbers. Under great duress the men worked to build their boat while keeping the aggressors at bay, and the moment it was finished they set off, only to discover they could not find a way through the reef and the boat had to be abandoned.

The Captain, in true democratic fashion, called on his men to offer an opinion as to what should be done. In the meantime the islanders had increased in number and hostility, so as a last resort it was decided to use what planks were still available from the mother ship and build a flat-bottomed boat, or punt, which could be floated in shallow water. While this was being done two sentries posted as lookouts onboard the ship were speared by the islanders. Exhausted, demoralised and desperate, the crew pleaded with the Captain to leave the rock, ready or not. It was better to *'perish by the craziness of their punt'*, they said, than be murdered by savages.

The punt being finished, eighteen people, including the two injured sentries, their guts spilling, climbed on board and once again tried to make their way through the labyrinth. They took with them some muskets, a small amount of powder and ten gallons of water – enough for two wine glasses each *per diem* – which they had acquired by digging deep into the sand, which meant it was brackish. The moment they left the ship the islanders rushed on board and pillaged everything they could find.

This time the survivors managed to negotiate their way through the reef. The little punt was on the open sea for five days before it was finally spotted off the coast of Tahiti on 27 May, two months after they had first left the island to go trading for hogs.

Had the survivors arrived at any other island than Tahiti they would have almost certainly been speared to death. Had they arrived any later they would not have survived the storm that an hour later *'blew a tempest, accompanied with thunder and lightning, and torrents of rain, during the following night.'* And Lucy, John, little George and a whole line of Woods would have been wiped out.

On 2 October 1803 the *Sydney Gazette* reported that Mr Wood, *'mate of the 'Margaret', and Mrs Wood and her infant happily returned to Otaheiti on 27th May, in a very reduced state.'*

The lives of the two injured men, incidentally, were saved by local missionaries, who pushed their guts back inside their stomachs and roughly stitched them up.

That was not the end of the story. Lucy and company were now stranded on Tahiti, with no money, or the wherewithal to make any, and no means of returning to Port Jackson. Having lost their ship, Turnbull and Buyers had evidently lost all authority, and the crew effectively deserted, leaving only the cook, the mate (John Wood), the Captain and Turnbull himself *'united in a common cause, that of returning to our native country.'*

For three months they sat it out. Then just as they were beginning to completely abandon hope the brig *Dart* sailed into port, on its way to Port Jackson. She picked up as passengers *'Mr Turnbull, Captain Buyers formerly of the ship 'Margaret', Mr Wood, wife of the mate Mrs Wood, and her infant child'*, and set off for Port Jackson. The journey took five weeks as they sailed again via Norfolk Island, this time to collect Captain Foveaux (then Lieutenant-Colonel in charge of the island). They eventually arrived at Port Jackson on 30 September 1803, sixteen months after they had originally set out. By which time Lucy would have realised she was pregnant again.

Oddly enough although Turnbull's accounts of his adventures are minutely detailed he never once mentions John or Lucy by name, let alone their infant son. The only evidence we have that they were on board throughout both the voyage and the shipwreck, and that they arrived back at Port Jackson on board the *Dart* is from the report in the *Sydney Gazette.*

~

By now the longing for adventure that I ascribed to Lucy was probably well and truly sated. She never accompanied John on any subsequent voyages. Perhaps she hoped that her husband's love of the sea would have been equally satisfied and that he would have been happy to settle down on their farm and become a farmer, like the rest of her family. But unfortunately that was not to be.

Less than a month after arriving back in Sydney John Wood signed up as a member of the crew of the schooner *Endeavour*, which was taking convicts from Port Jackson to Hobart in Van Diemen's Land (now Tasmania).

The ship left Sydney on 20 October to sail south. Off Botany Bay a storm began to get up. John and the first mate, a Mr Higgins, were working up on the deck, ignoring the distant rumble of thunder and the gathering clouds. The sky turned black and lightning hit the water with a resounding crack, but still they carried on, until a bolt of lightning struck them both at the same time, hurling them backwards onto the deck. John Wood was severely burned and Mr Higgins was blinded.

The *Sydney Gazette* on 30 October 1803 reported the following:

'Off Botany Bay during a thunderstorm on the evening of the preceding Thursday, Mr Higgins, mate, and Mr Wood, formerly of the 'Margaret' were severely hurt by lightning which we before remarked was extremely vivid, and the flashes of unusually long continuance. The former was for some minutes deprived of sight, but afterwards tolerably recovered his right eye, the left continuing much inflamed. Mr Wood's hurt was in the loins, and was so severe as to render it necessary that he should be brought ashore immediately for the benefit of medical assistance. As the vessel sustained no damage and none of the people embarking for the settlement at Hobart on Van Diemen's land were at all affected she weighed the morning after her arrival, but Mr Wood was unable to accompany the voyage.'

What happened to John next or how permanent his injuries were is not recorded, although as it has been pointed out elsewhere he and Lucy never conceived another child. He may or may not have been present when Lucy, with the help of Margaret Catchpole, gave birth to their daughter Sophia on 5 May 1804, this time on dry land at Green Hills. In July that year Lucy and John were granted 100 acres across the river from Mary and Thomas.

There is a blank in John's life between October 1803 and August of 1806, when his signature appears on a memorial sent to Governor Bligh from the Hawkesbury settlers. Maybe during that time he decided to settle at the Hawkesbury and try his hand at farming. Or maybe ...

In my search for John Wood's missing years I came upon his name scribbled in the margin of a letter written by a Lieutenant Fowler: *'John Wood one of Capt Flinders' Boats crew now prisoner in the Isle de France.'*

The explorer Matthew Flinders, on his way from Port Jackson to England on board *HMS Cumberland*, had stopped at the Isle de France (now Mauritius) for repairs to his ship and promptly been arrested for spying. The island being French territory and Britain being at war with France, he was held there, to his outrage and against orders from above, for seven years.

Was the John Wood of Flinders's crew 'our' John Wood? It made sense: those missing years could well have been spent cooped up as a prisoner on the Isle de France along with the renowned explorer. It could be another thrilling discovery, another famous name to add to the Pitt collection. John's injuries may not have proved too serious and he may well have signed up with Captain Flinders soon after his accident at Botany Bay; and he had obviously been released before his boss, which accounted for why he was able to be at the Hawkesbury to sign the welcome to Governor Bligh in 1806. Flinders had been arrested in December of 1803. Would there have been time for John to have recovered from his injuries in October of that same year to join the expedition?

The answer, after a lot of hunting, turned out to be *not quite.*

HMS Cumberland left Port Jackson on 20 September 1803, according to Flinders's own account, just over a month before Wood had been struck by lightning. After all that I had to concede there must have been another John Wood, seaman, thus ending what could have been a good tale.

There is evidence John did go to sea again, in 1809, on board the sealer *Active,* and later that year on *Perseverance,* another sealer, from where he was put ashore with seven other men on an uninhabited island south of New Zealand – named Campbell Island in honour of their employer – with orders to club, skin and boil the carcasses of seals for their oil. John and his gang were left there for ten months in freezing temperatures, surviving on nesting sea birds when their supplies ran out. He eventually arrived back at Port Jackson in January 1811, over a year after he'd left. The following month he was off again on a mission to Newcastle, and again a few months later to Macquarie Island, returning to Port Jackson at the end of October 1811. All in all, in those three years he was home for just a few months. He spent the early part of 1812 trying to sue his employers Robert Campbell & Co for a number of things, not least for compensation for his ten months living on a freezing cold uninhabited island with no provisions.

John Wood's life deserves a book on its own. And his absence from home may not have mattered quite so much for Lucy except, as she was not yet to know, her married life was going to be cut short before its time.

Chapter 21

1803: William Faithfull

WITH ALL THE TALK of my Pitt ancestry I should not forget the other side of the family.

My four times great grandparents Thomas and Hannah Laycock were earlier European-Australian pioneers even than Mary. When the New South Wales Corps was formed back in England with the express purpose of replacing the First Fleet marines as policemen and guards in the new colony, Thomas – who had been a sergeant with the 2nd Horse Grenadier Guards before being pensioned off on half pay – was the first man to enlist. He and his wife Hannah travelled to New South Wales in 1791 on the *Gorgon*, along with their five eldest children – Sarah, William, Thomas junior, Samuel and little George (who died the following year).

Quartermaster Laycock was a larger-than-life character in more than one sense: he was six feet six inches tall, and he had a propensity for becoming involved in noisy confrontations, the most notorious of which became known as the incident of Boston's Pig.

On 29 October 1796 Thomas spotted some pigs trespassing on land belonging to Captain Foveaux. He summoned William Faithfull, who was then a private in the corps, and ordered him to shoot one of the pigs. Whether by chance or otherwise, Faithfull shot the heavily pregnant prize sow, at which point the pigs' owner, a free settler called John Boston, appeared on the scene and demanded to know *'Who was the damned rascal who shot my sow?'*

Outraged that any member of his regiment should be labelled a 'rascal' Laycock ordered Faithfull to retaliate. Before he could do so Boston set about Faithfull with a length of sugar cane, which he had grabbed off a bystander. Faithfull then clocked him on the back of the head with the butt of his loaded musket, so hard that the ramrod fell out. Boston cried out *'Murder!'* Still Laycock urged Faithfull to *'thresh'* Boston till he could no longer stand, at which point Mrs Boston appeared on the scene and started screaming, and Boston escaped through a neighbour's garden.

Boston subsequently sued Quartermaster Laycock and Lieutenant McKellar, Faithfull's senior officers, for assault. He claimed that Laycock had ordered the pig to be shot in revenge for a personal grudge he had against him concerning a loan. The trial, which was presided over by the best brains in the colony under Governor Hunter, lasted over seven days and covered ten pages of the *Historical Records of New South Wales*. It was a *cause célèbre*, the first civil case ever heard in the colony, and it established an important precedent: members of the New South Wales Corps were subject to the law of the land just like anyone else; and regardless of whether or not they were entitled to shoot a trespassing pig, being called a 'rascal' did not entitle them to lay about anyone – not even a Jacobin such as Boston – with a loaded weapon.

The court found for Boston, and Laycock and Faithfull were fined 20s each.

Faithfull was then advised by his friends to appeal against the verdict – again a first – although as Governor Hunter pointed out he did not appear to know the meaning of the word. The appeal was turned down.

~

The story became legend and was still being talked about some seven years later. Susanna, out walking with her mother in Green Hills one spring morning in 1803, on seeing a young man across the road tip his hat to her, and enquiring of Mary, 'Who is that?', and on being told, 'He is the man who shot John

Boston's pig,' knew exactly what her mother was talking about.

The following afternoon I see Susanna and Faithfull being introduced at the house of a mutual friend.

'I have heard of you,' Susanna found herself saying. 'You are the man who . . .'

'. . . shot Boston's pig.' Faithfull sighed. 'My reputation goes before me, as always.'

'I do beg your pardon,' Susanna flushed. 'I did not intend any . . .'

'Don't apologise.' He smiled at her in a weary sort of a way. 'It's just that it was, what, seven years ago now and a man has done a thing or two since for which he would far prefer to be known.'

'Such as?'

'Such as . . . let me see now. Such as being the man who stood in a room one bright spring afternoon talking to the prettiest girl in Green Hills.'

'Oh.'

He said this in such an odd way – swivelling on his heels as he spoke and appearing to absent-mindedly scan the room, as if his mind was elsewhere – that Susanna wasn't at all sure she had heard right. It wasn't until his gaze returned to her and the corner of his mouth twitched in what she assumed was meant to be a smile that she found herself flushing, again.

'So,' she said after a slightly awkward silence. 'What brings you to Green Hills?'

His mouth twitched again. He is laughing at my feeble attempt at conversation, thought Susanna.

'I'm looking after Captain Foveaux's farms,' Faithfull replied.

'Captain Foveaux?'

'Yes. He was my commanding officer in the Corps when I first arrived here.'

'And it was on his land, was it not . . .?'

'Where I shot the wretched pig, yes.'

'Oh dear.' Susanna bit her lip. 'So this Captain Foveaux,' she continued, nervously. 'You manage his farms now?'

'I do. While he is in Norfolk Island. I have a piece of my own land as well.'

'How very interesting.'

'Now I am no longer with the Corps.'

'And so, as well as looking after Captain Foveaux's land . . .'

'I farm.'

'I see.'

'And you live nearby.' He said it as a statement.

'I do.'

'With your mother and two sisters and a brother.'

'You know all about us!'

'Of course. It is a very small place.'

'What else do you know about us?'

He pivoted again, appearing to give the question a certain amount of thought.

He wasn't particularly handsome, thought Susanna. His head was too square, though his features were relatively refined. He stood very upright – his army training she presumed – and when he turned his head his body went with it, as though the two were bolted together. In contrast to his rather formal bearing however he had an oddly casual manner that she found both disconcerting and endearing.

'I know,' said Faithfull eventually, still looking away from her, 'that your mother is a widow, you lost your father some years ago, you came here from Dorset and you are related to Admiral Nelson.'

He turned back to look at her. Her heart sank a bit at the mention of Lord Nelson.

'Only very distantly,' she said, in a rather small voice.

He laughed.

'What . . .'

'I'm sorry,' he recovered himself. 'Your face, when I mentioned Admiral Nelson.'

'My face?'

'It fell a thousand miles! I know exactly what you were

thinking.' He leaned towards her and all but whispered in her ear. 'This wretched man only monopolises me because of my family connections.'

'Well, I . . .'

'He's nothing but a fortune-seeker. He's not interested in me in the slightest.'

'I thought . . .'

'Admit it. Go on.'

She looked directly at him. Despite herself she started to laugh.

'You are . . .' she began, shaking her head.

'I am what?'

'You are the most surprising man I ever met.'

'Excellent! Then you will remember me when we next meet.'

~

And she did. She went to bed that night dreaming of him.

Susanna, as it happens, was almost the same age as Jane Austen, who of course never married. Ms Austen's heroines flew into a panic if they were not hitched by their early twenties, and Susanna in 1803 was already twenty-nine. She had been in the colony now for nearly two years and with men still outnumbering women by at least three to one she was no closer to finding a husband. A certain anxiety, not to say desperation, must have entered her mother's head from time to time; her eldest daughter could not have been short of suitors and the following year she would hit the dreaded thirty which, as any woman was aware, was getting on for middle age.

And now here was William Faithfull, ex private with the New South Wales Corps. Of all the men Susanna had been introduced to in the colony he was by far the most unusual, and interesting. There was no one else who had begun to set her heart racing. Which was unfortunate, because for a number of reasons he could not be regarded as suitable husband material.

Chapter 22

1804: The Palmers

AFTER A SHORT TIME in the new colony one thing had become obvious to Mary: Background was Everything.

You might have thought that this tiny group of people, not even the population of a small town in England, finding themselves in the same leaky boat so to speak would want to pull together and work shoulder to shoulder for the benefit of the community as a whole. After all life in 1804 New South Wales was still tough. The colony was still a place of risk and hard graft and a long way from an obvious land of golden opportunity.

However the free settlers were only too aware that they were living in an open prison surrounded by convicts and emancipists, who vastly outnumbered them. Already the people were forming themselves into clearly defined Clubs, with Labels.

As described by Peter Cunningham, surgeon with the Royal Navy and author of *Two Years in New South Wales*, the top club comprised the Pure Merinos (thoroughbreds, named after the sheep), which included the governor and his family and some of the top officials, among them the John Macarthurs. Next came the Exclusives, or Illegitimates – free settlers who had travelled to the continent for reasons other than law, among whom could be numbered Mary Pitt and her family. Below them were the military and the emancipists and at the bottom of the heap were the convicts.

(Except they were not referred to as 'convicts'. It was *'a word too ticklish to be pronounced in these sensitive latitudes'*, said Cunningham. One emancipist was even awarded 50 shillings against a libeller who had called him a *'d-d convict'*. The preferred term, other than on official records of course, was *'government man'* (or woman). The colony was already creating its own subtle and complex language, bound to confuse and unsettle the outsider in much the same way as the word 'native' – used by early colonists to describe an Aboriginal person – is now also considered 'ticklish'.)

Each Club stuck to its own and rarely socialised - let alone spoke - with anyone below them, except to give orders. It was like a microcosm of Georgian English society, only more so: in order to avoid the smallest possibility of being mistaken for a convict the upper echelons created their own exaggerated rules of behaviour, which made society back home seem downright democratic by comparison. These were the roots of the colonial snobbery that lasted well into the 20th century.

Like many other free settlers the Pitt family had taken a step or two upwards since arriving in the colony. It's true to say, and Mary would have realised this, that the colony was still too raw and primitive to attract people of the top rank. Its appeal lay more with the desperate, the freeloaders, the ones who'd failed back at home and whose friends were probably glad to be rid of; profligate young men who'd squandered their inheritance; men and women who having enjoyed the indulgence of the free passage, grants of land and all provided out of government stores, had little knowledge of farming and a disinclination for hard work, and often became a burden on the colony.

That's not to say all the free settlers in the early 1800s were ne'er-do-wells. There were the brave and enterprising, often younger sons who'd missed out on the family inheritance and decided to chance their luck in an unknown territory. And of course there was Mary and her family, and others like them, 'respectable' people who'd fallen on hard times back home through no fault of their own. Here a person could leave her own background behind, and to some extent that is what Mary and her family had done. She'd been reincarnated as a gentlewoman, no longer a yeoman's wife, and fully allowed to be addressed officially as Mrs Pitt. Here they were entitled to mix with the best. Their lack of money meant nothing – such a thing did not exist yet in New South Wales – but their connection to the Nelson family meant everything.

Mary Pitt had never met Horatio Nelson, but he knew about her. In 1804 he wrote to Governor King from the deck of *HMS Victory* asking after the Pitt family and received the following reply:

> [They] *'are comfortably settled and will be as they have been, the peculiar object of my care, which they have rendered themselves highly deserving of, and are the best examples as settlers of any sent here.'*

~

Thus it was that this exemplary member of the settler community found herself standing in the gardens of Woolloomooloo House in Garden Cove on this balmy late afternoon in autumn, her three daughters beside her. They were guests of Mr John Palmer and his American wife Susan.

The Palmers were regarded as prime movers among social circles in Sydney and hosted grand dinners for carefully selected guests. John Palmer was typical of the kind of man who had arrived in the colony in the early days with the navy – in his case as purser on *Sirius* in the First Fleet – and decided to settle there and make a considerable name and fortune for himself as a businessman, farmer, explorer and ship owner. As Commissary he was responsible for the government stores and the colony's banking system: a kind of Chancellor of the Exchequer, Minister of the Board of Trade and Governor of the Bank of England combined. It was the Palmers to whom Margaret Catchpole had first been assigned as cook, although by 1804 she was elsewhere, attending to the birth of little Sophia Wood at the Hawkesbury among other things.

Mary would have considered herself a worthy guest of one

of the most influential and successful men in the colony, and as she gazed around at her fellow visitors she may well have been thinking how very different the cream of Sydney society was to back home. Very few of the assembled company for instance would have frequented the Assembly Rooms in Bath or the salons of Almack's; they could hardly be expected to know their *contredance* from their *cotillions*. And while the men were vastly superior to the women in quantity, when it came to quality it was a very different matter.

Woolloomooloo House was one of the grandest buildings in the colony. Built and named by John Palmer some years before, the long low brick building lay close to the harbour's edge near Garden Island. In front of the house where Mary and the others were now standing, beautifully tended gardens dotted with fruit trees sloped gently down to the water. On the far side of a protective fence cows grazed, and the barns, stables, workmen's huts and piggery were reminders that this was not just a place of social entertainment but a working farm.

On a patch of grass at the edge of the orchard a band of the New South Wales Corps was playing a medley of patriotic British songs.

(Mary found herself suddenly transported to the Assembly Rooms in Bath. She was visiting the town with her two elderly aunts. There was music playing in the next door room. The three women had a pack of cards between them and were pondering the possibility – or as they were beginning to discover, the improbability – of finding a game that could be played by three people. They had tried quadrille, with no success, piquet was impossible, as was cribbage. They were on the verge of giving up when . . .)

'Mother, I have someone I'd like to introduce you to.'

Mary blinked. It took a moment to flip from 1769 Bath to 1804 Sydney.

Her son Thomas was standing right in front of her. By his side was a good-looking young man she had not met before. He wore a frock coat and a serious expression.

'James Wilshire – my mother, Mrs Pitt.'

'Delighted to meet you, Mrs Pitt.' He bowed, in a very formal manner.

'I am most interested to meet you, Mr Wilshire,' responded Mary, resisting the urge to curtsey back.

'Mr Wilshire works for Mr Palmer as his deputy.'

'Is that so?'

Mr Wilshire inclined his handsome head. 'Among other things.'

'And how do you find New South Wales?'

'I find it the most delightful place on earth.'

'Really?'

'Do you not agree?'

'I – on an evening like this, in such a place as this, why yes, who could not?'

'A man is very lucky.' Wilshire caught the eye of the two younger girls and nodded gravely to them.

'Oh – allow me to introduce my daughter Jemima, and Hester, my youngest.' Of Susanna there was, mysteriously, no sign.

'James Wilshire.' He clicked his heels together and bowed again.

'Were you in the army, Mr Wilshire?'

'Gracious no, Mrs Pitt.' He laughed, then checked himself.

'Mr Wilshire is a businessman,' said Thomas. 'He owns a tanning factory in Brickfield Hill.'

'What a busy man you are.'

'One must make the most of opportunities Mrs Pitt, do you not agree?' He smiled at the girls, who smiled politely back. 'I came here on a whim, you could say. I'd heard good things about the place and considered, if a man cannot make it here he cannot make it anywhere. I feel privileged,' he addressed this rather obviously to Jemima, 'to be given such opportunities.'

Jemima stared back at him, as only Jemima could.

'We've come to escort you ladies into the dining room,' said

Thomas. 'Dinner is to be served directly.'

Mary bowed and smiled. 'Please, go ahead. I will join you in a moment.'

She had spotted Susanna. Or rather she had heard her laugh, which was unusual. She was approaching her mother slowly through the orchard, her arm linked with William Faithfull's. She was wearing a pale pink muslin dress, nipped in above the waist and with tiny white roses sown into the lace around her neck. She looked, her mother could not help but notice, radiant.

'Look who is here, mama,' said Susanna. Her eyes were shining.

'Mr Faithfull.'

'I'm very glad to see you Mrs Pitt,' he said with surprising warmth.

'Mr Faithfull said he will go out of his mind if he hears one more person discussing the drought or the latest price of wheat.'

'I'm sure you have much more interesting things to talk about.' The corner of Faithfull's mouth twitched.

Mary smiled slightly.

'We were just talking, Miss Susanna and I,' he glanced at her eldest daughter in what Mary thought was a surprisingly intimate manner, 'about the Irish. I gather you have a Defender working for you?'

'Oh, you mean James Horse. Yes I do. Why?'

'Was he caught up in the troubles at Castle Hill?'

'No, not to my knowledge.'

'I'm glad to hear it. We were also arguing about . . .'

'Discussing,' Susanna interposed.

'Discussing the pros and cons of the New South Wales Corps. Which I am no longer a member of but remain loyal to, as is only right.'

'In what context?'

'In the context of the Castle Hill rebellion. Put down in a most efficient manner by the vastly outnumbered and unfairly maligned and aforementioned New South Wales Corps. Not a bad band either Mrs Pitt, what do you think?'

'Goodness me, I . . .'

'I'm sorry. You . . . ?'

'You switch about so fast, Mr Faithfull. One moment we are talking about the Irish, the next you are discussing music.'

'It is my brain you see, Mrs Pitt, it runs away with me. I apologise. What was I saying?'

Susanna laughed. 'You were talking about Castle Hill.'

'Ah, yes. Did you hear of it, Mrs Pitt?'

'I certainly did. They got within a few miles of us.'

'What I cannot understand is why the Irish should consider themselves – and only themselves – above the law.'

'I'm sorry Mr Faithfull, I don't follow you.'

'Why is it always the Irish who are so quarrelsome? What about everyone else? What makes the Irish so special?'

Mary smiled slightly. 'To be honest with you I believe the Irish are quite special. I was born there.'

'Oh. My apologies. I did not mean . . .'

'No, I know you didn't. The Irish consider themselves special because the rest of the world thinks of them as beyond the pale. And the prejudice has arrived in the colony along with them.'

'I have nothing against them, believe me. But they got a good routing, that's for sure.'

'So I heard,' said Mary. 'Thanks to Major Johnston and – the other one.'

'Quartermaster Laycock.'

'Quartermaster Laycock?' Susanna came to life suddenly. 'Wasn't he the one who ordered you to . . .'

'Yes, he was.'

'To what?' Mary looked quizzical.

'Shoot John Boston's pig.' They said it together, and together they laughed.

'You see, Mrs Pitt?' Faithfull expostulated. 'The darned thing follows me everywhere. Can you not see it?'

'See what?'

'The ghost of John Boston's sow. It haunts me, everywhere I go. There it is, over by the fence, d'ye see? Staring at me. Miss Susanna,' he turned to Susanna in mock terror, 'take me away from here – ask me to dance – anything – just get me away from those accusing eyes.'

'*Me* ask *you* to dance?'

'Why not? We are not in England now.'

(We are not in England now.)

'You do dance, don't you?'

('Do you know gleek, Miss Matcham?')

'Well!' Susanna covered her mouth with a gloved hand.

Mary turned and nearly dropped her cards.

'What's the matter? Am I being forward?'

('I do beg your pardon, I didn't mean to surprise you,' said the young man. 'Robert Pitt. At your service, ladies. I hope I'm not intruding.')

'Did you hear that, mama?' Susanna was laughing.

'I'm so sorry Susanna, my mind was . . .'

'Elsewhere. Back in the old country no doubt.' Faithfull turned to look about him, in that rather odd way he had.

'How did you know?'

'Just a guess, Mrs Pitt.' He turned back to look at her. 'And not such a clever one. I've no doubt most people's minds are on the old country a good deal of the time. Except mine of course. I can barely remember the place.'

Susanna laughed again.

'Isn't it the best thing in the world,' Faithfull went on, looking from one woman to the other, 'to be able to make a woman laugh?'

What a strange young man, thought Mary. But he certainly could make Susanna laugh, and that was something.

'And now if you will excuse us, Mrs Pitt.' He bowed in that rather stiff military way he had. 'Miss Susanna is about to save me from being stared to death.'

Mary watched for a moment as the two young things

wandered off, arm in arm and still laughing, seemingly oblivious to everything around them, phantom pigs included.

The late afternoon sun was low in the sky, spreading its golden light across the walls of the building and dancing on the water. A little band of ducks stood in noisy conference on the shore in front of Mary and she idly wondered if they were natives of the country or if they'd been forced to come here like virtually everyone else.

(He had sat down next to her and tried to teach them the rules of gleek, but they never got around to playing it. Instead they got talking and quickly established that he, Robert Pitt, lived in Child Okeford in Dorset and only a stone's throw away from Mary and her aunts. And that moreover they were related! They shared an aunt, so he believed.

Then they danced. It was the first time she had ventured onto the floor in the Assembly Rooms and she was as nervous as a child. But he guided her firmly and whispered instructions into her ear and laughed when she went wrong, which was often. They laughed all evening. And when it was all over he asked, quite naturally, if he might be permitted to call on them one day in the near future. Which of course he did.)

'Mrs Pitt.' A small, stocky, smiling middle aged man was approaching Mary across the lawn.

'Hello Mr Palmer.'

'Why are you standing here all alone?'

'I wasn't alone Mr Palmer. Far from it. But then nor was I exactly here.'

'Ah.' Her host's smile wavered for an instant.

'I was a long way away and a long time ago.'

'Ah,' he said again, this time with understanding. 'Then, if I am not intruding . . .'

'Not in the least,' said Mary, smiling warmly.

'Allow me to escort you inside.'

Two long tables ran the length of the room. John Palmer sat at the head of one, with Mary on his left, in the honoured position. Hester and Jemima sat at the far end of the table with

James Wilshire between them. Susanna was halfway down, opposite William Faithfull. There was a small altercation with another young man about their positions. Faithfull, it transpired, had done some switching of place names.

The following day Mary and Thomas had a serious discussion.

'William Faithfull was a private with the New South Wales Corps,' said Thomas.

'So he told me.'

'You know they are a bunch of ruffians. Recruited from the lowest of the low, the sort of men who couldn't make it into the regular army, and that's saying something. You only have to look at what they've been up to in the colony.'

'He's no longer with them, he told me.'

'Moreover he is illiterate. And he was involved in some notorious incident a few years ago.'

'John Boston's pig.'

'You know about it then.'

'Doesn't everyone?'

'I do not believe he is a suitable escort for Susanna.'

'Oh Thomas, how pompous you sound!'

Thomas sighed heavily and looked away.

'Thomas,' Mary reached out and touched her son lightly on the hand. 'This is New South Wales, Tom. It isn't Dorset, or Bath or London. He's a pleasant young man in his own way and he shows spark.'

'This is not like you, mother. You said you wanted only the best for your daughters.'

'And so I do. But we have to adapt, Tom. It isn't just background that counts, not here, it's not even education. What matters here is enterprise, courage, imagination, that's what this place needs. Besides,' she murmured to herself, 'he reminded me of your father.'

'What did you say?'

'Besides,' she said, a little louder, 'have you seen the way Susanna's eyes light up when she is with him? Have you seen how she laughs?'

'You are beginning to sound sentimental, mother.'

'I hope so. I do hope so.' She smiled fondly at her son.

'Anyway,' she went on, 'do remember he was Colonel Foveaux's batman and extremely highly thought of. He is not unconnected. And he has property.'

'Nonetheless.'

'And what of James Wilshire?' said Mary. 'What have you discovered about him?'

'He has an excellent position as Acting Deputy-Commissary. He came to New South Wales free four years ago. He owns land in Lane Cove and a house in Chapel Row, and he has established a tanning factory at Brickfield Hill. His people are from Berkshire I believe. Or maybe it's Buckinghamshire. I understand he decided to come here when his father died. He is not the eldest son, you see.'

'And he can read and write.'

'Of course.'

'Admirable. But can he manage Jemima, do you think?'

'Jemima?'

'She is a handful, you must admit that, Tom.'

'Who mentioned Jemima? It's Hester he's set his cap at.'

'Hester? My baby?'

'She's eighteen, mama. Hardly a baby. Barely two years younger than I was when we arrived here, remember?'

Mary looked closely at her son. He was only twenty-three but he looked older. It was not so much the physical work as the anxiety and the responsibility of being the head of the family since the age of seven. He's becoming middle-aged, thought his mother, and I never even noticed.

'And what about you, Tom?' she said.

'Me?' He looked at her blankly.

'Don't forget yourself. You must find someone too you know.'

'There's too much to do first.'

He had to see his three sisters married, and married well.

Now they were no longer on government stores there were four women and three convict workers to be provided for, and their 230 acres to be properly established. By then, he may be too old. He might never find a wife, and the family name would die with him. That would be sad. That would be too great a sacrifice.

Mary reached out and took her son's hand between hers and squeezed it hard.

~

On 21 November 1804 Mary's eldest daughter Susanna, aged thirty, married William Faithfull at St Mary's, Parramatta.

Two months after that, in February 1805, her youngest daughter Hester, aged eighteen, married James Wilshire at St Phillip's Church in Sydney.

In the case of Susanna Mary had, effectively, taken a gamble. She had agreed to the marriage of her eldest daughter to an illiterate ex-private, something she may not have conceived of back in the old country. But she was sufficiently far-sighted to recognise the rules were different in her adopted home, and that the two new members of her family were both ambitious young men setting out to make their own way in a colony where enterprise and spirit meant more than background. Only time would tell whether or not the gamble was to pay off.

Chapter 23

1809: Jemima

IN 1809 A YOUNG MAN called Robert Jenkins arrived in the colony on *Atalanta*. He was from Gloucestershire, well educated, a good rider and hunter, of impeccable stock. He was acting as agent for a London merchant called William Wilson, who owned the ship he arrived on. He had a splendid future ahead of him and he was the perfect match for Jemima Pitt.

Then a few months after he arrived Jenkins's employer went bankrupt, leaving Jenkins, in his own words,*'almost penniless and in a state of mind not at all enviable'*.

Out of the window along with his finances went all hope of marrying Jemima.

~

'Jemima, there is someone I want you to meet,' said Thomas.

Jemima turned from the stove upon which she had been preparing the family supper.

Since the weddings of her two sisters she had kept house for her mother and unmarried brother at Bronte. She cooked for them and kept the larder filled, she handled the books and still found time to help out on the farm when things were busy. She was showing herself to be a hard-working, capable and alarmingly self-sufficient woman, but in 1809 she was twenty-six and still no nearer finding a husband.

It was not for want of offers. In 1809 New South Wales the men still outnumbered the women, and someone of Jemima's resourcefulness (and wealth) would have been much sought after. But she was still smarting from the recent and sudden ending of her relationship with Robert Jenkins and had, to Thomas's consternation, stubbornly refused to show any interest in any man since.

'His name is Austin Forrest,' said Tom. 'He was a captain with the East India Company but he's been working for Robert Campbell for the past few years, captaining his trading ships between Calcutta and here. Wilshire has done business with him, and now apparently he has decided to settle in the colony.'

Jemima sat down opposite Tom and began eating.

'Did you hear me?'

'How are you to know whether this one is suitable?' she asked.

'Don't be difficult, Jem. Look – I only did it for the best. Jenkins was not a good prospect, you know as well as I do.'

'It was through no fault of his, you know as well as I do.'

'I am not passing judgment on him, I am asking you – urging you to forget him and move on. You are after all . . .' he hesitated.

'. . . not getting any younger.' Jemima looked up at her brother as she chewed. 'You are absolutely right dear brother, as always. What did you say his name was?'

'Captain Austin Forrest. He has acquired huge amounts of land here – '

'What colour are his eyes?' asked Jemima.

' – most of Governor Hunter's old properties. He is a man of considerable means. And I can't see what the colour of his eyes has to do with anything.'

'Age?'

'I've no idea. He is mature, that I do know.'

'Demeanour?'

Tom frowned in irritation. 'Look, I don't recall. He has a moustache, that's about all I remember of him.'

'Tom you are a hopeless marriage broker. If you can tell me the colour of his eyes, his approximate height and his age within a year or so I will consider meeting him. But not before.'

'Jemima you are completely impossible.'

'I know,' said she with a sad smile.

~

Jemima took a good hard look. Captain Forrest was engaged in what looked like an intense conversation which allowed her to appraise him at length and quite openly.

Her first impressions were not good. He was old, far older than her, perhaps by twenty years. His hair was beginning to thin and to go grey. His moustache was of a completely different colour to what was left of his hair and had the appearance of being stuck on.

He stood with his hands clasped firmly behind his back. His manner when addressing others was deferential – body tilted slightly forwards, head on one side, a bit like a bird. He had a hearty laugh and she sensed it might not be quite real. He was a good listener, that was a definite plus, and he seemed to be known and obviously liked by most of the other men in the room. They were virtually lining up to speak to him.

The conversations were genial, and often loud. There was a lot of laughter and slapping of backs. In none of the exchanges was there ever a woman present. A man's man, concluded Jemima. He probably didn't even like women.

'Has he been married before?' she asked her brother.

'Not to my knowledge,' said Thomas.

'Hmm.'

'Look,' he continued, 'are we going to stand here all day or will you allow me to introduce him before he disappears altogether?'

'Perhaps that would be for the best.'

Thomas sighed heavily.

Poor Thomas, thought Jemima. He looked so worried. And why should he be so anxious to marry her off? Wasn't she a precious companion and housekeeper for a man who, by the way, was not yet married himself?

Then suddenly, and for no apparent reason, Captain Austin Forrest turned to look right at Jemima and gave her a broad smile.

The following year, on 18 April 1810, Captain Austin Forrest, aged 47, married twenty-six-year-old Jemima Pitt. It was the first marriage to be officially registered in 'the Parish Church of Hawkesbury' and the witnesses were James Wilshire and Thomas Pitt.

Soon afterwards Forrest bought Swilly Farm, from James Badgery. It was close by the Hawkesbury/Nepean River just down the road from Bronte, and it was there that Jemima gave birth on 14 April 1811 to her first child Eliza, who survived a month and died on 15 May.

In November of the same year Captain and Mrs Forrest announced in the *Sydney Gazette* their impending departure for England. It looked as if Jemima was to be the first and only one of her generation to turn her back on the new country, and what a wrench that would be for her mother and her siblings. Whether it was her idea to go home, or her husband's, we will never know. Because late on Christmas Eve of the same year little Eliza died, and less than two years into their marriage, Austin Forrest, on returning home from a trip to Windsor, took a fall from his horse and was killed.

On 28 December 1811 the *Sydney Gazette* carried the following announcement:

'At a late hour on Christmas Eve, as Captain Austin Forrest of Richmond, (formerly of Calcutta) was returning home from Windsor, he was unfortunately killed by a fall from his horse. The body was found between 12 and 1 on Christmas morning shortly after the melancholy accident had taken place, and on Friday the remains of this much connected gentleman were interred at Windsor . . .

The deceased has left a widow to lament her loss, and we may add without a danger of contradiction that everyone who had the slightest knowledge of Captain Forrest will sensibly participate in the feelings of his afflicted widow.'

So ended, sadly, the Forrest line. And Jemima's future, once again, lay in the balance.

Chapter 24

1812: Robert Jenkins

THERE WAS ONE MAN in Sydney who read Forrest's obituary with a particular interest.

In 1812 Robert Jenkins was living in a 'handsome' rented house fronting the harbour in George Street, along with one male convict servant and a boy clerk.

I would imagine Robert immediately sent widowed Mrs Forrest a card expressing his deepest condolences. Then he would have waited a couple of months for the sake of decorum before sending her another letter requesting he pay her a visit at her home C/o Swilly Farm, Richmond.

So it was that one mild day in March 1812 Robert Jenkins travelled by carriage from his house at Sydney Cove to the Hawkesbury. At the entrance to Swilly Farm he was greeted not by Jemima but by another young woman, whom he took, rightly, to be a sister.

'Do come in Mr Jenkins,' said Lucy, rather flustered. 'She is expecting you. She is around somewhere. And do, er, take a seat.'

He did.

The room in which he sat was neat, bright, and impeccably ordered. More like a town house than a country farm, Robert thought to himself.

'And you are?' he enquired politely.

'Mrs Wood, Lucy, Jemima's sister.'

'Do you live here too, Mrs Wood?'

'No no, I live nearby, just across the river from my mother

and my brother, and from my older sister and her husband. We are all still here, save Hester.'

'The whole family lives in Richmond still?' said Robert. 'How very pleasant. Or is it? One never really knows with families these days.'

'It is. Particularly in these – unhappy circumstances.'

'I heard of her loss,' said Robert gravely. He looked down and away for a moment. 'A double loss I believe.'

'Yes.'

There was a brief moment of thoughtful silence.

'And how is she?'

'She is – how can one say? She seems to be coping, in her own way. She is very strong.'

'I remember.'

Another moment passed.

Robert got to his feet. 'Perhaps I should come back later?' He bowed slightly.

'Oh no! That's to say – she is out there somewhere.'

'Then perhaps I may be allowed to go look for her?'

'Well if you like. She really is . . .' Lucy sighed.

'She is what?'

'Sometimes . . . Oh Mr Jenkins sometimes I cannot understand Jemima at all. She is . . .'

'Wilful?'

'Wayward is the word I was looking for. She knew you were coming. I told her she should be here and looking, well, not as if she's just come in from the paddocks, if you see what I mean. She just gave me a look.'

'I can imagine.' Robert smiled. 'All the same, if it is inconvenient. If she is busy.'

'Upon my word no, I shall go find her myself.'

Jemima was standing in her orchard, peering closely at a fruit tree. She wore gardening gloves and heavy boots, into which she had roughly tucked her skirt to keep it from the dirt.

'Yes?' she said, without turning round.

'What are you doing?' cried her elder sister.

'What does it look like? I'm examining the apples for blight. So far so good it seems.'

'Your paramour is here.' Lucy sighed.

'My what?' Jemima turned to look at her sister for the first time.

'You knew he was coming. Don't be coy. He's sitting there like patience on a monument, waiting to see you.'

'I'll be in directly.' Jemima turned her attention back to the tree.

'Oh nonsense. Stop playing hard to get.'

'No such thing. I have work to do. He can wait.'

'It's extraordinarily rude. He wrote to you and you agreed to see him and now he's . . .'

'Right here.'

They looked up to see Jenkins approaching across the paddock. He bent to avoid a low branch of a fruit tree, removed his hat and smiled at Jemima.

'No!' cried Lucy. 'You cannot see her yet!' And she stepped in front of her sister in a ridiculous attempt to shield her outlandishly rustic sibling from the sight of the snappily dressed young man from the city.

'Oh. And why is that?' said he.

'Because she's . . .'

'I am not presentable,' said Jemima, edging around her sister and brushing at her skirt. 'As Lucy would have me be. Dressed to the nines and coiffed to within an inch of my life.'

'And you're not even wearing a hat!'

'And I'm not even wearing a hat. Good day to you Mr Jenkins.'

She extended a hand to him, which was gloved, and covered in a layer of gardener's dirt.

'Oh,' she said. But before she could withdraw it Jenkins had taken the offending hand in his and was brushing it very lightly with his lips.

'It is good to see you,' he said.

'You'll have to forgive the, er, I've been inspecting the

apples.'

'And the prognosis?'

'Well, so far so good, but one can never assume anything. Last year it was greenfly and this year there's been some form of blight, so one cannot take chances.'

Robert smiled. And then he looked grave.

'I heard of your loss, your double loss. I am deeply sorry.'

'Thank you, I received your card.' Jemima looked at him steadily. 'Life goes on.' And then, without turning towards her sister she said, 'What is it Lucy, why are you sighing?'

'Is that all you can say?' Lucy was gazing at her sister in frustration. 'Mr Jenkins has come a long way and you cannot even offer him a cup of tea.'

'Well that's easily fixed,' said Jemima. And pulling off her gloves she led the three of them into the house.

~

It was nearly three years since they'd last met and Jemima did not seem much changed, thought Robert. Slightly thinner perhaps, and older, in maturity rather than appearance. She had grown up, he thought, with a touch of regret. Yet despite her eccentric manner, and dress, she was still a handsome woman.

Lucy poured the tea.

'Sugar, Mr Jenkins?'

'Ah no, Mrs Wood, thank you.'

'Lucy's husband,' said Jemima by way of explanation, 'is a mariner, hence his almost continuous absence.'

'That must be hard for you.' Robert smiled at Lucy. 'It must be hard for both of you.'

'Strangely enough much can be achieved without male company,' said Jemima. 'Is your tea strong enough, Mr Jenkins?'

'It is, thank you. The farm, for instance?'

'The farm included. It's hard work, isn't it Lucy, but we manage. And I was never afraid of hard work.'

'You have helpers, of course.'

'Of course. But one must keep an eye. You must know that for yourself. When the river deigns to stay within its appointed banks,' Jemima went on, 'which I'm happy to say it has for a year or so, then life is quite tolerable.'

'The farm looks magnificent.'

'There you are then,' she said.

They drank their tea in silence for a moment.

'And how has life been for you, Mr Jenkins?' asked Lucy from the corner of the room to which she had removed herself in an uncharacteristic attempt to appear invisible.

'Life?' Robert turned to see where the voice came from. 'Ah, life – has been interesting, you could say.'

'I'm surprised you chose to stay in the colony after your – unfortunate beginnings,' said Jemima.

'So was I,' said Robert, turning back to address her. 'The truth is I had no choice. I was penniless, not to put too fine a point on it. But necessity being the mother of enterprise I was forced to go into business on my own account and, bit by bit, I have built myself up. And since what sets this country apart from any other is that a man of initiative may make something out of nothing – a fact of which I am living proof – I fully intend to stay the course here.'

'Indeed,' said Jemima.

There was a short pause.

'And if I may be allowed to boast for a moment ...' he continued.

'Absolutely not.'

'I beg your pardon?' He looked to see if Jemima was smiling, and saw she was not.

'You may give me a factual account of yourself, if you wish to. I can't abide a boastful man.'

'Then I will do my utmost, humbly, to explain that thanks to – good fortune – and my eagerness to grasp opportunities where I see them – which is itself dependent on a certain good luck you could say, in that such opportunities do not present themselves to everyone, as I fully appreciate, so I count myself fortunate in that instance, I ... Where was I?'

'Talking in riddles,' said Jemima, smiling slightly despite herself. 'Where do you live?

'Ah. I live in a handsome – no, splendid – or perhaps large – is large acceptable? – house with a magnificent – ah, a pleasant, yes, a pleasant view of Sydney harbour.'

'And in what are you engaged at present?'

'Engaged? You mean work. Oh, you would find it dull and insignificant.'

'That's a shame.'

'I am engaged in a profitable if – unexciting, at least to the layman – albeit prestigious, I think I can say in all humility, task of auditing the books of a company called Kable, Lord and Underwood.'

'I've heard of them.'

'Appointed by the Court of Civil Jurisdiction. If that is not to sound presumptuous, or indeed pretentious.'

'So you've become a respectable citizen at last.' Jemima smiled faintly. 'Are you married?'

'No I am not.'

'And what is the purpose of this visit?'

He felt like a schoolboy under interrogation. A bit of him wanted to get up and walk away. And then he remembered it had been Jemima's directness that he has always found so enticing. Not say challenging.

'I came to pay my respects,' he said, with a hint of archness. 'And to remind you of my existence.'

Jemima turned away from him and appeared to look out of the window for some time.

'Are you ambitious Mr Jenkins?' she said, still gazing out of the window.

Robert frowned. 'Why 'Mr Jenkins'?'

'Robert then.' She turned to look at him again, her eyebrow cocked in enquiry.

'Naturally I am ambitious,' said he. 'Who in this colony is not? Is that so bad?'

'Not in the least.' She gave him a smile, but it was a wary one. And then rather abruptly she said, 'Talking of hard work, if you will excuse me I have plenty of it.'

There was a little gasp from the corner.

Jemima rose and held out her hand. 'Forgive me,' she said to Robert, 'but as you yourself pointed out a woman without a man is a helpless thing, so she must work all the harder to keep the home fires burning, so to speak.'

'I understand,' muttered Robert, bending over her hand.

'Especially considering what lies ahead.'

'To what,' said Robert, 'are you specifically referring?'

'To my departure to England. Did you not know?'

Robert's face froze momentarily.

'Er, no, I had no idea.'

'Postponed somewhat. This country has not been a lucky one for me, Mr Jenkins.'

'I am – forgive me,' Robert coughed into his hand. 'I am extremely sorry to hear that, Mrs Forrest.'

'So you see your journey was rather wasted. I apologise, Mr Jenkins. Robert.'

It was Lucy who accompanied Robert outside. As they stood waiting for the horses to be harnessed she said, 'You must not take her manner to heart, Mr Jenkins.'

'She is still in mourning of course.'

'That's not it. Well yes she is, but she's afraid people are only after her money. She doesn't just own Swilly Farm you know, she has another 500 acres in Liberty Plains.'

'I know.'

'All of which makes her a highly desirable prospect, and she's only too aware of it.'

'I did love her once.' Robert removed his hat for a moment and smoothed his hand over his hair. It was brushed forward across his brow, quite *à la mode,* as Lucy could not help but notice, approvingly.

'And she loved you too. But since the accident, she has become – altered.'

'I noticed.' He replaced his hat on his head.

'Not to say insufferable.'

'And is she really . . .' he cleared his throat, 'really planning on going back to England?'

Lucy didn't immediately respond.

'I mean, if I had realised . . .'

'She threatens it.' She wiped away a tear. 'She says she has no reason to stay here now. As if the family were not reason enough.'

'So you think, if there were reason enough, perhaps beyond family . . .' He let the suggestion dangle.

'Of course. But you will need to be determined. And you will need to be thick-skinned, and not easily thwarted.'

'That I can manage.'

Lucy was crying openly now. 'If you can persuade her . . . Oh Mr Jenkins you have no idea how happy that would make us all. It makes no sense at all for her to go back to England but she seems to think this country only brings her bad luck.'

She looked into the distance for a moment. 'She needs to know it is possible to be happy again. She needs – to let other people in, if you see what I mean.'

She turned and tried to smile.

'Thank you, Mrs Wood,' said Robert. He looked at her gravely as he took her hand and bowed over it. 'You have given me food for thought.'

He turned to step into the carriage and as he did so Lucy reached up and touched his arm.

'You will come again, won't you Mr Jenkins?'

'Rest assured.'

~

In November of that same year, 1812, Robert Jenkins wrote a long letter home. It took nearly two years to arrive and would not have arrived at all had it not been for the extraordinary tenacity of its bearer.

In the early 19th century there was no official postal service between New South Wales and Britain, so letters were carried aboard whatever ship happened to be making the journey and the delivery at the other end was often quite random. For some reason Jenkins's letter, along with others, found its way into the hands of a General Joseph Holt. Holt was an Irish emancipist who had been transported to Botany Bay for leading insurgents on behalf of the United Irishmen in the Irish Rebellion of 1798. He had received a full pardon in January 1811 and was returning to Britain on the *Isabella*, leaving Port Jackson in December 1812.

The ship was wrecked off the Falklands Islands. Holt hung on there till April 1813 and then managed to hitch a lift, but to America rather than England. He did not arrive in Britain until the following February, fourteen months after he had left New South Wales; and amazingly, he was still carrying the 54 letters from New South Wales, some of which he insisted on delivering personally. So in early March he hired a coach to take him to every address he needed to visit in London. Among them was Number 18 Wells Street, Cripplegate.

On arriving at the house he rapped on the door and a young woman – whom he rightly assumed to be Jenkins's sister – answered. On being handed the letter and told it was from her brother, she fainted. Moments later an elderly lady appeared and on being told the same thing, did likewise. It transpired they had been told Robert had died two years earlier.

> *'You will be surprised to hear me talk of making a home in such a terrible country as New South Wales* [Jenkins wrote], *but when I enquire into the state of trade and general affairs in England, I receive from those lately arrived from that country such unfavourable intelligence that I really conceive I am better here, where I am well known and know everybody, where I am generally well respected . . . I fully intend, when I can scrape up money, to purchase some cows and let them breed.*
>
> *. . . upon the whole, I do not think that the circumstances of having been kidnapped into the colony will be one of the greatest misfortunes of my life.'*

He described his handsome house fronting the harbour,

where he led a bachelor existence. And then:

'As a secret, I will also acquaint you that I am courting a rich widow, young, rather handsome, very good-tempered, a great economist, and therefore very desirable. If we do say the crooked words, I will let you know, but this is at present a great secret.'

The rich widow, of course, could not have been anyone other than Jemima Forrest.

Chapter 25

An ideal husband

MARY WOULD HAVE WATCHED Robert Jenkins's courtship of her only remaining unmarried daughter with keen interest.

Of Mary's three sons in law only James Wilshire could have been considered, by the standards of early 19th century New South Wales, ideal husband material. Yet the assumption is – since there were no signs of family rifts – that Mary Pitt had given her blessing to both John Wood, a humble mariner, and William Faithfull, the illiterate ex-private.

It has been a long time since a mother could dictate who her offspring should and shouldn't marry, although no one could ever stop a parent from voicing an opinion. Mrs Bennet in *Pride & Prejudice* declared no man with less than four thousand a year could possibly be acceptable for any of her five daughters. We may scoff, as we are invited to do, at Mrs Bennet's apparent mercenary ambitions, but despite her flightiness she was only too aware of the precariousness of an all-female household. It was not simply snobbery, it was a question of survival.

My mother had different priorities. She used to tell me she didn't mind who I married so long as he was white, he wasn't an actor and his eyes were not too close together. In this she was thinking both of herself and me – she knew what actors were like. So I spent years looking for a non-white actor, without success, and ended up marrying a white journalist with normal eyes who was, not to put too fine a point on it, a notch or two down in the social scale. My mother, unsurprisingly, disapproved, claiming he wasn't good enough for me, by which she meant he was not good enough for her. It was not because he wasn't intelligent, or mature, or in a steady, well-paid job. It was because he spoke with a south London accent. It was a question of class.

My mother herself married Mr Ideal: a decent, quiet, intelligent businessman of old, upper middle class English/Irish stock. It's said he introduced her to income tax, which doesn't sound very romantic. They stayed together throughout their lives, and despite what seemed to me to be important differences they were entirely interdependent and in their own way, devoted.

For my part I have always maintained that I don't care who my children marry or end up with so long as he or she makes them happy. But that is because I am an Enlightened 21st Century Person who cares not a hoot for a person's race, class, background or financial situation. More to the point, my kids have careers which one way or another they should be able to continue when or if they find partners and have children. Which gives them an independence and freedom even I didn't really have thirty years ago. It's a question of happiness.

But Mary's situation was not mine, nor my mother's – and nor, strictly speaking, Mrs Bennet's.

Money, class and happiness meant very different things in early New South Wales. To begin with until Governor Macquarie introduced a form of currency for the first time in the 1810s there was no such thing as money. People traded using promissory notes, and barter, and labourers and junior soldiers, notoriously, were often paid in rum. Moreover a rich person setting foot on colonial soil – which not many of them did in those early days – would not have been able to hang onto his money unless he was prepared to work hard and use his initiative. Money could buy a person land and labour to work it, but even owning land was not much use unless you knew how to make it productive.

As for class: there was no landed gentry; no Mr Darcys or

Mr Bingleys, or even Mr Matchams, men of inherited fortune who spent their time on gentlemanly pursuits such as hunting, shooting and socialising. Everyone from the governor down had to work for his living, no matter who he was or where he came from. Some of the colony's most significant characters, including many governors, army officers and men such as John Macarthur, came from quite lowly backgrounds.

As for the luxury of marrying for happiness: Australia is rightly proud of powerful women pioneers such as Elizabeth Macarthur, Mary Reibey and Hannah Laycock (my four times great grandmother). But in each of these cases while the women may have shown as much if not more enterprise and business sense than their husbands, they still depended on them for their beginnings. Mary Pitt and Hannah Laycock were among very few women to be granted land in their own right. Hannah's was given to her by Governor King ostensibly as part compensation for her husband Thomas's doubtful behaviour. Yet in a codicil to his will Thomas bequeathed this same grant to his wife, so technically it belonged to him. Ironically a later grant promised to Hannah by King did not materialise because of a change in the law regarding women's land rights.

So finding ideal husbands was crucial for the Pitt girls. However enterprising and clever they were, they depended on men to get them off the starting blocks. They did not have the luxury of being able to marry for love or happiness alone.

Family lore says it was Thomas who disapproved of Jemima's initial liaison with the bankrupt Robert Jenkins. Jemima, as I've painted her and as she turned out later in her life, was not the sort of person to be dictated to and she was not under age, so maybe she saw sense in her brother's objection at the time, who knows.

When James Wilshire married Hester he was acting deputy commissary and running his own tannery business. He owned a house in Chapel Row (now Castlereagh Street), which he sold for £100 soon after his marriage, and he had also extended his early grant in Lane Cove to 245 acres, which was leased out. As these things went, he was as ideal as they came.

At the time of marrying Susanna William Faithfull already owned 118 acres at Petersham Hill, plus stock given him by his ex commanding officer, Colonel Foveaux. He also had a share in a 125 acre grant in Richmond, about which he was in dispute and which he sold soon after his marriage. The 100 acre block of land he and Susanna went to live on next to Mary at Green Hills was leased. Faithfull's background may have been lowly but his connection with Foveaux proved significant.

John Wood was a seaman who despite his 100 acre grant continued going to sea for the rest of his life, which suggests he either didn't take to farming or felt he could not rely on it to support his family. Robert Jenkins, at the time of wooing Jemima for the second time was on his way to becoming ... but that's to give the game away.

Ideal husbands or not, in early 19th century New South Wales, Mary must have been sleeping better at night.

Chapter 26

1809: The settler and the convict

'Old Mrs Pit is very fond of me,' wrote Margaret Catchpole in a letter to her uncle and aunt in October 1809, *'. . . but I shall I believe soon goo to live by myself.'*

By then they would have known one another for around five years, the settler and the convict, most probably ever since Margaret helped deliver Lucy Wood's daughter Sophia. Whenever Mary's health faltered she was there, this strange, dark-haired woman, ministering to her with her strange herbal remedies, the ingredients of which she kept a tight secret.

But Mary Pitt must have wondered about her. About how such a sober-minded, conscientious and resourceful woman could have been led into stealing a horse and finding herself transported to Botany Bay.

'Were you a firebrand in your youth, Margaret?' she asked her one day.

It was June, early winter on the Hawkesbury. There was still a bit of warmth when the sun was at its height, but the ground frosts were hard at night. Yet nothing would stop Mary from spending the morning, as she spent most mornings, sitting on the veranda of the house that came to be known as Bronte.

Margaret flushed. 'I'm sure I don't know what you mean, madam.'

'Don't you? You say very little about your background, and that is your privilege, of course. And I know you have good connections and faithful friends back in the old country.'

'And how do you know that?'

'All those parcels and letters you receive.'

'Ah, those. They took long enough. Some of them took two years to get to me.'

'I know. The postal service here is almost as bad as in England. And while I don't mean to pry . . .' Mary paused for a moment, but nothing was forthcoming.

'I heard about the Dight family. That you saved the lives of Mrs Dight and her three children in the floods,' she continued. She was talking of the floods that in March of that year came higher than they'd ever been since the Pitts went to live there.

'I only did what anyone would do, madam,' said Margaret.

'That's not strictly true, is it?'

'Are you quite comfortable, madam?'

'Stop trying to change the subject. And do sit down.' Mary indicated the chair next to her.

'Mrs Dight said the water came up into the house faster than she'd ever believed possible,' said Mary, as Margaret took the seat next to her.

'That is true. Up to our middle in less than two hours.'

'And where was Mr Dight meanwhile?'

'He'd gone down with his men to release the pigs. When the rains first started coming. But he wasn't to know, none of us was to know how quick. So then, I could see we couldn't make it out through the door and in floods, they tell you always to go upwards, if you can. So that's what we did.'

'Up into the roof?'

'And we weren't there more than a moment when the chimney went and then the middle wall and I thought we'd be crushed to death, me and Mrs Dight and the three little children, all of us. And you could hear, it was dreadful, the screaming of the poor people riding on their houses crying out for God's sake to be saved. Others firing their guns. And then providence turned up a boat to save us from a watery grave, and I was more frightened then than ever before.'

She paused and brushed her skirt for a moment. Mary turned to look at her.

'Mrs Dight said it was not the first time you've saved the lives of other people, and their children.'

'Did she say that?' Margaret continued to look down at her lap.

'I suppose life here must be quite dull for you compared with your life back home.'

'Oh no,' Margaret looked up. 'That's not true at all, not at all.'

A small tear had appeared in the corner of her eye and she brushed if off, crossly. 'I'm trying to lead a good life, madam,' she said.

'I know you are, Margaret.' Mary leaned over and placed her hand over the other woman's. 'And so you do. Ever since you arrived here, at the Hawkesbury, you've made yourself an indispensable member of the community and I don't know what we would do without you, any of us. Which is what makes me all the more curious.' She smiled and squeezed Margaret's hand. 'But I have no right to ask you these questions in the first place.'

It disturbed her to see Margaret so discomfited. This private woman, private and independent and unmarried woman – three things that singled her out from almost every other woman in the colony, convict or free. And it was not for want of offers – there had been a gardener, and several sailors, and she had turned them all down.

After eighteen months or so with the Palmers Margaret had gone to work for the Bowman family on the Hawkesbury, and thence to the Rouses – whose baby she had helped deliver on board *Nile*. She was even asked to look after their property when Richard Rouse was relocated to Parramatta, but she found it a 'lonesome' job and quit to go and live on her own, along with a few sheep and goats. Since then she had gone from one family to another in the Hawkesbury district, mostly to help deliver their babies. The following month, October, she went to help Susanna give birth to her firstborn, William Pitt.

~

As for Margaret's history, the truth, according to her confession to the magistrate after she was apprehended, and which Mary probably never did get to learn, went like this:

It was 1797, when Margaret was around thirty-four years old. She was at a loose end during a rare spell of unemployment and was wandering the streets of Ipswich when she'd bumped into a man called John Cook. He claimed to have known Margaret from before, a claim she denied, yet she agreed to meet again and on one of those occasions he'd proposed marriage, which she declined.

It was his idea she dress up in boy's clothing and steal her ex-employer Mr Cobbold's horse, ride it to London and sell it. She told the magistrate Cook threatened to kill her if she did not. It was Cook who released the coach horse from the stable but it was Margaret, an expert horsewoman, who rode it all the way to Aldgate in east London, by which time word had got out and a notice posted about a stolen horse, and she was apprehended and taken into custody and later tried. Of John Cook there was no sign, then or later.

There were holes in the story which the Reverend Cobbold attempted to fill in in his book. Why having stolen the horse against her will did Margaret not give herself up before she arrived in London and explain her story? According to the Reverend, Cook had shown Margaret a forged letter claiming to be from Will Laud which said he would be waiting in London for her in order to marry her. However Margaret did not mention Laud in her confession, nor did she refer to a letter, so that was presumably the Reverend's embellishment.

Whatever the circumstances she took the rap and despite her good character she received the mandatory death sentence for horse stealing, commuted to transportation. Then after three anguished years in jail waiting to be transported she was urged by Will Laud, who happened to be languishing in the debtors' prison next door, to escape, and during the ensuing chase he was killed.

Of John Cook there was no further mention, until in a letter to her uncle and aunt Margaret wrote, intriguingly, *'I hope you will see my John Cook and give my love to him.'*

The truth will probably never be known.

The story may seem the stuff of high drama to us now, but in her letters home Margaret makes it very clear she was doing all she could to put her past behind her and lead an honest life, socialising with her 'betters' and working her way to a full pardon so she could do what she always wanted to do, return home to her family and friends.

> *'I mind that my company is good always, better than myself, and if anything I go smarter than ever I did. I look pretty well but I have lost one of my front teeth and a good many of them are broken away.'*

So she wrote to her uncle and aunt in 1807. She had been back to work for the Palmers but had suffered sunstroke walking thirty miles in the blazing heat on an errand for them; so while she said Mrs Palmer was *'a very nices ladey'* and was sorry to part with her, she felt the work there was too hard. She talked of the high price of wheat, stock, tea and shoes, and the toll the heavy floods took on herself and others, both physical and financial. She said the country was still full of *'wicked people'* – she felt unsafe travelling about on her own, and a parcel that had been sent to her from home was stolen – but the natives were becoming less troublesome. The weather, she claimed, was responsible for the enduring fertility of older women – *'Very old women have them* [children] *that never had none before'* - and the precociousness of the younger - *'the young girls that are born in this country marry very young at 14 or 15 years old.'*

She rented a farm of around fifteen acres and lived there alone *'except a little child or two come and stop with me'* – quite possibly children she had helped deliver, who she regarded as her grandchildren. One of the last things she wrote was, *'I am living all alone as before in a very honest way of life – here is not one woman in the Colony live like myself.'*

After her adventurous beginnings not a whiff of scandal

touched Margaret while she was in the colony. She would have been mortified to know that some time after her death, later in the 1800s, she was to become the subject of so much speculation and gossip, and all thanks to the Reverend Cobbold's book.

Chapter 27

1810: The Laycocks

ONE YEAR LATER, on another veranda in another part of Sydney, my fourteen-year-old great great great grandmother Elizabeth Laycock sat looking out over the scrap of land they called a paddock at King's Grove Farm.

After arriving in the colony in 1791 Thomas and Hannah Laycock had produced two more children to add to their existing four, both of them girls. It was the younger of the two who now sat, her legs swinging beneath her, struggling to come to terms with the country she had just arrived in.

The outlook did nothing to lift her mood. It was September, which Elizabeth had to remind herself in this topsy-turvy country was spring. The ground beyond the veranda was a sort of dull brown, like straw, which is pretty much what it was. The trees were a washed-out green, more silvery grey than green really, and many of them looked half dead, branches broken off and hanging, the bark peeling off and drooping like sad strips of old rag. There was a line of them by the stream, or creek, as they called it here. It went on, the land, more scrub than land, in all directions, up the hills and down again, on and on, the same greyish-greenish-brownish, all the way to the horizon. The only real colour to be seen was in the sky, a brilliant blue, very different from home and, like everything else, it looked foreign, all of it. Foreign and weird. And then there was the scrawtch of the birds – there was no other way to describe the horrible noise they made – scrawtch scrawtch scrawtch scrawtch, on and on and on.

Two days before, Elizabeth Laycock had arrived back in the colony in which she'd been born, but had barely lived, with her mother Hannah and her elder sister Rebecca. At the age of not quite five years old she had been sent back to the old country to be educated, along with her sister and her brothers William and Samuel, and she had lived there ever since.

The first mention of the two Laycock girls in England comes from a letter written by their guardian in September 1801 to William Balmain, New South Wales's chief surgeon, which said, *'Tell Mr Laycock his two girls are hearty and well and the boys was very well a few days ago when I heard from them.'*

(The boys were obviously living separately from the girls and there is an unconfirmed report they went to Eton.) On his return to England the following year Balmain himself wrote to D'Arcy Wentworth – assistant surgeon and one of the colony's more colourful inhabitants, who bought his property at Homebush from Quartermaster Laycock – saying, *'Tell Laycock's family I kissed his two daughters. They are delightful girls and . . . I shall ride to see his sons the moment I have time.'*

The two boys had returned to New South Wales in 1804, and then in or around 1808 their mother had left the colony and gone to join her daughters in England, where she had stayed for two years. It has been suggested that she did so to get away from her ne'er-do-well of a husband, and since in the governor's statistical report of 1807 he was listed as 'living with a concubine' one can hardly blame her. The year before that Thomas had been court martialled, along with his son Thomas junior, and dismissed from the New South Wales Corps, after thirty-three years of service, for threatening his commanding officer Major Johnston and publicly proclaiming he would call him out and take a shot at him. In his will, drawn up not long before he died and which Hannah may or may not have had sight of, Thomas referred to his wife as *'now residing in England or elsewhere'*, so there had obviously been little or no communication between Mr and Mrs Laycock since Mrs Laycock had been out of the colony.

Inside the house a conversation was in progress, which Elizabeth was part eavesdropping through the mesh of the open window behind her. Her brothers were talking to her mother and sister, filling them in on the latest news in the colony. Bits of it reached her. There was 'a new governor . . . sorting out the chaos . . . since the rebellion.'

'Father was unwell.' It was William talking.

Her ears pricked up at the mention of her father. Quartermaster Laycock, the man she never really knew, who she hadn't seen since she'd left the colony and had only the vaguest recollection of – hugely tall, rather loud, quite fierce but quite a character too – and now he was dead. They'd come all this way without even knowing that he had died before they had left home.

'What do you mean, unwell?' asked her sister Rebecca.

'For the past few years.'

'He went mad.' She recognised Sammy's voice. 'Frankly. Barking. He picked quarrels all the time. He went out of his way to insult everyone. He called Thomas a bugger and a rascal. Accused him of 'walking out' with the housekeeper. In public.' This was Thomas junior, Elizabeth's brother, also of the New South Wales Corps.

'What housekeeper?' asked Rebecca.

'Mary Sargent her name was. He left her £200 in his will,' said Samuel, with meaning.

There was a silence.

'He was accused of treating His Majesty's Service with contempt by declaring he didn't give a damn for his commission,' Samuel went on. 'In public.'

'Who is this Mary Sargent?' Rebecca asked again.

'And what else was there? Yes, drinking in public houses with known prostitutes and Irish rebels.'

'The charge was cancelled,' said William.

'So it was.'

'This all happened years ago, Samuel,' said Elizabeth's mother.

'I know. But in the last year or so he became – what's the word, Will?'

'Irrational. According to Wentworth.'

'That's the word he used.'

'Wentworth? D'Arcy Wentworth?' Her mother sounded concerned. 'Why should he have anything to do with it?'

'He was helpful to us', said William. 'He's a good and useful friend when you need one. It was he who advised us to take over father's affairs.'

'I see.'

There was a short pause.

'I'm sorry if you find all this distressing, mother,' said William.

Elizabeth thought she could hear her mother sigh, and her next remark was spoken so softly she could barely hear it.

'There is nothing I didn't already know, William.'

'And you do have to remember his better side. Let's not forget the astonishing acts of bravery at Castle Hill, for which he was officially commended.'

'By Major Johnston of all people,' said Samuel, and laughed loudly. 'You know about Castle Hill, Becky?'

'A little.'

'The Irish convicts rebelled. Or tried to. Ha! Typical of them, messed it up completely, fortunately for us. And it was father who was instrumental in putting them down.'

'What did he do?'

'He was in charge of a detachment of the New South Wales Corps. They marched through the night, from Sydney to Parramatta and on to the Hawkesbury. Fifty soldiers against two hundred rebels. And routed them. Major Johnston said no amount of praise could adequately reflect Quartermaster Laycock's outstanding bravery.'

'Your father was an immensely courageous man,' said Hannah.

'He was also a drunk and a philanderer,' said Sammy.

'What's a philanderer?'

It had become altogether too interesting. Elizabeth was standing in the doorway of the room. There was Sammy, his legs hooked over the arm of his chair, and William, next to him, sitting bolt upright.

Sammy unhooked his legs and lent forward. 'A philanderer, Lizzie, is someone who . . .'

'Thank you Samuel, there is no need.' said his mother.

Elizabeth perched on the arm of the settee, next to her sister. She wasn't sure she wanted to be part of the conversation but neither did she want to miss anything.

'Father and Thomas were banged up for bad behaviour on a public street and he was dismissed from the Corps, Lizzie.'

'Like someone else I know,' said William.

'And as you also know, brother, that was for playing cards.'

'You were dismissed from the New South Wales Corps for playing cards?' Rebecca stared at her brother in dismay.

'With a private,' Sammy shrugged. 'Such is the way of things. As for papa – he was a rubber ball, Lizzie, he always bounced back.'

'Wasn't there something' Rebecca wrinkled her eyebrows, 'about a pig?'

'Boston's pig!' Her younger brother kicked up his heels in joy. 'What a story! Boston's prize sow, grazing on Foveaux's prime land! He ordered some underling to take a pot shot at it and, pop! Landed himself in a whole pile of sh . . . trouble and got himself a fine in the bargain. A long story, Lizzie. Another time.'

'Indeed,' said their mother firmly.

Elizabeth may not have been following every detail but she'd got the gist. Her father was a hero, a rogue, a drunk and an all-round embarrassment.

'Time will tell,' said William in his measured tone, directing himself towards his younger sister. 'But I believe history will speak well of father. He was a loyal member of the New South Wales Corps, Lizzie. And a member of the Court of Jurisdiction. He was not without faults, but he was at the same time a brave, generous, clever man who will be remembered above all . . .'

'Who will be remembered,' said Elizabeth, more or less to herself.

'. . . as a man of significance, a pioneer, who played a crucial part in shaping the future of this colony,' concluded William.

'Thank you William,' said his mother, with a smile. 'That was gracious of you.'

'RIP,' said Samuel.

~

It's true to say Quartermaster Laycock was quite often in the headlines, either for ordering William Faithfull to shoot John Boston's pig or for mutinous and disorderly behaviour on the streets of Sydney. At the same time over the years he managed to acquire 1655 acres of prime land in and around Sydney, from Parsley Bay (now the site of Vaucluse House) to Liberty Plains and beyond. In the end he did seem to go off the rails and his affairs were handed over to his sons William and Thomas Junior, with the aid of D'Arcy Wentworth.

King's Grove Farm had been granted to Hannah in 1804 by Governor King, hence its name. At 500 acres it was the second largest grant of many that were given that day and one of only two granted to women. On the same day both William, aged around nineteen, and Samuel, aged around sixteen, were granted 100 acres each close by. They were the first grants to be allocated in what subsequently to be known as, oddly enough, Kingsgrove.

At a time when education was only generally available to families of 'quality' and, of those, rarely for their women, for the Laycocks to have gone to the trouble and expense of sending not only their sons but their daughters to England for this purpose was significant. It suggested that Hannah and Thomas, and I would hazard a guess it was mostly Hannah, had aspirations for their daughters – social if not intellectual. And it's more than probable Hannah carried these aspirations with her when she brought Rebecca and Elizabeth back to New

South Wales.

However in my story Elizabeth had been in a sulk from the moment she boarded *Canada* (coincidentally the same ship that had brought the Pitts to the colony on its first journey nine years earlier). She could see no reason why she should be forced to uproot herself from the only country she knew and transported, like a convict – or so she saw herself – away from her friends and everything familiar. The one thing that had kept her going had been the prospect of seeing her brothers again and, most important of all, of meeting the father she barely knew. And now not only was that denied her, but the man she had hero-worshipped from afar turned out to be a scoundrel – if what her brothers said was true – and known to virtually every person in the colony except his two younger daughters.

Chapter 28

1810: The visit

IN THE EARLY AFTERNOON of Thursday 13 December 1810 the Laycocks had visitors.

Elizabeth watched them through the window at King's Grove Farm. There were two of them, a man and a woman, and they were strolling around in front of the house with her mother. He walked upright, ramrod stiff. The woman, his wife presumably, walked alongside him, nodding occasionally and pointing at things. Fragments of conversation drifted Elizabeth's way.

'It's not much of a garden I'm afraid.' It was her mother speaking. 'We've been away, the girls and I, we only arrived back quite recently.'

'Back from where?' asked the woman. She had an accent, Scottish, Elizabeth surmised.

'England.'

'Ah, England. And are you glad to be back?'

Her mother's answer came through loud and clear and turned Elizabeth's heart to ice.

'Oh yes. This is our home now.'

'Allow me to introduce you,' said Hannah Laycock, as she entered the house with her guests. 'My younger daughter Elizabeth and my elder daughter Rebecca. Governor and Mrs Macquarie.'

Elizabeth did a half-curtsey and her elder sister gave a little bow. The governor returned the bow and smiled.

He had greying hair, combed forwards strand by strand in

neat little waves that rested on his forehead a bit like seaweed, thought Elizabeth. He had a long, rather noble nose. His eyes were like rocks but when he smiled, they smiled too.

His wife seemed to take her cue from her husband. She was not by any stretch of the imagination a beauty but she looked friendly enough, if rather pale. She had the same nose as her husband (they were cousins, though Elizabeth was not to know this), and she held a fan, which from time to time she waved, in a desultory attempt to seek relief from the fierce December heat.

'The girls were born in the colony,' her mother was saying. 'However they have spent most of their lives in England and are most pleased to be back.' She looked meaningfully at her younger daughter. 'Do sit down.'

'Thank you,' said the governor. He spoke like his wife, with a brusque Scots accent, but lilting too.

'May I offer you refreshment?' said the lady of the house.

'That is very . . .' began Mrs Macquarie.

'No no, thank you,' interrupted her husband. 'We'll not be staying long.'

He lowered himself into an upright chair and turned to peruse the room and its contents.

'To what,' asked Hannah, 'do we owe the pleasure?'

'We're doing the rounds of the colony,' said the governor. He crossed his ankles in a manner that was almost prim. 'Checking up on you all, you could say.'

'And how do you find us?'

The good man shook his head. 'A bit of a curate's egg, Mrs Laycock, you could say. On some of the farms the pasture land is excellent, the rest of it – little better than a slum, to tell you the truth.'

'Oh!'

'The official buildings in particular, most of them, in a state of total decay. Streets no better than sheep's tracks and some of the farmhouses little more than huts. I wonder any person can live in this country with any pride.'

'We have seen some places in a shocking state of disrepair,' said Mrs Macquarie, almost apologetically.

'I do not include you in this Mrs Laycock,' the governor continued.

'I'm relieved to hear it,' said she.

'On the contrary I find you in an excellently forward state of improvement.'

'He's referring to the farm of course,' said his lady wife, with a little laugh. 'The house itself is charming, if I may say so Mrs Laycock, and most comfortable.' She waved her fan and looked about her.

'It's been too long,' the governor went on, 'far too long since this colony was properly managed. Ever since the rebellion the place has gone to rack and ruin, and I . . .'

'What rebellion?' asked Elizabeth.

'Hush Elizabeth, the governor is speaking,' said her mother. 'I apologise Mr Macquarie, do go on.'

'She doesn't know her own country's history?' He raised an eyebrow. 'Then you have some teaching to do, Mrs Laycock.

'In this country,' he continued, 'emancipists outnumber free settlers – did you know that, Mrs Laycock? And yet no one will allow them a proper place. They have never been received into society, nor given positions of authority, and why not? Why should a convicted felon who has served his term not be allowed to redeem himself by doing good works for the benefit of the community? It's a scandalous waste. There are good men, and women too, who could be useful members of the society if they were allowed to be.'

'I think,' Hannah began, with some trepidation, 'you might encounter some opposition to this theory, Mr Macquarie.'

'Opposition? Tcha!' It was an odd sound, a bit like a small explosion. 'What opposition? This country has had no proper leadership for two years - two years, Mrs Laycock. Since the appalling deposition of His Majesty's governor this country has been ruled by a small group of usurpers for the benefit of themselves and their kind only. And not for the first time. I am revoking every land grant authorised during the illegal interregnum and I am replacing everyone in authority with those properly qualified to hold such offices, whatever their background.'

There was silence. The women looked at him wide-eyed.

'As for the opposition – I have every respect for those people who came here of their own free will but this country is to be run for the benefit of everyone, not just to appease a few. Emancipists are the future of this country Mrs Laycock. That is my belief and my determination.'

'I see,' said Hannah. And then, partly by way of changing the subject, 'And where else have you visited, in your tour of the colony?' she asked.

'We've been west to Parramatta, Toongabbie, Baulkham Hills,' said the governor's wife. 'Where else, dear?'

'The Hawkesbury, Castle Hill, south along the George's River,' said the governor. 'Not forgetting,' he said with a smile, 'Liverpool'.

'Liverpool?' Hannah raised her eyebrows.

'Mr Macquarie has been naming some new townships,' said his wife. 'I believe we've visited most of the colony, haven't we dear?'

'Such as it is,' said her husband.

'While you were at the Hawkesbury,' said Hannah, 'did you, by any chance, happen to encounter anyone of the Pitt family? Mary Pitt, and her son and daughters?'

'Mary Pitt, now,' the governor pondered. 'I believe we did, yes. By Green Hills that would be, would it?'

'Richmond, dear,' said his wife with a smile.

'Ah yes, indeed. Richmond,' he chuckled. 'Bronte. Yes, I remember. Nelson. The Nelson connection. Yes indeed.'

'And how was she?'

'Who? Oh, Mrs Pitt. She was well. Yes. As I remember. The widow with the daughters ..?' he looked at his wife.

'Many daughters,' said she. 'All married now I believe.'

'I am so glad,' said Hannah. 'I must arrange a visit.'

'I've christened the new townships of the Hawkesbury, Mrs Laycock. Green Hills is now Windsor, from the similarity of its situation to that of the same name in England, and Richmond, after Richmond Hill.'

'A little touch of England on the Hawkesbury.' Hannah smiled.

'Precisely. Moreover . . .'

'Dearest,' interrupted the governor's wife, glancing at the clock on the wall. 'We should not take up the time of these good ladies any longer.'

'Indeed. Indeed,' said the great man, getting to his feet. 'We have other places to visit, Mrs Laycock. May I say it has been the greatest pleasure to have met you.' He bowed, first to Hannah, then to the girls.

'It has been an honour, sir,' said Hannah. 'And perhaps you will tell me if I passed? Will we get a good report?'

'My dear lady, of course,' said the governor with a smile.

~

'Well my dears,' said Hannah as she closed the door on the visitors. 'That was a surprise.'

She brushed the dust from her skirt, sat herself down and dabbed delicately at her face with a handkerchief.

The heat hung heavily. Elizabeth leaned back in her chair. A fly buzzed. She followed its progress, cross-eyed, as it circled annoyingly and pointlessly around her head.

'That man is exactly what this country needs,' Hannah pronounced.

'I thought he was odd,' said Elizabeth.

'In what way?' asked her mother.

'Arrogant.'

'Arrogant? He's the governor of the colony, he has every right to be arrogant. What this country needs,' Hannah repeated, 'is a man of vision and vigour. He seems exactly that sort of man. And his wife was charming.'

'What did he mean about the country having no proper leadership for two years?' asked Rebecca.

'He was referring to the deposing of Governor Bligh. Something you should know about. Your brother Thomas was closely concerned with it.'

'Thomas was responsible for deposing Governor Bligh?' Rebecca's eyes widened.

'Not on his own, of course not.'

'And what did the governor do to get himself deposed?'

The fly came to rest on Elizabeth's forearm and she made a desultory attempt to swat it. But the heat had got to her and she was too slow.

'In a nutshell,' said Hannah, 'he upset some of the most powerful people in the colony, and so they petitioned to get rid of him.'

'Who did? Who wanted rid of him?' asked Rebecca.

'Members of the New South Wales Corps, in general. And John Macarthur in particular.'

'Isn't arresting the governor,' ventured Rebecca, 'a bit like arresting the king?'

The fly was off again, back to the same business, the same silly routine.

'In a sense yes, the governor is the King's representative.'

'Which makes John Macarthur a sort of colonial Oliver Cromwell.'

'Yes, you could say that, in fact - Elizabeth,' Hannah interrupted herself suddenly. 'Are you listening to this or is that fly more interesting than our conversation?'

'I'm listening,' Elizabeth turned to face her mother. 'You said brother Thomas arrested Governor Bligh and deposed him.'

'No, dear.' Her mother could not resist a smile. 'I said Thomas was among the party of men who arrested him.'

'That's how he hurt his back.'

'How do you know about that?'

'Sammy told me. He fell off a ladder or something. Hunting for the governor.'

'So you do know about it?'

'Not really. Only the interesting bits. And they found him, the governor, hiding under a bed.'

'I wouldn't believe everything you hear, dear. Macarthur drew up a petition declaring the governor was unfit to lead the country, and claimed it was signed by all the respectable inhabitants in the colony.'

'Did father sign the petition?' Elizabeth asked.

'I believe he did, yes.'

'And did you? Or would you have done if you'd been here?'

There was a pause. 'I would probably not have been asked,' replied Hannah eventually. 'I am not important enough. Besides, I am a woman.'

'But if you had been, important enough,' Elizabeth persisted, 'would you have signed it?'

'Lizzie,' said Rebecca sharply.

'What?'

Her elder sister glared at her.

Elizabeth pursed her lips and looked down at her lap. But she was watching her mother out of the corner of her eye.

It was a bit much to take in, the history lesson. But it intrigued Elizabeth, fascinated her even, to think that her own family, her own brother – who let's face it she knew as well as she had known her father, which was not at all – were so closely connected to important goings on in this strange alien country of theirs.

She wondered what her mother made of it all. Which side she was on. And that was another curious thing, to think there were 'sides', as there were in the Civil War in England, which is something Elizabeth did know about, seeing as she was brought up there. She could have told you everything you needed to know about Oliver Cromwell, but as for New South Wales ...

'So, whose side are we on, mama?' Elizabeth asked.

Hannah ave her daughter a long look. 'We are on the side of government, Elizabeth, so long as it has the best interests of the colony at heart. But I'm glad,' she continued, with a smile, 'to see you taking an interest in your country at long last.'

'I never said it was my country,' mumbled Elizabeth.

~

The Rum Rebellion, as the deposing of Governor Bligh came to be called many years later, threw an already divided colony into complete turmoil.

William (*The Bounty*) Bligh had been sent to the colony with the express purpose of wresting control from the hands of the New South Wales Corps. Governors Hunter and King before him had done their best to bust the military monopoly but they were only partially successful. Bligh arrived with all guns blazing, as was expected, and alienated pretty well everyone except the Hawkesbury farmers. When Bligh was deposed the cat and mouse game began all over again: the Corps immediately replaced everyone of authority with men of their own, granted land to whoever they chose and so on. Their enemies, of which there were many, were punished for their lack of support by imprisonment or confiscation of their lands or their convict workers, or even, ironically, with threats of deportation.

However as in the English Civil War the divisions among the people were not always clearly defined. Hannah Laycock's family had had long connections to the New South Wales Corps, and in addition under the illegal regime her eldest daughter Sarah's husband Nicholas Bayly was made Secretary to Major Johnston and Acting Provost Marshal, which made him one of the most powerful people in the colony. Yet Hannah owed her grant of land to Governor King, as did her sons.

At the same time, despite his repeated declarations of loyalty to Governor Bligh Thomas Pitt, along with his sisters Susanna and Jemima, was happy to receive handsome land grants from the very regime that deposed him.

Life and loyalties, you could say, were not clear cut.

Chapter 29

1808: Thomas Pitt and the Rum Rebellion

AT 6PM ON 26 January 1808, twenty years to the day after Governor Phillip had first planted the Union Jack into the turf at Sydney Cove, 300 soldiers from the New South Wales Corps, led by Major George Johnston, marched with full colours and military band playing 'The British Grenadiers' up Bridge Street to Government House in Sydney to arrest Governor Bligh. The only person who turned out to try and stop them was Bligh's daughter Mary, armed with an umbrella.

The governor could not immediately be found so a small search party, which included Lieutenant Thomas Laycock Jnr, was sent to hunt for him. They discovered him eventually *'in a situation too disgraceful to be mentioned'* (upstairs in a *'scalene'* under a bed, allegedly, according to Lance-Corporal Marlborough, who found him). Laycock fell off a ladder during the search, injuring his back, and subsequently became known as the only physical casualty of the otherwise bloodless rebellion.

The immediate cause of the coup was the settler John Macarthur's refusal to pay a shipping fine and his further refusal, when arrested and ordered to attend court, to have the case heard by the judge advocate. Criminal courts then consisted of *'the judge advocate and six officers of his majesty's service by sea and land, who sit also by precept from the governor'* (according to John Turnbull). In this instance since there were no naval officers the tribunal was made up of New South Wales Corps officers, among them Thomas Laycock junior.

Unsurprisingly, being military men, they sided with Macarthur and were consequently accused by Bligh, a naval man, of treason, which was a hangable offence.

The event came to be known as the Rum Rebellion. It wasn't about rum however. It was the culmination of a long-running power struggle between His Majesty's government represented by the governor on the one hand, and private enterprise represented by the New South Wales Corps on the other. It was 'a fight over the future and the nature of the colony', to quote Michael Duffy in the *Sydney Morning Herald* (2006).

~

By 1808 Thomas Matcham Pitt was an established and respected member of the Hawkesbury community. He owned, with his mother, 530 acres of land. In addition to the two original 100 acre grants in Green Hills he had acquired 300 acres in what is now Kurrajong, and a further thirty acres near the Hawkesbury. He had also assumed a new middle name.

When Governor King was replaced by Governor Bligh in 1806 Thomas was one of five men chosen to represent the Hawkesbury settlers in an official letter welcoming the new governor, pledging undying loyalty – something they frequently did in those days: flatter first, make demands next – and requesting such things as freedom of trade, an open market and an end to the monopoly exercised by the New South Wales Corps.

Just 26 days before the rebellion, on 1 January 1808, Thomas wrote again to the governor, with 832 other settlers from around the colony, to

> '. . . *express the fullest and unfeigned sense of gratitude for the manifold, great, and essential blessings and benefits we freely continue to enjoy from your Excellency's arduous, just, determined and salutary government over us . . .* [and promising once again] *at the risque of our lives and properties, at all times, as liege subjects, to support . . . your Excellency's gracious government over us.*'

They went on to request free trade, once again, and trial by jury.

These letters, also known as petitions, or 'memorials', were the only formal way the settlers could make their demands known. There was no parliament in New South Wales at the time. The effusiveness of the praise and the fulsomeness of the language were at least partly a formality.

~

On the evening of 26 January 1808 and on many evenings following, an inhabitant of Sydney may not have been too surprised to hear gunshot and see fires burning in the distance, even if few people in New South Wales yet thought of the founding of the colony twenty years earlier as cause for celebration.

If a settler at Green Hills had ventured out to see what all the fuss was about, as Thomas may well have done, he would have seen a large crowd, very much the worse for drink, gathered round a bonfire on Ham Common, upon which were placed effigies of the governor and William Gore, the provost marshal. Directing proceedings was Sergeant Lowther of the New South Wales Corps, assisted by several others including Robert Fitz and Thomas Hobby. The chief constable, Andrew Thompson, whose job it was to keep some kind of order, stood by looking on, completely powerless.

Martial law had been declared and all roads out of Sydney blocked. If Thomas had stopped to ask what was up he would have been told the governor had been arrested and Major George Johnston declared lieutenant governor in his place. He may have been more or less surprised. He would have known that Bligh, while a good friend to the Hawkesbury settlers, had upset virtually everyone else in the colony with his heavy-handed behaviour and dangerously antagonised the still-powerful New South Wales Corps. But he would never have imagined a group of Corps officers, goaded on by John Macarthur, would have had the temerity to arrest His Majesty's representative and replace him with their own selves.

Thomas would have been astonished to learn that over the

following few days every single official who had been appointed by Bligh – secretaries and magistrates, provost marshals and judge-advocates – would be replaced by members of the New South Wales Corps, or their friends; and that Governor Bligh was held under arrest and, it would transpire, would never govern the colony again.

But how was it that, less than a month after pledging total loyalty to the governor, Thomas's signature appeared on the following letter, sent to Lieutenant Governor Johnston on 30 January?

'Impressed with the highest sense of the obligation due to you for having come forward at this momentous crisis to extricate the loyal inhabitants of the colony from that dread and horror which the recent arbitrary measures had caused . . . Now that we can freely express the sentiments of our minds, we gladly beg to assure you that we are ready to support you with our lives and properties, conscious that every act of your administration would meet His Majesty's approbation.

We cannot in language sufficiently praise the meritorious services of the New South Wales Corps on this memorable occasion.'

The letter was signed by 'sixty-six persons', including Robert Fitz, Thos Hobby, John Brennan, James Badgery, Thomas M Pitt, Thomas Arndell and Wm Faithful [sic].

~

Perhaps the story went something like this:

It was early on the evening following the coup and Thomas was alone at Bronte with his mother. Hearing a noise from outside the house, he took up his gun and went to see what was going on.

He was used to trespassers. They were usually escaped convicts, lurking in the trees and occasionally trying to bed down in one of the outhouses. But these intruders were approaching him quite openly along the track right up to his front door.

'Good evening, Tom,' said the man in front. He recognised

John Brennan, a neighbour. He was drunk.

'John,' said Thomas. He lowered the gun.

'Howareya?' said his neighbour. He was grinning, not pleasantly.

'What can I do for you?'

'Something here we want you to sign.' He was waving a piece of paper.

'What is it?'

'Just sign it.'

Thomas stared at Brennan. He'd always had his doubts about Brennan.

'If you know what's good for you!' came another voice. Thomas Hobby, lieutenant with the New South Wales Corps, another neighbour. He was drunk too.

'What do you mean?'

'No more nor less than what I said!'

'Are you threatening me?' He didn't like Hobby's tone. He was trying to see past him to make out who else was in the party when Hobby, closely followed by Brennan, pushed right past him and into his own front room.

'That's better,' said Brennan. 'Cosier, if you get my meaning,' he added, sweetly.

'Let me read it.' Thomas put the gun down and tried to grab the piece of paper that Brennan had thrust in front of his nose.

'No need. Just sign.'

'I'm not signing anything I'm not allowed to read.' He stood there with his hands on his hips, staring at the two men.

'Or,' continued Brennan, 'what we can do, we can arrange to have your convicts taken away from you. That's for starters.'

'And we can relieve you of your farm,' said Hobby. He laughed, hiccupped, and took a swig from a bottle.

'You can't do that.' Thomas laughed, tightly.

'You'd be surprised,' said Hobby. He lurched and staggered against the wall and the whole house shook. 'We have means.'

'What in God's name . . .'

'It's just a letter,' said Brennan. 'Addressed to Major

Johnston.'

'Saying what?'

'Saying this and that,' said Hobby. 'Arndell's signed.'

'Arndell?'

'So you see it's all above board and hunky-dory.'

'Then let me see it.'

'You don't need to do that,' said Hobby, and burped loudly. At which point Mary Pitt appeared from the inner room.

'What's going on?' She looked back and forth at the two men. 'Thomas Hobby are you drunk?'

'You betcha.'

She turned to her son. 'Did you invite these men here?'

'I did not. Mother go back in, I'm dealing with it.'

'Then how dare they? How dare you?' She stepped right up to Hobby, wincing as she got the full waft of his breath. 'I'm ashamed of you Thomas Hobby, and surprised too. What is your business?'

'My business,' Hobby put his face close to hers and breathed right at her, 'is not to do with you, Mrs Pitt. Our business is with your son here.'

By now they were all there, all five of them, surrounding Thomas in his own front room, which suddenly seemed very small. They were his neighbours and, by definition, his friends. Or so he had thought. Yet not one of them would look him in the eye.

'Get out of my house.' Thomas spoke quietly.

'Or? Or what? You'll call the constabulary? Andrew Thompson?'

They were laughing now, laughing and swigging and jostling one another.

'Come on, just do it,' Hobby snatched the piece of paper from Brennan and waved it in Thomas's face. 'Just do it. Sign.'

'Sign, sign, sign . . .' it became a chant.

'Or,' Hobby scratched his head. He pretended to be thinking. 'Tell you what, we could have you placed on the next ship and sent back home. Back to mother England. Now that would be a lark, wouldn't it?'

'On whose authority?'

'On the authority of the powers that be. Which is us. Authority's different now,' said Hobby. 'Authority's all topsy-turvy now. Believe me.'

Thomas looked from one to the other. He knew them all, some better than others. Lieutenant Thomas Hobby of the New South Wales Corps, John Brennan, the Irish emancipist, Thomas Biggers, likewise, one of the largest landowners on the Hawkesbury, hero of the 1806 flood; William Cox, whose father was one of the most respected men in the colony; James Badgery – friend of Colonel Paterson, he wasn't surprised to see him there. They were his neighbours, fellow farmers mostly, people he'd sat around a campfire with, people he thought he could trust.

He glanced down at the paper before him. A million thoughts flashed through his mind.

'We need 500 signatures before the end of the night,' said Hobby, between burps. 'We've got Arndell, and Mason, and let's see now, who else - Skinner, and Carver . . .'

'Thomas Rickerby, William Addy . . .'

Hobby was swaggering around the room as if it was his. He walked up to Thomas's mother, who was standing arms akimbo, unmovable, and once again thrust his face close to hers.

'The people,' he said to her, 'who don't do the right thing, end up as Marked Men. Or in prison. With their rights taken away from them. And all for want of one little signature. Because, you see, the people who were in charge yesterday are not in charge any longer. That's the way of things. That's how things can change so quick here, you never really know where you are, do you?'

'Thomas Hobby you are a disgrace to your regiment.'

There was a dramatic and concerted intake of breath.

'Mrs Pitt,' said Hobby, his face still almost touching hers, 'if you was a man, I would take issue with you for insulting an officer of His Majesty's realm.'

She ignored him. She moved away and confronted the others. 'And you, Thomas Biggers,' she said. 'Who put you up to this? And you, William?'

Young William Cox stared at her and then looked away. The others began moving towards her, almost imperceptibly.

Thomas grabbed the piece of paper from Hobby's hand, signed it and thrust it back at him.

'And now get out of my house,' he said.

'There, thought you'd see sense.' Hobby had the temerity to tip his hat to Thomas. And then to his mother.

'You did right. Pardon for the interruption, Mrs Pitt, Mr Pitt.'

And they were gone.

There was a silence. Mary looked at her son.

'What was that all about?'

'I suspect it's a petition in support of the coup, mother.'

'Why did you sign it?'

'I was afraid of what they might do. Of what they could do. They were not idle threats mother. They could . . . we could . . . they could have . . .' He sighed. He hadn't the energy to finish the sentence.

Mary stared at him a moment longer and then turned and walked away without another word.

~

Thomas's experience of early 19th century New South Wales would have been very different to that of the female members of the family. On his frequent business visits he had witnessed the stink and despair in the back streets of Sydney Town. He'd seen brawls breaking out on the street, or in pubs, over the most trivial matter, or over nothing at all. He'd watched convicts flogged until their backs were sheets of blood and observed men previously known for their honesty openly cheating. Every day he'd seen cunning and deceit triumph over common integrity and humanity. He had struggled to retain the principles he'd lived by all his life and often, more often than he cared to admit, been forced to compromise them simply in order to survive.

He had witnessed the antagonism between convict and settler, between military man and convict, and it appalled him. He was disgusted at the lack of regard for the law of the land, or for common sense, or for the well-being of one's fellow man or the colony as a whole. Above all he was infuriated at his inability to do anything about it. At its worst, which it often was, he felt the colony was turning into a lawless pit of degradation and despair, a hell on earth.

None of this, needless to say, he was prepared to divulge to his mother or his sisters.

Most crucially, at this point, Thomas knew the strength of the New South Wales Corps. And he knew the power structure had changed overnight, literally, much the same – only quicker – as it had after the departure of Governor Phillip.

It was like living in quicksand. One false move and you could be sucked right in. He did not feel ashamed so much as despondent. It was back to the bad old days and there was not a thing anyone could do about it. Sometimes the whole place sickened him.

Three months later, on 11 April 1808, Thomas Arndell – one of the Hawkesbury's most influential and prominent landowners, who had arrived in the colony as surgeon with the First Fleet and had been, until relieved of his duties by the new regime, a magistrate – wrote the following letter to the governor's (ex-) secretary Griffin:

> *'I signed a paper a few days subsequent to the 26th January*, expressing my Disapprobation of a Paper which I signed not long before, which Paper Contained thanks to Governor Bligh for his kindness to the People and good Government of them. I now most solemnly declare that I signed the paper subsequent to the 26th January through fear, and without so much as knowing the contents at the time I signed it. It might have contained more than I have expressed but I don't know what they are.'*

(*The 30 January letter to Major Johnston.)

A footnote in the Historical Records of Australia expresses astonishment that a man of the intelligence and education of Thomas Arndell should sign a paper without knowing its contents. It (the footnote) suggests he did not regard these petitions as important.

On the 28 April 1808 John Brennan wrote to (by now ex-) chief constable Andrew Thompson to say:

'Mr Arndell informed me you wished to have a copy of the letter addressed to Major Johnston, which I was unfortunately concerned in, by going amongst the settlers to get their signatures thereto, and to which I sincerely repent in my duplicity in taking the advice of others, in doing which I ought not to have done – I am happy to have it to send to you and herein enclose it.'

John Brennan's 'confession' was the first indication that the signatures on the 30 January paper in support of Major Johnston had been obtained at least partly under duress. It goes some way to explaining why so many people who put their names to the memorial in praise of Governor Bligh (Thomas and Arndell among them), also signed the paper condemning him barely a month later.

And then there was James Wilshire.

Wilshire signed both the petition written to Major Johnston asking him to arrest Governor Bligh (possibly obtained after the event), and another declaration written the following day in support of the coup. And yet when Bligh was making plans to return to England after his deposition in order to present his case, one of the men he asked to accompany him as a witness on his behalf was James Wilshire. (The journey did not happen until some years later and Wilshire ended up not going.)

Wilshire was also made a Deputy Commissary on 2 September 1808, a position he seemed to share with Robert Fitz, who was one of the instigators of the rebellion. When Palmer was arrested and stripped of his position by the military regime Fitz took over. A month later Wilshire received a handsome land grant from the same regime. It's probably not fair to say he played for both sides, or that he was prepared to sign anything that was put under his nose; but it does suggest either that people were threatened into signing papers or that those same papers were not considered to have much import. Or, perhaps most likely of all, most people wanted to get on with their lives and their jobs and didn't too much care who was in charge.

For the next few years Thomas seemed to have kept his head down. While other settlers from the Hawkesbury and elsewhere in the colony fired off letter after letter to everyone from Colonel Paterson to Viscount Castelreagh, protesting in the strongest terms at the methods used to gain their signatures on the letter of 30 January, denying they had anything to do with the coup and deploring the conduct of the illegal regime and the outrageous treatment given to anyone who opposed it, Thomas remained quiet. His signature is not to be found on any more official letters until the arrival of Governor Macquarie.

When we look at what happened to some of those who opposed the coup and refused to recognise or take orders from the new regime – men such as John Palmer, John Bowman and George Suttor, all of whom were stripped of their positions and imprisoned – no one could be blamed for keeping quiet at such a time.

Robert Fitz, who had been made high constable in place of Andrew Thompson, *'offered a free Pardon and a Passage to England for any Convict for Life who would give any information'* about any settler who was a party to these pro-Bligh addresses. Interestingly no one ever came forward to claim the reward.

~

Bligh was subsequently placed under house arrest and one way or another it was two years before he returned to England. Major Johnston and John Macarthur were also recalled to England but it was not until 1811 that Johnston was court martialled. He was cashiered, yet allowed to return to New

South Wales as a free citizen and to keep his properties – an astonishingly lenient sentence for mutiny, regardless of the provocation. The unrepentant John Macarthur meanwhile was told if he returned to the colony he would be tried there for insurrection, so he was effectively exiled until 1817, when the charges were dropped.

Chapter 30

1812: Thomas and Elizabeth

IN 1812 THOMAS, now thirty-one, was very different from the boy who had arrived in the colony eleven years before. Physical labour had put years and muscles on him and the weather had tanned his already tough Dorset skin into hardened antipodean leather. He looked older than he was, and when he allowed himself to stop and think about it he darn well felt older too.

The challenges never let up. It was a constant battle against the wretched climate, which he loved and hated equally. He'd witnessed floods, droughts, hailstorms, watched helpless as plagues of caterpillars devoured his crops, and fought running battles with ants and locusts. He had survived sunstroke, dehydration, and the terrible sun blight that rendered people virtually blind for weeks on end.

Just occasionally, probably not often enough, he allowed himself a smidgen of satisfaction, knowing he had turned these 230 acres of forest into a living and breathing farm. When the land was not under flood the soil was lush and richly fertile. He was now growing wheat and maize and had an increasing number of sheep and pigs, and a horse. He had four convicts working for him, all of them off the government stores. Having survived the debacle of four years ago, he was now an established Hawkesbury landowner and farmer.

The extended Pitt family had not done badly under the military regime. Lt Colonel Foveaux, the initial acting governor, granted land in Liberty Plains (now Strathfield) to his ex-batman William Faithfull and his wife Susanna, to James and Hester Wilshire and to Jemima Forrest, partly thanks to Admiral Nelson's letter of recommendation to Governor King. Lt Colonel Paterson, who took over from Foveaux, gave Thomas 300 acres 'bounded by South and Badgery's Creeks', south of Sydney town and way outside Thomas's catchment area, so he would have hired an overseer to manage it. When the new governor arrived in January 1810 the Pitt siblings must have held their collective breath, knowing that grants allocated under the illegal regime could have been rescinded. Fortunately for them Governor Macquarie considered theirs to have been fairly given and validated them. They were lucky where others were not.

In December 1810 Thomas, along with 93 other Hawkesbury settlers, had emerged from his shell to write to the new governor congratulating him on his arrival in the colony. In the intervening two years Governor Macquarie, who later was to become known as the 'Father of Australia', and with good reason, had with great subtlety and intelligence reinstated the members and some of the methods of the old regime, introduced new stringent standards of hygiene and begun a far-reaching plan for the construction of towns, roads and public buildings. He had also, more controversially, appointed a number of emancipists into official positions, just as he promised the Laycock women he would do. After two years under his governorship the colony was shaping up to be a place of stability and consequence.

~

By 1812 it was just Thomas and his mother living on the Richmond farms. Mary of the 'weak constitution' was now 64 years old. She had outlived her own expectation but she stooped now, and walked stiffly. Thomas saw the suffering in her face, but she never complained. They rarely spoke about the old country. Mary did not encourage it and Thomas's memory of it became hazier every day.

There was another subject they no longer discussed, and

that was the business of Thomas's wife. The wife he hadn't yet met. The wife he knew he ought to have, that more than anything he knew would bring the greatest happiness and relief to his mother. He was aware of all of this, as he was aware of a niggling, almost irritating little sensation which may or may not have to do with a kind of loneliness. In the evenings, especially after his mother had retired to bed, which now her eyes were fading she did more or less as soon as the sun went down, he was aware of a profound and almost deafening silence, both outside him and within. Always inclined to be serious, he was beginning to forget the last time he laughed out loud. He was becoming, though he did not like to admit it to himself, dull.

~

It was August 1812 when Hannah and Elizabeth Laycock eventually got around to visiting the Pitts on their farm on the Hawkesbury.

Hannah Laycock had always had an especial admiration for Mary Pitt. Unlike most women in the colony she had not come to New South Wales as some man's wife. She was one of a small number of independent women who'd chosen to migrate of their own volition, in this instance with several children in tow. She felt an affinity with the older woman, despite the eleven-year age difference.

They had met only once before, but Hannah remembered there were several Pitt girls. She couldn't recall precisely how many, but she was fairly sure that the two youngest were much the same age when they came to the colony as her own two younger daughters were now. She had some idea the Pitt girls were now married, and she also had the faint memory of a boy, Thomas, who presumably was married also, although that particular piece of news had not yet reached her.

Thomas knew of the impending visit but showed little interest. He knew of the Laycocks – who didn't – and of their connection with the New South Wales Corps. But when he saw the carriage arrive at the house and from it step a middle-aged woman and a young girl, he was glad to be working some distance from the house and thereby not obliged to join in the socialising.

Mary led her visitors into the front room of her newly-built two storey brick house with its plastered walls and glazed windows. It stood atop the rise looking down over the flood plain and beyond it the hazy blue mountains that still formed a barrier between the tiny settlement and whatever lay beyond. It was a mild winter day and the women were in good spirits. Following the usual pleasantries they moved swiftly on to the fascinating topic of family.

Mary learned that Hannah Laycock was the proud mother of six: three boys and three girls, the youngest of whom was in the room with them right there, only half listening to the conversation. Hannah's second son Thomas - the first European to cross Van Diemen's Land on foot by the way, from Port Dalrymple to Hobart and back again - was now a captain with the 98th Regiment of Foot and currently on duty in England, where he had been for two years, along with his wife Isabella, daughter of Captain Eber Bunker of Nantucket Island, and their child.

Hannah learned that Mary Pitt's daughters were indeed all married now – although one, Jemima, was sadly already a widow. Mary also had a son named Thomas, who was still living with her on the Bronte property and 'was out there somewhere, working,' as the older woman explained to her companion apologetically, peering through the window. 'I can see him now. I was hoping I might be able to introduce you but it's more than my life is worth to interrupt him.'

Elizabeth's ears pricked up, and she was through the door and into the paddock before the two women had time to notice the gap in the room.

~

He looked like a convict worker, with his moleskin trousers and his heavy, mud-stained boots. He was picking at something with a hoe. She took the chance.

'Hello, I'm Elizabeth,' she said.

The man looked up, straightened, removed his hat, wiped his brow, and stared down at the young girl squinting up at him. She was wearing an unusual bonnet from which, slightly chaotically, some ringlets were fighting to escape.

'Ah, yes. You would be,' he said. 'Thomas Pitt.' He bowed, rather stiffly, and replaced his hat. Elizabeth giggled.

'My mama is talking to yours.'

'I know,' said Thomas.

'You know? Yet you don't come to join us? That's not very sociable of you.'

'I'm not a very sociable person.'

There was a little pause. He really wanted to get on.

'Don't you have people to do your work for you?'

'I do,' he said. 'But there's always more to be done.'

'Oh,' said the girl.

She stood there, hands tucked behind her back, tracing circles in the ground with her big toe, like a child. And a child is what she was – she could not have been more than fifteen or sixteen. Quite pretty, with large imploring eyes and an odd, rather sudden smile that came and vanished in a moment, as if she was not quite sure. Her skin was very pale and her voice refined, of a kind he'd not heard for some time. He guessed she had not been in the colony very long.

'It's beautiful here,' she said at last.

'Glad you find it so.'

'You can see for miles. Are those the Blue Mountains?'

'They are, yes.'

'What do you think is beyond them? Do you think it's China, or a great sea? Or do you think it's a kind of El Dorado and there are people living among palm trees anointing themselves with oil and eating grapes all day?'

He laughed. 'I have no idea. I don't give them a lot of thought.'

'They say they swallow the cattle. If I were a man I'd be packing my bags and following them, see how they work their way through. And on the other side I imagine huge plains, luscious and green, and a sea of some kind or maybe a huge lake, and the cattle grazing around the water, big and fat and supremely contented. May I sit down, Mr Pitt?'

'Oh. Yes, of course.'

She'd spotted a bench, the one Thomas had set up so his mother could watch the sunset. And before he had time to aid her or to stop her she'd seated herself and was patting the bench next to her.

'Come,' she said, in a tone of voice that was not used to refusal.

He did, not without reluctance.

'Are you glad you came here?' she asked after a while.

He made a noise between a snort and a grunt.

'What does that mean?' she said.

'It's what a pig might say when he's asked if he prefers it in or outside the sty. "It depends what else you're offering."'

She laughed at that.

'You are funny.'

He shrugged.

'I hated it when I first got here,' she said. 'Hated it. There was no culture, I thought, no spirit, no life.' She screwed up her face. 'Poor mama. I swore the moment I was of age I was going to leave, go home, for good. I even began counting the days, carving them on the tree outside my window, like the convicts do. I got as far as three hundred and then I stopped.'

'You took pity on the tree perhaps.'

'Not really. Or maybe yes, in a way. You must feel very proud.' She turned to him but did not wait for his answer. 'All this – this beautiful garden, these – whatever they are, crops, are they?'

'Wheat and barley.'

'To be living off your own land. What was it like when you first came here?'

'It was a wilderness. Trees as far as the eye can see. You could not see the river. You wouldn't even have known there was a river. Except when it flooded.'

'It is impossible to imagine. What did you live in?'

'In a hut, of sorts, made from canvas. Then from bark. Then slabs and finally' – he gestured towards the house – 'as you can see.'

'You built this house?'

'With help, yes.'

'It's splendid.' She turned to gaze at the little two-storey brick building.

'I'm not sure that splendid is the word.' He smiled. 'But it is an improvement on the first.'

'How did you know how to build a house?'

'I found out, the hard way.'

'In London,' said Elizabeth, 'we lived in a terraced house in Clement's Inn. Do you know Clement's Inn, Mr Pitt?'

'I have never been to London, Miss Laycock.'

'Never been to London?' Her eyebrows shot up. 'No matter. It was a place of much merriment, believe it or not, particularly at weekends.'

'All those lawyers, eh?'

'Oh yes. They certainly knew how to party. So we would dress up, my sister and I, and parade up and down the streets in our ridiculous bonnets, fancying we were the smartest young ladies in town and all those young men would have nothing better to do than gaze upon us.'

'And did they?'

'Who knows? So the moment we arrived here I asked mama, where is Clement's Inn? And she said – There is no Clement's Inn here, Elizabeth, nor anything like it. So you'd better get used to what there is.'

'And you found that unacceptable.'

'Completely. I went into a major sulk for a whole year and filled my time desecrating a tree.'

'And then what happened?'

'I said goodbye to Clement's Inn,' she said. 'And instead of destroying the tree I decided to draw it. I had always wanted to draw but there was no one to teach me. So one day I just got out my crayons and began. And as I drew, I forgot about marking off the days, or anything else really.'

There was a short and thoughtful pause.

'Did you know there are over a hundred species of eucalypt?' said Elizabeth.

'Are there?'

'At least. And every one of them different.'

'Well now.'

'I think,' said Elizabeth, sitting suddenly upright and looking down at her lap, 'perhaps you are laughing at me.'

'I'm so sorry if I give you that impression, Miss Laycock.' He turned to look properly at her. 'It was not my intention.'

He wanted to put a comforting hand on hers, but he didn't want anything misconstrued.

'Did you know my father?' she asked the question suddenly.

'Quartermaster Laycock?' Thomas laughed. 'Everyone knew Quartermaster Laycock.'

'Except me.' She was looking into the distance. 'My mother won't talk about him.'

There was a moment, and he looked at the young girl thoughtfully. 'I barely knew my father either,' Thomas spoke gently. 'Only by reputation. And hard though it is you have to ignore the reputation, especially here.'

Elizabeth frowned. 'It's all I have,' she said in a small voice.

'It's not all you have. You have a courageous mother, as have I, exceptionally so.'

'You think so?'

'Two of the most remarkable women in New South Wales are together in that house right now. And neither of them has had an easy time of it.'

Elizabeth nodded thoughtfully.

'It is impossibly difficult for a woman alone in this country,' Thomas went on, 'and the older they are the harder it is to let go of the old place.'

'If you had known . . .' Elizabeth began, and hesitated.

'If I'd known how it was going to be, would I have come here in the first place?' He pondered on this for a while. 'Yes. Absolutely.'

'Oh.' She was taken aback by his intensity.

'Absolutely.'

Thomas wandered into his own private world momentarily.

'You asked me how I went about building a house and I say the same way you went about drawing a tree,' he woke out of his reverie. 'By making it up as I went along. That is the way things work here. Only in my case I was being overlooked. Constantly.'

'By?'

'By the convict workers, watching my every move and waiting for me to slip up.'

'And did you slip up?'

'All the time, all the time.' He laughed briefly. 'Every single thing I have ever done here has been an experiment – every seed I've planted, every structure I built – exactly like everyone else. We're all experimenting. There are no instruction books telling us what to do.'

'It's a challenge.'

'It's certainly that.' Thomas smiled. 'What worked in the old country doesn't necessarily apply here. And so in this ramshackle, random way we are building a country from scratch, novices, all of us. It's . . .' He stopped.

'It is what, Mr Pitt?'

'Well if you really stopped to think about it, the responsibility would be overwhelming.'

'It's an adventure, is that what you're saying?' said Elizabeth.

'That's it exactly. An experiment and an adventure.' Thomas turned to look at the young girl next to him, and as he spoke he wondered at the things he was saying, because they were not things he had ever properly articulated before, even to himself.

An hour later Mrs Pitt and Mrs Laycock, who'd been so

absorbed in their conversation they had forgotten about Elizabeth, set off in search of her and found the two young people still sitting together on the bench.

The women were astonished in quite different ways – Mary Pitt to see her son doing something other than working, and Hannah Laycock to see her daughter talking and laughing so freely with a man to whom she had not been formally introduced. But the same thought, unspoken of course, may well have entered their heads at the same moment.

~

On 15 February 1813 Thomas Matcham Pitt was married by licence from his Excellency Governor Macquarie to *'the amiable Elizabeth Laycock'* (so said the *Sydney Gazette*). The ceremony was conducted by the Reverend Samuel Marsden at St John's Parramatta, and the witnesses were John Wilshire and Rebecca Laycock.

Thus were two of the colony's earliest pioneering European families united.

~

A few weeks later, on 22 March, Jemima Forrest and Robert Jenkins were married by Special Licence granted by His Excellency Governor Macquarie, again at St John's and again by the Reverend Samuel Marsden. The witnesses were Lucy Wood and Eber Bunker.

Chapter 31

September 1815: Reflections

MARY PITT SITS on the very same bench at Bronte where Thomas and Elizabeth first made their acquaintance and gazes across the steep slope of the paddocks to the river. It is a gentle spring day. Above her cockatoos cry, not as loudly as they used to, it seems. The river is calm.

Mary is now 67 years old. Her job, the reason she came to the colony, is over. The last of her children has married and new grandchildren are appearing almost every year – at last count there were twelve of them, and another one on the way for Thomas and Elizabeth, their second.

This new generation – 'currency lads and lasses', so-called – the ones born in the country, free from the spectre and judgment of the old place, are already showing themselves to be an altogether different breed. Mary watches her grandchildren growing tall, straight, fearless and optimistic, and running around barefoot. There is even a new twang to their speech. They are the ones who will shape this new country, thinks Mary, when she and her generation are long gone and forgotten.

It is thirteen years since my ancestress first came to the Hawkesbury, and the farm is unrecognisable. Around twenty acres of land have been cleared and the grass on this September day grows a confident, lasting green. In front of the house is Mary's pride and joy: her garden where, to everyone's surprise, roses thrive. Beyond it is a little orchard of peach and apricot trees. Behind the house wheat and maize grow and on the lower paddocks sheep and cattle are grazing. It is a scene of such stillness and permanence that Mary cannot believe the times when she has looked down on these same paddocks and watched them disappear under floodwater.

Mary is used to floods. Back home in Dorset the river Stour paid frequent uninvited visits right up over her threshold into her living room. It was inconvenient, and dirty, and left an unpleasant residue and a smell that lingered for weeks sometimes, but it was never life-threatening.

Here it is a different matter. Like everything else in this continent the floods are that much bigger and more brutal. Six times in the past thirteen years the Hawkesbury has burst its banks. The first was in March 1806 when the river rose forty-five feet in the space of two days and devastated 36,000 acres of the surrounding country. Thousands of farmers lost their stock, their crops and their buildings and seven people lost their lives. There was *'not a house except at the Green Hills to be seen'*, said the *Sydney Gazette,* and only the roofs of the highest buildings on the far side of the river remained above water. It was then that Margaret Catchpole helped save the lives of the Dight family. Mary was lucky on that occasion.

The worst was in June 1809. There had been a drought earlier in the year and the ground was cracked-dry and as hard and impermeable as rock.

The rain began falling in solid, unrelenting sheets. In a few hours the dips in the lower paddocks had filled with water and Mary watched as the dips became pools and the pools spread and joined to become lakes. By late the same afternoon the lower paddocks were completely under water and she continued to gaze in quiet and helpless horror as the river crept on upwards towards the house, like some ghastly, unstoppable monster, all day and the day after without remission, several feet an hour until all around her, from Green Hills to South Creek, was one giant sheet of water. There was always a moment in heavy rain when a decision had to be made to leave or to stay put, but the water rose so rapidly there was no question of escape and now she was trapped, with Thomas and their workers and what stock they'd managed to rescue, isolated on higher ground. And still the rain kept on coming until at last, the sky began to brighten and the rain ceased. But the monster crept on until it reached halfway up the hill and then quite suddenly it stopped, and hesitated, as if making up its mind, before it slowly began to recede back to its rightful home, taking with it a year's worth of Mary and Thomas's grain.

Then barely two months later the rains came again.

It began on Saturday 29 July and it kept on furiously and without a break for two days. Once again the flats were under water but this time the monster came twice as fast and many times more vengeful, as if on a mission to destroy everything it had failed to destroy two months earlier. On the third day the rain eased and the floodwater began to abate, and so Mary gave a sigh of relief and went on with her business.

But the rain had not yet done with them. Late that afternoon it resumed, this time with doubled energy, and above the roar of the flood Mary could hear the blood-chilling sound of men, women and children, stranded on the roofs of their houses, or clutching desperately to trees, crying out to be rescued and firing muskets to attract the attention of the few brave rescuers in too few boats. She watched, transfixed, as the river tore through her property, taking everything with it – stock, sheds, trees, what was left of her crops – and moved inexorably on towards her house. And she wept with frustration and dismay and horror, silently cursing the day she'd decided to come to this hellhole of a country.

The river never quite reached the house, thank God. Yet Mary railed against it, and against the monstrosity that caused this devastation: the antipodean climate. So harsh, so utterly inhuman; one day blasting you with heat so fierce it knocked the breath right out of you and the next chucking down the rain as if some delinquent up there had pulled the plug out of some gigantic bathtub.

Some years the rain didn't come at all and the ground dried and shrivelled and shrank and refused to allow anything to grow in it, anything at all. At times like these she wondered at herself, at the stupidity of thinking she could come to live in a country where the weather made ordinary life so impossible. It was simply not a country fit for human beings. No wonder no one had bothered to come here before. No wonder the natives had kept it to themselves; only they knew how to live here and how pointless it was building houses and growing crops only for the elements to take everything away. God, in His wisdom, had passed this country by. That's what Mary thought at times like these.

~

Floods still happen today, in the 21st century, and not just at the Hawkesbury. The extreme climate of the world's oldest continent never lets up. For years droughts devastated the countryside in New South Wales, while floods wreaked equal damage in Queensland. In the late summer of 2012, after a decade of drought, 70% of New South Wales was under flood or threatened with flood. The people are used to it and nowadays there are rescue services, and insurance, and telephone communication. It is rare for people to drown in floods nowadays.

For Mary and others however there was no safety net. Even back home in Dorset there was the security of knowing that in *extremis* someone, or something, the parish or even Lord Rivers himself, would come to her rescue. Here everything was too new, too improvisatory. The nearest to an emergency service was a neighbour who was brave enough to risk his life saving others. Thomas Biggers, villain of the Rum Rebellion petition, was one. Margaret Catchpole was another. Otherwise they were totally, horrifyingly, on their own.

~

It's been three years now since the river flooded. The rain has fallen, but in solicitous amounts, enough to nourish the grass and paint the paddocks green. In calm moments, like now,

Mary knows she made the right decision to come here. But they've been tough years, tougher than she ever imagined.

She has never got used to the vast distances. In Fiddleford just about everything a person needed was within walking distance of May Cottage. Here it is half a day's walk to visit a neighbour and a day's journey, by dray, to Sydney or Parramatta, to visit her friends or her daughters.

She has never got used to the climate. Even when the river isn't flooding she misses the softness of the air back home, the sweetness of the birdsong, the delicacy of the English landscape. If England is a watercolour washed in pastel New South Wales is a vast canvas, splashed with broad, brash strokes in primary colours: birds screech, the rain buckets, the sun blazes, all in a massive assault on the senses. There are times when she wishes she could throw a gauze over everything, quieten it down, blur the edges, make it less.

But now that she is older and her eyes are clouded by cataracts and her hearing dulled, these things don't bother Mary quite so much. Time, familiarity and old age have done what her imagination could not do: transformed the crude coarseness of the place into something subtler, something more like home. It is one compensation for old age perhaps. But it's been hard work and nothing but hard work, and now she is no longer able to do much at all – even to prune the roses and tend to her little orchard – she begins to reflect on what it has all been for.

~

In 1802 Green Hills was virtually non-existent except in name: a couple of decaying granaries, a dilapidated government house and a falling down store. The settlers were scattered all over the countryside and there was no such thing as a local township until Governor Macquarie created Richmond in 1810. The only medical assistance to be had locally was from an unskilled convict called John Molloy, who in time was replaced by a skilled surgeon, Thomas Arndell. Now, thirteen years on, one floor of a three-storey building that was built as a brewery acts as the nearest thing to a hospital.

The first school had been run out of his own house by a Mr Harris, a missionary, where he also held services. When a schoolhouse was built in 1805 he swiftly moved into it, but purpose-built buildings were a luxury then and, to the annoyance of Mr Harris's successor, the same building had to serve as a chapel and courthouse; just as the little hut where John and Lucy Wood were married was also a carpenter's workshop.

Until the arrival of Governor Macquarie the building of churches was not considered to be of prime importance; previous governors were more concerned for the physical survival of the people than for their spiritual growth. The first church services were conducted under a tree by the Reverend Richard Johnson, who arrived with the First Fleet, and the first church was built at his own expense in what is now Phillip Street in Sydney. To the reverend's annoyance he received very little assistance or interest from Governor Phillip, who was agnostic or even, secretly, atheist. So Mary and her fellow worshippers had to make do, attending services held either in one of these multi-purpose buildings or in one of her neighbour's houses.

In her years on the Hawkesbury the local population has tripled, from around 1,000 to over 3,000, and the European population of New South Wales as a whole has gone from just over 5,000 to around 11,000. The previous year three men, Gregory Blaxland, William Lawson and William Wentworth finally found a way through the Blue Mountains and discovered neither China nor an inland sea, but vast new expanses that farmers of the future will flock to. For now, the colony still comprises the few hundred square miles surrounding Sydney Town, bordered on the west by Parramatta and the north by the Hawkesbury. But people are continually moving outwards and in time, thinks Mary, Thomas, or more likely Thomas's sons, will be pioneers in that new country beyond the Known.

For the first time since the arrival of the First Fleet it is beginning to look as if the colony will have a future. Thanks in part to the new governor there is a sense of order and permanence. People of substance are choosing to come here voluntarily, to live off the backs of the earlier generation of escapees. For they have all been escapees of one sort or another: convicts sent to rid the old country of its lowliest life form, and migrants, like Mary, who were unable to thrive back home. It was a country of the mediocre and the mindless. And yet out of all of this is beginning to emerge something glorious.

God is here after all.

~

A month later Mary made her final journey to see her new granddaughter Elizabeth Wilshire at her daughter Hester's home in George Street in Sydney. She died there on 7 November.

Her obituary appeared in the *Sydney Gazette* on 18 November 1815:

> *'Died on the Tuesday, the 7th instant, Much Lamented. Mrs Mary Pitt, Richmond Hill, aged 67 years. She lived highly respected by all who had been gratified in her acquaintance and died in the arms of her family, in whose remembrance her maternal care and tender solicitude will ever remain a theme of grateful contemplation.'*

There is no record of where she was buried.

On the same day Mary died her daughter in law Elizabeth Pitt gave birth to a girl and named her Mary Matcham. Thus was Mary Matcham Pitt reincarnated.

Chapter 32

1813–1821: Mr and Mrs Thomas Matcham Pitt

AT THE AGE WHEN most young things in England are just starting to think about their A levels, and in Australia their HSCs, young Elizabeth Pitt, aged not yet seventeen, was beginning her new life as the wife of a farmer and landowner of 630 acres near the Hawkesbury river. (In 1812 Thomas had been granted another 100 acres in Kurrajong.)

Up until his marriage Thomas had invariably had a spare sister to look after him, usually Jemima. His mother, when she was there, would have done what she could for him domestically, and it is possible that Lucy dropped by to lend a hand on occasion. But to find herself mistress of the household would have been quite a shock for young Elizabeth. She would have had to assert considerable authority and housekeeping expertise, at an age when her 21st century counterpart is probably still living at home and learning how to order takeaway pizza.

What kind of a man had Elizabeth married?

Many years later, in 1885, Thomas's eldest son GM said in a letter to his cousin Matilda Warren Jenkins,

> *'From what I have heard of my father, he was a man amongst men, of a noble and generous heart; he was one of nature's Noblemen. I always believed he came from Noble stock . . .'*

The records reveal an upright citizen and a philanthropic and conscientious member of the community. One of six men chosen to represent the Hawkesbury settlers in a letter of welcome to Governor Bligh in 1806, and signatory to three further letters to the governor expressing thanks and support; signatory to a letter from the Hawkesbury settlers welcoming Governor Macquarie in 1810, and three years later, steward at a dinner in Macquarie's honour hosted by his brother in law Robert Jenkins in a tent in the garden of Jenkins's house in George Street.

One of a group of men called upon by Governor Macquarie in 1816 to discuss an average wage rate, which was part of an ongoing discussion on the issue of currency. Up until then citizens of New South Wales bartered, or used foreign coins or exchanged promissory notes or relied on the old standby, rum. Out of these discussions was formed the Bank of New South Wales, of which Robert Jenkins was one of seven directors.

In September 1809 Thomas was foreman of the jury at the inquest into the death of little George Rouse. George, who had been brought into the world just four years earlier with the aid of Margaret Catchpole fell off a bridge on his father's property and drowned. (It was a crying shame that the woman who over the years had saved so many children from drowning was not there to do the same for poor George.)

Along with William Faithfull and others Thomas joined a committee and donated towards the building of a new school at Windsor in 1811 – an altruistic gesture for a man with no children, not to mention a wife, at the time. The existing school had been built six years previously under the auspices of Governor King with the proviso that local settlers contribute towards paying for a teacher, which they had failed to do; which meant, as the incumbent Mr Harris pointedly declared, *'I preach a free gospel and run almost a free school.'*

On two occasions Thomas testified to the character of his convict workers for mitigation of their sentences – one in 1816 for John Weston and the following year for Darby Ryan – thus enabling them to obtain their pardons. Then in January 1819 Thomas was elected onto the Foundation Committee of the brand new Hawkesbury Benevolent Society.

There was not much in the way of charity or benevolence in

the early days of colonisation. The colonisers were far too preoccupied with their own survival to give much thought to the less lucky, or healthy, or generally advantaged. After the Hawkesbury floods carts were sent from farm to farm, asking for donations of grain or meat or anything anyone could provide; the deprived were being asked to donate to the destitute. The purpose of the Hawkesbury Benevolent Society was to identify the needy, and instead of relying on donations they had the inspired idea of acquiring a herd of cattle, which they farmed on land donated by Governor Macquarie. This kept the organisation going for forty-five years.

Then in the Colonial Secretary's papers I came upon a reference to a James Scott, of Windsor, orphan, aged seven: *'Surviving parent or guardian: Mr Pitt'.*

On 1 January 1819 young James was one of the first boys to be admitted to the newly created Male Orphan School, which Governor Macquarie had set up in the premises of the Female Orphan School in George Street, Sydney. (The female orphans meanwhile having been relocated to Parramatta.).

So who was this James Scott? And what was his connection to Thomas?

My curiosity had partly to do with his name. I thought he might have been the younger brother of William Scott, who later came to work for Thomas and later still was to play an important role in the lives of both Elizabeth and her son George. William and his sister Margaret came to the colony, aged fourteen and nine respectively, on board *Surry*, from Cork. According to the ship's log, *'On 20th October 1816 Mrs Joan Scott departed this life . . . leaving three small children on board.'*

Assuming this was William and Margaret's mother I surmised the third child might have been James.

However according to another family genealogist, Janelle Cust, while James Scott had indeed travelled to the colony with his mother and she had died during the journey, the boat they were on sailed from Scotland rather than Ireland. There was no mention of a brother or sister, and when the young lad arrived at Port Jackson he was placed in the care of his father, also called James, who had been transported earlier for an unknown felony and served his time. Old habits appeared to die hard however and in June of 1818 James senior was sent up to the Coal River for theft, leaving little James in the care of, presumably, Thomas and Elizabeth Pitt.

Despite the similarities in stories it appears I was wrong, and exactly how 'Mr Pitt' got to be named as little James's guardian and parent remains a mystery. Thomas described James as *'a very nice boy . . . quite destitute and a real object of charity'*; all of which goes to show him, in my view, as a man of compassion and sensitivity, always keeping an eye out for others less fortunate than himself.

There is Thomas the enigma, who signed contradictory letters in support of both sides in the Rum Rebellion; who testified at the trial of John Macarthur for sedition following the coup of January 1808 (during which Macarthur claimed Thomas had previously referred to the emancipist solicitor George Crossley, a good friend of Governor Bligh, as *'a perjured old Villain'*. There is Thomas the litigant, who sued Thomas Biggers for non-payment of a promissory note for £157 (and lost on a technicality), and who issued a writ for the arrest of the store-keeper at the Hawkesbury, Andrew Thompson, for £50 (what for, and what the outcome was, is unknown).

Finally, there was Thomas the family man. It had taken him over ten years to find a suitable wife. It's reassuring to know Mary saw all her children married before she died (although by 1813 the first to do so, Lucy, was by then a widow), and she'd have been gratified to see Thomas adopting the middle name of Matcham, and thus beginning a tradition in the family that has continued down the generations right up to the present day, perpetuating the memory of our great ancestress. And quite right too.

On 5 January 1814 Thomas became a father for the first time when Elizabeth gave birth to George Matcham Pitt.

The seventeen-year-old mother would have been congratulated on producing such a healthy child; and my great great grandfather and future mayor of East St Leonards would have lain in his cot and gazed around him in innocent wonder at the various aunts, uncles, cousins and grandmothers who gathered to admire the strapping little boy who, they declared, would one day grow up to be successful in everything he did, just as his father had done.

How satisfying it must have been for Mary to have seen her only son produce an heir; to know the name of Pitt was to survive at least another generation. How heartening to watch her young daughter in law handling her new life with such confidence.

Less than two years later, on the day Mary died, Elizabeth gave birth to child number two, named Mary Matcham in honour of her grandmother. Three more children followed. The last, Eliza, was born on the 1 November 1820. Seven weeks later, on the 28 January 1821, Thomas Pitt was dead.

He'd been on his way back to the Hawkesbury from a business meeting in Sydney. It had been a typically hot summer day and he may have been travelling in an open carriage when, as so often happens in the country of extreme weather, the wind changed and from what had been a clear blue sky came a torrential downpour. By the time he arrived home at Richmond, Thomas was drenched through and shivering.

Elizabeth ordered him out of his sodden clothes and into a tub of hot water and then straight to bed. She gave him a kiss and a tot of rum to stop the shivering, and left him to it.

The following day he was feverish. Elizabeth urged him to keep to his bed until the fever subsided. But it would not go away.

On 20 January the Reverend Henry Fulton and neighbours Archibald Bell and John Dight came to the house to witness Thomas's signature on his will:

'I Thomas Matcham Pitt of sound mind but labouring under

sickness do . . . bequeath unto my dearly beloved wife Elizabeth Pitt all my Estate and Effects personal . . . and in Trust . . . unto my eldest son George Matcham Pitt all those five farms which I now occupy in the district of Richmond . . . which he is to possess after the demise of his mother and not before . . . unto my second son Robert Pitt all those farms . . . containing about 400 acres (near Curryjong brush).'

Thomas lingered for another week. His wife sat by him constantly, watching as he grew weaker. At one point she drew her children into the room to say goodbye to their father, and I picture a scene of almost unbearable poignancy: six-year-old George and five-year-old Mary, Robert and William, at three and one too young to understand what was going on, and baby Eliza, in her mother's arms, gathered around the bed of their ailing father. I see little Robert and William staring in bewilderment as their older brother and sister break down in tears, and as their mother ushers them gently out of the room they turn to take one last look at their dying father.

Thomas was thirty-nine when he died. His obituary appeared in the *Sydney Gazette* on 3 February 1921:

'On Sunday morning last, in his 40th year, at Richmond, Mr Thomas Matcham Pitt, Gent, a distant relation of the late Lord Nelson, leaving a widow and five orphans to deplore the loss of a tender and affectionate husband and parent. His death was occasioned by a severe cold contracted in going home from Sydney; which terminated in a fever that brought his existence to a period in the short space of a few days. The relatives of Mr Pitt, who are most respectably circumstanced, sensibly participated in the unhappiness of his late happy family; and so likewise will all who had the pleasure of his acquaintance. The probity of his heart could only be equalled by the complacency of his manner; and as he was universally esteemed, so will he now be as universally lamented.'

He was buried at St Peter's churchyard in Richmond on the 30 January 1821. He left his twenty-four-year-old widow Elizabeth, mother of five, facing an abyss.

Chapter 33

1821: Elizabeth

THERE WERE OTHER DEATHS in the family around that time.

Three months before her brother, on 3 September 1820, Susanna died, aged 46, of causes unknown. She left her husband William with four children aged from fourteen to six years old.

By 1821 Lucy Wood was aged 44 and had been a widow for nine years, ever since the death – presumed to have happened at sea – of her husband John. Earlier that year the 100 acres she had shared with her husband were expanded by an additional grant of 175 acres next door – something her late mother had been requesting for years.

So I am imagining it to be highly possible that both William and Lucy, who were both neighbours, were among the first to call on the grieving widow – Lucy to offer comfort, William to offer advice. With five children under seven Elizabeth had inherited 630 acres of land – a big responsibility for a young woman of twenty-four. Two weeks after Thomas's death she advertised 200 acres of it for lease, which may well have been at her brother in law William's suggestion.

Young George Matcham Pitt meanwhile, aged just seven, was now head of the family. But along with his new responsibilities had come a sudden invisibility. While adult family members and neighbours crowded into the front room and his younger brothers hung around them until shooed away by a well-meaning servant, and only aunt Lucy and sister Mary, one year his junior, were allowed to minister unto her mother and her guests, George did what he thought any head of the household should do: he became his father.

He got up at the crack of dawn, as he had seen his father do, and he was out in the paddocks working till his back ached, as he'd seen his father do – in the old days that is, before he'd taken to donning smart clothes and attending meetings. George's responsibilities had been limited to feeding the pigs and occasionally helping to herd the cows, but he needed new ones now. Lacking instruction or ideas he looked around for a role model to replace the father he had lost, and soon found one.

At that time William Scott was working on the Pitt farms as a labourer. At nineteen years old he could have been George's older brother.

William was a free man and so entitled to sell his labour to whoever wanted to buy it. It might have occurred to him, possibly before anyone else, that the death of the master had left not just the family but the whole workings of the farm in limbo. There was no one to oversee the convict workers and no one to make decisions, and after a week or so it became obvious that things at Pitt and Nelson Farms could quite easily fall apart. Strictly speaking it was not William's problem, and while he enjoyed his work well enough, and his late employer had always been good to him, so long as the situation continued – which with the mistress of the house cocooned in her own misery it very easily could – it was time he thought about moving on.

He was locked into this thought one day while harnessing one of the horses to the plough when he looked up to see the new young master of the household standing just two feet away from him with a question mark on his face.

'Can I help you?' William asked George.

George thought for a bit, and then he said, 'What do I have to do?'

'What do you mean?'

George frowned. 'What do I have to do?' he repeated.

William frowned back at him. 'I don't know why you're asking me, lad. I don't even know what you're talking about.'

'You're in charge now, aren't you?'

'Me?' William laughed shortly, and pushed his hat back from his face a bit. 'Says who?'

'Well, who else then?'

William stopped what he was doing for a moment. 'Look, I'm just the hired help around here, I don't make decisions.'

'Then who does? You're the boss now, aren't you? Who else is going to tell people what to do?'

William looked down at the young boy as he stood there, bare-footed, arms folded, legs planted squarely in the ground, just as his father used to do.

'I have to get my instructions, just like anyone else,' he said.

'Who from? My mother?'

'Well, yes.'

'I'm the boss now,' said little George.

William chuckled, and then stopped. 'Well I guess you are. So it's you should be telling me what to do, not the other way around.'

'And I'm saying you should be - you should be taking charge. Otherwise . . .'

'The place could go to the dogs, is what you're saying.'

George nodded, and bit his lip, and William realised he was trying not to cry.

'Look, I'm sorry about your dad.' He spoke more softly and put a hand on the boy's shoulder, which George immediately shook off.

'I could do that,' said George. 'What you're doing.'

'Very well, you do it then.'

William handed the horse's harness to the young boy and stood back to watch.

George looped the collar over the horse's head, wrapped the strap around the horse's girth and the tug around the horse's belly, all as if he'd been doing it all his life.

'You want to do the ploughing too, do you?' William

laughed.

'If you like.'

William stopped laughing for a moment. 'I almost believe you think you could,' he said.

'I know what to do. And when I'm bigger . . .'

'When you're bigger I'll be long gone,' said William.

'You're not going anywhere.' George glared at him.

A short while later Elizabeth was alerted by shouts coming from the direction of the paddock behind the house and looking out, she saw her eldest son standing there, the plough positioned in front of him, and behind him shouting instructions was one of the farm workers, whose name she couldn't immediately recall. Then to her astonishment she watched as her seven-year-old, big for his age and strong too, but seven years old just the same, leaning with all his weight into the handles of the plough, which he could barely reach, and with one tremendous heave setting the whole thing moving; and she continued to watch with increasing disbelief as plough, horse, boy and man set off down the paddock in what was not quite a straight line, accompanied by shouts and whoops of laughter from both. She made a mental note to have a word with the young farm worker.

~

'What did you say his name was?'

George looked up at his mother and hesitated. There were rules in this new fatherless world that he was not yet sure of.

'Who?' he said.

Elizabeth sighed. 'My love, I am not going to get him into trouble. I just want you to tell me who he is. I've seen him around the farm, he looks like a capable man.'

'William. His name's William.'

'William Scott. I thought so. And what do you think of young William?'

George shrugged.

'Is he a capable man? In your opinion? As the boss of the household?'

George seemed to be mulling this over. 'I think so. He works hard. He seems to know what he's doing.'

Elizabeth nodded gravely. 'Then next time you see him be a darling and tell him to come and speak to me, would you do that? And I promise I'm not going to tell him off, or scold him in any way.'

'Very well, mama.'

'Oh, and George.'

'Yes, mama?'

'Just because you're the boss now, doesn't mean you have to be so very serious. Remember you are barely seven years old.'

'I will try to remember that, mama,' said George seriously.

It was not long after this that William paid the first of what were to become regular visits to the farmhouse. Initially, conferences with the lady of the house took place on the veranda, as was only right. But in time William was allowed into the front room, which surprised George, because the rules stated that only Certain People should be allowed to set foot inside the house, and a humble farm labourer was not one of them. But then perhaps William had by that time become more than just a farm labourer.

~

Later that year there was a brief cause for celebration.

When the other William – George's uncle, his late aunt Susanna Faithfull's husband – proposed to his aunt Lucy it seemed the most natural thing in the world. They had known one another ever since Faithfull came into the family, his four children were not that much younger than Lucy's two and knew each other well. It would be a comfort for Lucy to have a companion after all her years alone; and so they applied for a marriage licence on 26 September 1821 with the intention of marrying just three days later at St Peter's, Richmond.

It was the first time since his father's death that George had seen his mother truly happy, and he watched as she set to preparing the wedding breakfast with an energy he had quite forgotten she had.

It was Lucy who broke the news.

The local chaplain, the Reverend Fulton, had called the wedding off. Under what was colloquially known as the 'dead sister act', which forbade a man from marrying his sister in law, even though she was not a blood relative, he had revoked the licence.

It was a cruel blow for Lucy. It had been a rare chance of happiness for a woman who had not had an easy life. Despite outliving all her siblings, she never married again.

William meanwhile, undeterred, looked around for another wife and found Margaret Bringelly, and the two of them were married only two months later, in November 1821.

The following year George, aged eight, began school, along with his cousin George Faithfull. It was common in those days for children to put in several hours of work both before and after school, so George began each day as he had always done: feeding the hogs and moving the cattle if such a thing were necessary. In times of heavy rain he herded the animals onto higher ground without waiting to be told.

William Scott, though officially not yet named overseer of Pitt and Nelson Farms, was now effectively running things, which accounted, George surmised, for his almost daily presence in the house. George quickly became used to seeing his adopted elder brother about the place, in fact he welcomed it – it gave him someone to talk to about how the farm was going, what cattle they should sell and what they should keep, whether they should grow more maize or let the paddocks lie fallow that year, and other such adult things. He was pleased too to see how William brought a smile to his mother's face, a flush even. And he may or may not have noticed how his mother's girth was starting to expand, until one day in 1824 George was presented with a brand new baby brother.

Little John Pitt was followed three years later by Elizabeth Scott; then four years later along came Augusta and finally, two years after that, Frances. The last three children took the name of Scott and seem to have been incorporated into the family along with their step-siblings.

By this time William Scott was the fully-fledged overseer of the two properties. So why, the question begs itself, did he and Elizabeth never marry?

One can only imagine that Elizabeth considered the stigma of being the unmarried mother of four illegitimate children, which in those days was considerable, less burdensome than the prospect of her legitimate offspring losing out on her late husband's properties on her death. By law, a woman on marrying handed over the rights to whatever property she owned to her husband, including land she had been granted in her own name. Had Elizabeth married William he would have inherited all her property, rather than her sons, as stipulated in Thomas's will. If this is the case it says a lot for Elizabeth's courage that she was not prepared to take the risk.

~

In 1831 Hannah Laycock, Elizabeth's mother and my other four times great grandmother, that doughty woman who first arrived in the colony in 1791 along with her eccentric husband, from whom she spent a good deal of her life apart, died at the age of 71.

The two Laycock wills make for interesting reading.

When Thomas Laycock senior died in 1809 he left his cattle and livestock to his children and his wife. He left a 900 acre estate to his eldest son William, a gold watch and chain to his second son Thomas junior, and £200 to the mysterious Mary Sargent – so long as she was still working for him when he died. The remainder, whatever that was, was to be shared between his four older children.

By the time Hannah died only three of her children – William, Samuel and Elizabeth – were still living. Her eldest daughter Sarah and second eldest son Thomas junior had both died, as had Thomas's wife Isabella, and Rebecca had returned to England in 1816. Hannah had sold King's Grove some years before but at the time of her death she still owned Putty Farm, north of the Hawkesbury, and four houses in Pitt Street.

She left one of those houses to her granddaughter Eliza – Elizabeth and Thomas's youngest daughter, who in the 1828 census was registered living with Hannah in Sydney – along with personal possessions and trinkets. The rest of Hannah's estate, which included the 100-acre Putty Farm and some cows and horses, she bequeathed to her two sons and her grandchildren. All Elizabeth received was a portrait of her nephew Thomas Eber Bunker Laycock, a *'dressing glass and smaller family bible'*, the house in Pitt Street bequeathed to her brother William, but not till after his death – something that was to cause problems later – and a third share of the residue of the estate, which probably did not amount to much. (As it happens Putty Farm, which was bequeathed to Hannah's grandson Thomas WEB Laycock, ended up partly with the Pitt family when Thomas married his cousin Mary, Elizabeth's eldest daughter.)

What can one interpret from a will? Thomas and Hannah Laycock had obviously broken off all communication before he died, though precisely who Mary Sargent was and the nature of her relationship with Thomas is a matter for conjecture. As for Hannah, it's strange that all she could find to leave directly to her sole surviving (and widowed) daughter were a few trinkets and the smaller family bible (the main bible went to Eliza). Clearly there were divisions in this family, and one can only wonder whether Hannah's rejection of her daughter had anything to do with Elizabeth's relationship with William Scott.

~

In the 1828 census Elizabeth's holdings had increased to 730 acres (where the extra 100 acres came from isn't clear and may well be a mistake in the records). William is named as her overseer, Margaret his sister appears with *'no employer listed'* and there were four other male workers under her name, two of whom were convicts. The children, by both Thomas and William, are grouped together. There were twelve horses and 250 cattle. George by then had possibly left school since there is no sign of him or his cousin George Faithfull on the register after 1824. I like to think that Elizabeth and William and their extended family lived in busy but prosperous harmony at that time, blighted only by the death, aged fifteen, of Elizabeth's youngest (legitimate) son William, in 1834.

The first day of the following year Elizabeth herself died, aged thirty-nine, the same age Thomas was at his death. She was buried along with young William and her late husband in the churchyard at St Peter's in Richmond.

George was not quite twenty-one when he inherited his mother's properties. Later that same year he got married, and three years after that he set out from his property at Richmond and ventured, along with his de facto stepfather William Scott, to take up land in the outer reaches of New South Wales. But that is another story for another time.

Chapter 34

2009: Moving on

FOR TWENTY-FIVE YEARS the Blue Mountains formed a barrier between the European settled areas of New South Wales and the unknown territory beyond. Now there's a winding but comfortably-graded road that leads up the mountains to townships named after the three men who made the breakthrough: Lawson, Blaxland and, more to the point in our case, Wentworth, or more specifically Wentworth Falls. And here we are, the three cousins, one from England, one from Australia and one dithering between, united at last and on our way to the family reunion at a house called Coorah, built by our great grandfather Robert Matcham Pitt on land bequeathed to him by his father George, which is now the Blue Mountains Grammar School.

It is a typical colonial house with verandas and an iron roof, standing in a vast parkland of around 40 acres. It was built by 'RM', as he was called, in 1889, and he managed to turn what was completely infertile soil into a self-sufficient dairy farm, with cattle and home-grown vegetables, plus a golf course. It was, or he was, particularly famous for his daffodils, which he grew and bred with meticulous dedication. RM eventually gave the house away to the Country Women's Association – presumably because none of his offspring wanted it, which is a shame – his only stipulation being that it must be used in some way for children. So its current function is entirely appropriate but does not stop us from informing the school staff, half-jokily, that we're coming back to reclaim our family heritage, at which they laugh slightly nervously.

98-year-old aunt Barbara – too frail to make the journey – is the only surviving relative to have direct memories of the house. She and her sisters, my and cousin Frances's late mothers, spent many happy Christmases there with extended family; and there are photos of our mothers as babes in arms, beribboned children or sulky teenagers, arrayed in their best Edwardian garb along with sundry other family and friends on the front steps of the house.

This is where the family reunion is taking place. It is October, antipodean spring, originally planned to coincide with the daffodils but then, for more practical reasons, with the long weekend when the schoolchildren are away. So the daffs are over. The dust storm I arrived in the week before is a distant memory now and the weather is a spring-like twenty-five degrees.

Many woman hours have gone into this reunion. It was originally the brainchild of Salli Chmura, a Canberra relative, who coincidentally has also been working on a family history book, but my Australian cousin Libby took on the lion's share of the organisation. Without a database of family relatives she has relied on word of mouth and advertising to spread the word, but since this is the first Pitt family reunion ever no one expected to be able to muster more than around a couple of dozen people. Over the months however the list has grown to well over a hundred, drawn from all over the country and, if you accept the presence of myself and my English cousin Frances, overseas.

Libby has made name tags for everyone, colour-coded according to which branch of the family the invitee belongs to: blue for Thomas, yellow for Susanna, and so on. She has filled notice boards with photos and pictures of every generation, and where possible the houses they lived in (she was not a primary school teacher for nothing), created a collage to include everyone from great grandparents to our own children, and put together a book of photos and newspaper cuttings –

the pictorial version of my own written effort.

I have taken it upon myself to construct a map of Sydney and surrounds, including the Hawkesbury, with flags indicating all the places where our ancestors were granted land. (If just a tiny percentage of those grants were still in the family name we would be one of the richest families in New South Wales.) I have also printed out a basic outline of Mary's story, on the assumption that at least some of the people attending will know little about how they come to be where they are. None of us has ever organised a reunion before so like our ancestors we are making it up as we go along.

By Saturday, the day of the reunion, the spring weather has turned to winter, a chill mist has settled, as it often does in the Blue Mountains, the rain is pouring down and the temperature has dropped to nine degrees. Will anyone turn up?

The answer is – when did an Aussie let a bit of dodgy weather get in the way of anything? Among the 100 or so guests, many of whom are not grey-haired, there are people who haven't seen one another since childhood and others meeting cousins and other relatives for the first time. Many of them bring their own memorabilia – photos and family trees – all of which are displayed in rooms adjoining the main area, what used to be the living and dining room.

We had planned to spread out across the lawns of Coorah but the weather forcing everyone inside only seems to add to the conviviality. Photos are taken – of the group as a whole and of each branch of the family. Both Salli and Libby give speeches, and I say a few words about the woman who was responsible for all of us being Australian. As I stand there looking around at the room stuffed full of my very own Aussie rellies, I feel suddenly moved, and oddly grateful.

There is a cake with – an inspired idea – a quote from Mary's letter to her cousin George written while she was waiting to sail:

'I have brought my children up with fear and care . . .'

which is ceremonially cut by the eldest and the youngest (safe enough to wield a knife) person present. Finally we drink a toast to Mary Pitt, and if many people in the room had never heard of her before, they know who she is now.

~

I am finally reaching the end of part one of my family story, and with it the end of this part of my own personal journey. It is a sad moment.

In the course of the years of delving into my Australian family history I find I have dug my heels into the country in a way that I never really did when I was living here in my hedonistic early twenties. As I stand on Circular Quay, possibly for the last time, watching the traffic of ageing ferries, sailing boats and the floating cities that call themselves cruise liners, I think back to a time before the Harbour Bridge and powered ferries when my great great grandfather G M Pitt, who was rather a large gentleman apparently, used to travel from his home in Kirribilli to the city by rowboat, along with three 56lb weights brought along by the ferryman as counterweights.

I recall the 75th anniversary in 2007 of the opening of the 'coathanger', as the Harbour Bridge is colloquially called, which was a low key affair by comparison with its original opening in March 1932, an event my aunt Barbara remembers well.

She arrived home to be greeted by her mother, who had been following proceedings on the wireless, exclaiming in triumph, 'He didn't do it!'

'He' was Jack Lang, the New South Wales premier who, controversially, and to the dismay and disgust of my grandmother, decided that he rather than Sir Philip Game, Governor of New South Wales and His Majesty George V's representative, should be the one to cut the ribbon at the opening ceremony.

Despite threats of disruption from, in particular, a right-wing paramilitary organisation called the New Guard, nobody seemed to notice – not the organisers, nor the police nor the

50,000 people who turned out to watch the two-mile long procession – the lone horserider tagging along several yards behind the Governor-General's mounted escort. When it came to the moment of ribbon-cutting the lone rider spurred his horse, galloped past the official party and with a cry of 'I declare this bridge open on behalf of the decent citizens of New South Wales!' sliced the ribbon through with his sword.

It was a wonderful story and typically Australian, or so I thought, for its bloody-minded, larrikin mockery of officialdom. It was the New South Wales Corps all over again. On this occasion however it was not the lone horseman Frank de Groot who was the larrikin, or his fascist-leaning supporters, it was Jack Lang, who in the eyes of many people had betrayed his country by reneging on debts owed to Britain and generally thumbing his nose at the mother country, to the disgust not just of the New Guard but of the old guard of people such as my own family. (Not, I hasten to add, that my family were fascists.) It was an early example of the continuing tension between the old country – which my aunt, who spent just three of her 99 years there still referred to as 'home' – and the new.

This is the Australia that fought in both world wars on the far side of the world; that supported America in Vietnam, which the Brits did not, and the western coalition in Iraq and Afghanistan, which the Brits did. It is a country that has stayed loyal to allies living the opposite end of the world and yet has been largely ignored and even at times betrayed by them. It is a country that is closer to Asia than to any other continent but which, up until the middle of the last century, had a 'white Australia' policy that ensured no one but an educated white person was allowed to emigrate there. Things are very different now of course, as one look at the ethnic mix of the local people shows. It's a country that in a loaded referendum held a few years ago chose not to become a republic, but whose Prime Minister at the time of writing this, who was born in Wales, is a declared republican. It is a country that's a mix of

British self deprecation and American up-and-go; where trousers are 'pants' but pavements are pavements and a router – as in the device that connects your computer to the internet – is pronounced the American way, with an 'ow'. (And yes, there is a louche reason for that: 'Why would you never want to date a wombat? Because he eats roots and leaves.' A joke that only works in Australia.)

It is a country – or more to the point a state, New South Wales – that 40 years ago when I was living in Sydney set up an unpopular lottery in order to raise money for an opera house that nobody wanted, on a spot known as Bennelong Point, named in memory of the Aboriginal man befriended by Governor Phillip. My aunt remembers the site when it was a tram terminus. Before that – seventeen million years before, to be precise – it was a volcano. The first Europeans discovered the sites of three long-extinct volcanoes beneath what is now the city of Sydney, all of which is a reminder of how old this 'new' country actually is.

I have stood on beaches watching superhuman beings riding twenty-foot waves, and I've thought of Lucy and John Wood, with their tiny babe, out there on the ocean for months on end coping with hostile natives, shipwrecks and no satnav. I've sailed up the Hawkesbury River on a mailboat, delivering mail and other provisions to the dozen or so 'settlements', so-called – clusters of houses built beneath sheer cliffs and only accessible by water – and marvelled at the still untouched beauty of the river with its mangroves and swamps on one side and cliffs on the other, and thrilled at the thought that I am seeing it much as Mary and her family would have done two hundred years ago.

Mary and her family's new life began at a time when the colony of Botany Bay was still an experiment. By 1821, the year Thomas died and coincidentally the year Governor Macquarie retired and went back to live out the rest of his life on the Isle of Mull, it was a solidly established country with a new name and a positive future. Macquarie, sadly and like all governors before him did not leave in a blaze of glory. Despite taking the colony from an ad hoc, badly organised place of uncertainty and doubtful hygiene to a country of order, stability and good management he did not win the favours of the British government, partly because of his partiality for giving emancipists positions of authority and thereby upsetting the Exclusives.

The British Government's attitude to Botany Bay didn't often make a lot of sense. Having created a prison far far away where convicts could be sent to be out of sight and mind, the authorities back home then seemed to wash their hands of the whole enterprise, especially in the early days. At the same time they refused to allow the country its own currency, or parliament, or legal system, and if anyone in authority there showed signs of enterprise or initiative they seemed to do all they could to obstruct them.

In a way one could see their point: Botany Bay was set up as a place of correction, not opportunity. Or as our modern media would say it was a prison, not a holiday camp. It was not intended to be desirable. Why, soon criminals would be bribing their way there! (They did, though not till later on; money allegedly did pass hands on board the hulks in the old country.) They could even be tempted into crime with the sole purpose of being transported! (True again, though again not till later; it was openly acknowledged in the 1850s that some people were committing crimes such as arson as a way of engineering their transportation.) People were sent there to suffer. And if it was no longer possible to distinguish between the flawless souls who had migrated there unblemished by misdemeanour, or the need to commit misdemeanour, and the scum who had been forcibly sent there as punishment, then what was the world coming to?

No one who did not actually experience the early days of colonial Australia can possibly begin to imagine how the people – convicts and settlers, soldiers and governors – struggled, simply to survive. Nobody can possibly know what the Marys and Thomases went through each and every day in order to turn the barren, alien, unwieldy and remote landscape into the country it is now. They were helped by visionary governors such as Phillip, King and Macquarie; and even, in a different way, by the less organised but arguably further-sighted New South Wales Corps. They did all this at huge cost to the indigenous people, whose removal from the land they had successfully occupied for tens of thousands of years continues to cause problems in this otherwise relatively untroubled continent. But that is another story entirely, and not one I am qualified to pass judgment on.

Come to that, as a pom from London I am not really qualified to write my Australian family story in the first place. But there, it is done, and done as best as I've been able to do it. It has been a hugely absorbing experience and a humbling one, and by animating my ancestors and giving them characteristics they may or more likely may not have had, I have tried to bring the story alive; and to do justice, in some small way, to the astonishing courage and enterprise that enabled generations of their descendants to thrive and proudly call themselves Australian. As a half Aussie, half pom, I feel justified in being one of them.

Epilogue

Dynasties: The generations that came after

THOMAS AND ELIZABETH PITT between them had three (legitimate) sons and two daughters. Their eldest son George Matcham (GM) Pitt, he of the counterweighted ferries, became one of the first white settlers to take up land in the Moree district in northwest New South Wales in the 1830s. The story goes that he went all the way from his farm in Richmond on foot – which seems unlikely, not to say unnecessary – driving a herd of cattle. He also bought property in the Wellington district, but decided eventually to become a stock and station agent and founded the firm that became known as Pitt, Son and Badgery. (The 'Son' was his son Robert, my great granddad, who built Coorah.) He married the daughter of convicts and their ten surviving children were all born in Richmond.

GM and his wife Julia eventually moved from Richmond to Manly, and thence to Kirribilli, where he died in 1896 at the age of 82. He was Mayor of East St Leonards at one point and was partly responsible for the pipeline bringing mains water across the harbour to North Sydney. He is the subject of the book I or someone else has yet to write.

Thomas and Elizabeth's eldest daughter Mary Matcham, named in honour of her grandmother, went on to marry her cousin Thomas Laycock, grandson of Quartermaster Laycock, and Elizabeth's nephew. Their youngest daughter Eliza, who at some point had lived with her grandmother Hannah Laycock, married her cousin Austin Forrest Wilshire, Hester's son, who'd been named in honour of Jemima's first husband. This inter-marrying was partly the result of the limited gene pool, but it also suggests an enduring family connection.

~

SUSANNA and her husband William Faithfull had four children and lived throughout their married life next door to Mary and Thomas on the Hawkesbury, on land rented from a Thomas Spencer.

I have not been able to dig up much information on either of them, though there is a story about William dating back to 1805 – one year after he married Susanna – which nearly cut short their marriage before it had properly begun.

He was working on the property when he fell on a pitchfork, which penetrated his stomach. The report in the *Sydney Gazette* on 13 January did not expect him to survive, but somehow he did. Six months later however a friend called James Morris took out a case against him alleging that William, who had been a frequent guest in his house in Sydney, had spread a damaging rumour claiming Morris was planning to claim back a £200 loan from William's estate on the event of his death, even though no such money was owing. The case was brought not because of the alleged loan but because of the slur on Morris's reputation as a businessman. William admitted the rumour but said it did not emanate from him, and in trying to trace the source of the slander each person interviewed passed the buck to the next till it ended up on the shoulders of an eight year old child, *'who when challenged by her parents, denied it totally'*, said the *Gazette*. In the end both sides paid their own costs, and there is no record of what happened to that particular friendship.

Susanna and William's eldest son, also called William – after his father, as was traditional in various branches of the family and makes research that much more challenging – initially worked for his uncle Robert Jenkins, and then as overseer on his aunt Jemima Jenkins's property in Illawarra. William Junior was then given land on his own behalf near Goulburn which in time became one of the largest and best known sheep stations in New South Wales, by name Springfield. The property stayed in the family until a few years ago, when the Faithfull descendant, William Maple-Brown, retired to live in Goulburn with his wife Pamela. (Their son now runs the portion of the property that was not sold.) Springfield harboured generations of carefully preserved clothing and furniture, all of which was donated to the National Museum in Canberra. Thus was one of the better known and most successful farming dynasties of New South Wales descended from a man who arrived in the colony as an illiterate, eighteen-year-old private with the New South Wales Corps.

William married three times in all: he had two children by Margaret Thompson and when she died he married Maria Bell, daughter of Archibald Bell, who was one of the witnesses to Thomas's will, and after whom the oddly titled 'Bell's Line of Road', north of the Hawkesbury, is named.

Susanna died of unknown causes at the age of 46, in Richmond, three years after her near contemporary Jane Austen died, aged 41, in Winchester.

~

LUCY, after the excitement of her thirteen months at sea with her husband John and baby son George, lived the rest of her life on dry land. Following her aborted engagement to William Faithfull she spent the rest of her long life unmarried. Her daughter Sophia worked at the Female Orphan School before marrying Samuel Pinder Henry at the same church (St John's Parramatta) and by the same person (the Reverend Samuel Marsden) as her mother had done nineteen years earlier. Samuel, the son of missionaries based in Tahiti, became a sea captain, and Sophia died on Tahiti, where she had quite probably been conceived 47 years before. Lucy's son George Pitt Wood owned land near the Pitts on the Hawkesbury. He married the daughter of a convict and family rumour, unsubstantiated, says that George's mother disapproved of the match to the extent that when visiting her son she refused to get out of her carriage and demanded he come out of the house to speak to her.

Since this is only rumour it would not be fair to pass judgment on Lucy. Her nephew GM also married the daughter of convicts, but their parents Thomas and Elizabeth did not live long enough to know it. (And in any case Elizabeth as the mother of four children born out of wedlock was hardly in a position to make a moral judgment on others.)

Lucy eventually went to live and work with Jemima on her property in Illawarra. She died in Richmond in 1852, aged 75.

~

HESTER and James Wilshire had nine surviving children – two died when they were just weeks old. Their second son, James Wilshire Jnr, became the second Mayor of Sydney. Their third son Austin Forrest married Eliza Pitt, Thomas and Elizabeth's daughter; their daughter Matilda Pitt Wilshire married William Jenkins, Jemima's son; and their son Thomas Matcham Pitt Wilshire married Helen Faithfull, William's son by his second wife Margaret. The naming of Hester's children, and their inter-marriages, suggests she was very much a family person.

Hester's husband James held the position of Deputy Commissary on and off for many years. His tanning business, which he ran from premises in Brickfield Hill (now George Street) in Sydney was so successful it produced enough leather to fulfil the colony's needs and export the surplus. Hester, aka Esther, died in 1836, aged 49, again of unknown causes.

~

JEMIMA's second husband Robert Jenkins, the man her brother had allegedly disapproved of when he became bankrupt soon after arriving in the colony, went on to become the third richest man in New South Wales. He was an adept wheeler-dealer and in his relatively short life he had his fingers in many pies and became an intense patriot, hosting anniversary dinners for Governor Macquarie, for which he composed a ditty set to the music of 'Rule Britannia'. (He fell out with the governor later, who described him as 'fractious'.)

He was a director on the board of the first bank in Australia, the Bank of New South Wales. In 1817 Robert and Jemima were given 1000 acres in the Illawarra district, which Robert named 'Berkeley' after his home in Gloucestershire in England. He never lived there apparently. It is now a steel works, but nearby is the Berkeley Pioneer Cemetery where Robert, Hester and the Jenkins descendants are all buried.

Robert, like Jemima's first husband Austin Forrest, died from a fall from his horse. He was in Sydney, returning home from an auction, when his horse took fright and threw him.

Jemima went on to manage their properties on her own, with the aid of her nephew William Pitt Faithfull and her sister Lucy. She increased her holdings at Illawarra and elsewhere, and died suddenly on her property at Eagle Vale in Campbelltown, aged 58. There is a Jemima Park nearby named after her.

Jemima and Robert had two boys, the younger of whom, William Warren Jenkins, married Matilda Pitt, Hester's daughter.

~

With the exception of Lucy none of Mary's children lived to the age that she did. Causes of death weren't recorded at that time, unless they were dramatic, as in the case of Jemima's husbands. Jemima died 'suddenly', which suggests a heart attack, or stroke. Susanna and Hester died relatively young, which suggests possibly cancer. We will never know.

There tends to be much more information to be had about the men than the women unless, like Jemima, they were property owners. None of the female members of the Pitt family was honoured with a detailed obituary for instance. However when it comes to stories handed down through the generations orally there is more about Lucy than any of the others, perhaps because she lived longer than any of them. While one branch of the family claimed she refused to speak to her daughter in law, another maintains she was much loved. Of course both stories could be true, and everyone likes to think that their own particular ancestral line was peopled by charitably-minded, generous, compassionate, successful and upright citizens. The fact that there were convicts in the family, in the Pitt line and in the Wood's, was kept very quiet until a couple of generations ago.

Family ties appeared to have been strong. James Wilshire and Robert Jenkins were often involved in the same business ventures, and Thomas too on occasion. Thomas Pitt and William Faithfull were both members of the Hawkesbury Benevolent Society and sent their two sons, both called George, to the same school. Lucy lived with Jemima for many years, and Hester paid tribute to her brother in law and her brother by naming two of her children after them. I imagine this would have made Mary very happy.

~

MARGARET CATCHPOLE did not achieve legendary status until some time after her death, and thanks mostly to the Reverend Cobbold's book, which was published in 1845.

In order to turn her story into a morality tale the Reverend, despite declaring his narrative to be as true as he could make it, invented most of the latter part of Margaret's life including, and especially, her marriage to a wealthy businessman. This led to some confusion among the citizens of New South Wales and there was a belief he may have mistaken Margaret for Mary Reibey, who had also been transported for horse stealing. Mrs Reibey, then a prominent and prosperous member of Sydney society – thanks partly to her marriage to a wealthy businessman – had gone to some lengths to conceal her convict background and threatened to sue the Reverend for defamation. (She retracted when he managed to convince her any confusion was unintentional.)

But the story was out: in 1890 a *'party of literary gentleman'* made a pilgrimage to Richmond in the belief that Margaret's grave had been discovered at St Peter's graveyard, only to find it was someone else entirely. Another distant Pitt relation, G B Barton, wrote a series of pieces on Margaret for the *Evening*

News, which after his death was published as a book entitled *The True Story of Margaret Catchpole*. My great great grandfather G M Pitt, in a letter to the *Evening News* dated 2 December 1890, unwittingly fuelled the rumour there was more than one Margaret Catchpole:

'To the Editor.

Sir, - As you have been making enquiries of the Margaret Catchpole who was buried in Richmond churchyard in the year 1819, she was a nurse to my mother previous to her death. My father had a flock of sheep at Bronte, shepherded by a man named Tom, who died, through catching a heavy cold, from diarrhoea. Margaret attended him, and she caught the same complaint, and it carried her off. I believe this same woman to be the veritable Margaret who was transported from England for horse-stealing; and she never was married. That other Margaret Catchpole, spoken of by the Rev.Mr. Cobbold, had no connection with my mother's nurse. I was quite young in the year 1819, and I, therefore, cannot give you any more information. – Yours &c., GEO.M.PITT'

(Friday 5 December 1890 edition)

No one is completely sure where Margaret is buried. She is somewhere in St Peter's Cemetery in Richmond, where many of the Pitt family were buried, but her grave is unmarked. There was talk of her being interred in the Pitt family vault, or even with the Dights. Everyone, it seemed, wanted to claim her, even after her death.

~

GEORGE MATCHAM, that progressive visionary, died in 1833, aged 70 years old. He and Kitty had eleven surviving children over a period of twenty years, and after Lady Emma Hamilton's death they became foster parents of her daughter by Nelson, who was called Horatia.

George wrote copiously on all sorts of subjects from the doubtful necessity of having to eat meat to the taking of snuff which, he considered, was a good appetite suppressant but could be harmful if taken in excess. Smoking, which at one point was banned in England, served a useful purpose as punctuation in conversation in order to give a person time to think before speaking, and to check the consumption of alcohol. George and Kitty lived in Paris at one point but ended up in Holland Park in London, where in his dotage George indulged his hobby of inventing steam baths, playing with his grandchildren and spying on the men working on his house through a telescope. He was obviously much loved by his family and his grandchildren, and he had nothing but good things to say about his brother in law Horatio, both as a man and as a naval hero.

George's son, George Matcham junior, was the central character in a play by Terence Rattigan called *A Bequest to the Nation,* in which Nelson and Emma Hamilton are seen through the eyes of their nephew when he was a boy. It was made into a film starring the Australian actor Peter Finch (an acquaintance of aunt Barbara's, as it happens) as Nelson, Glenda Jackson as Lady Hamilton and Nigel Stock as George Matcham senior. (Incidentally round about the same time I appeared in a play in which Nigel Stock played Churchill and I his secretary. It toured briefly and then died quietly. Unfortunately I didn't then realise the man Nigel had been impersonating was my distant relative.)

There is no existing record, so far as I am aware, of any letters written between George and his cousin Mary after she arrived in New South Wales. The only surviving letter written by him to the Pitts was addressed to Thomas in 1828. He began by saying:

'My recollection of you is very slight. From your good mother I sometimes received a letter . . . I have now to recommend to your good advice and friendly attention my second son Charles Horatio Nelson Matcham who is going to Port Jackson to take up a grant of 2560 acres . . . He has never before left us and is now for the first time set afloat . . . One more favour I have to require that is to write me a line giving me an impartial account how these children go on.'

Unfortunately by 1828 Thomas had been dead for seven years, so obviously communication between George and the Pitts had fizzled out. There is no knowing whether or not Thomas's widow responded to the one letter that made its way into posterity.

As George had stated back in 1792 he always intended sending his 'younger son' to the colony, but it was nearly 40 years before his sixth – and third surviving – son actually set foot on antipodean turf.

~

CHARLES HORATIO NELSON MATCHAM (quite a name to live up to) arrived in Australia in 1829, aged twenty-three. His 2560 acres were near Gosford on the central coast north of Sydney, and on the map it appears there is a town named after him. My Australian cousin and I went in search of it and found just a piece of countryside, but no town.

From there Charles, who did not appear to have inherited his father's optimistic and sunny nature, wrote to his brother George to say, rather sourly:

> *'I candidly confess I see no prospect of honourably benefiting myself in this colony or of acquiring any degree of importance in the society in which I move. As for settling it appears to me a ruinous speculation, you invest the whole of your capital without deriving any return to enable you to carry on the current expenses of yr farm – this leads of course to borrowing and from thence to a sheriff's execution and there ends the unfortunate settler ... a young man of my age looks forward to obtain some degree of consideration in society, corresponding to the rank of his own family, which never can occur to me situated as I am, for the term settler is synonymous with that of blackguard.'*

On another occasion he wrote, *'it certainly is a peculiar country . . . single men are quite on the pave and miserably at a loss for society . . .'*

He was worried about the Depression, bushrangers, the state of the country's finances and its lack of defence against enemy invasion. In 1839 he said:

'. . . five American ships of War were found one fine morning anchored under the Town, not a soul having known of their having come in during the night and without a pilot.'

In 1838 he moved to Yass, south west of Sydney, where he complained about the poor state of the wool market and the dire shortage of labour. He kept his properties on the central coast and at one point he owned stations on either side of the Murrumbidgee and was living nearby, at Bogolong, around twenty kilometres from Yass. He died, unmarried, on 11 March 1844, and was buried in an obscure corner of the graveyard of St Clement's Church in Yass in what was, until the women of St Clement's clubbed together in 1922 to give him a tombstone, an unmarked grave. The heavily worn inscription reads:

CHARLES HORATIO NELSON MATCHAM
OF BOGOLONG MURRUMBIDGEE N.S.WALES
GENTLEMAN SETTLER
Died March 11th 1844
Aged 39 years

Interestingly there is no mention at the site of his famous uncle, and when I visited the local information office in 2010 they had no idea of the connection with Admiral Nelson.

CHN Matcham did not seem to do too badly so far as properties were concerned, which was only to be expected for someone arriving in the colony with thousands of acres of land and money in his pocket, not to mention an illustrious name. But he comes across as a sad and lonely, curmudgeonly figure who found it difficult to make friends or to find a wife. He died the same age as Thomas Pitt, whose son GM was off speculating in the Moree district at the same time Matcham was moving to Yass. There is no evidence the two men ever met.

~

At various times in the past our ancestors were in possession of a good part of Sydney and its surrounds. Quartermaster

Thomas Laycock owned 80 acres at Parsley Bay, now one of the most exclusive parts of the exclusive Eastern Suburbs. He was also the first to own land at a place he named Home Bush, famous now for the 2000 Olympic Games stadium. His wife Hannah's grant gave the name to the suburb of Kingsgrove, as did the Jenkins's grant, Berkeley, at Illawarra.

Pitt Street in Richmond is named after Thomas, and Pitt Street in Kirribilli after his eldest son GM. Pittwater and Pitt Town on the other hand were named after the Prime Minister of England, and Pitt Street in Sydney after Pit's Row, from the days when the water running through what was known as the Tank Stream was collected in pits for the use of local residents. Springfield station near Goulburn still exists and there is a Holbrook Street in Kirribilli which is named after the house owned by great great grandfather GM Pitt.

Thanks to Margaret Betts the original Pitt family property at the Hawkesbury retains the name Bronte. There is also a Bronte Park in Tasmania, named after the famous admiral by George Matcham's son in law Lt Arthur Davies, who married his daughter Elizabeth.

One way or another Mary Pitt and her extended family live on in 21st century New South Wales.

~

Interest in the Pitt family history goes back generations. Mary Eyre Matcham, George's great granddaughter, who wrote the wonderful *The Nelsons of Burnham Thorpe*, corresponded prolifically on the topic of family history with Matilda Warren Jenkins, who was granddaughter to both Jemima and Hester. (Matilda's father William married his cousin, also Matilda, Hester's daughter). It was probably Matilda who 'edited' Mary's letters.

However she was not the only member of the Jenkins family to take an interest in our genealogy. In 1859 Jemima and Robert Jenkins's elder son Robert (Matilda's uncle) sailed to England on board *Royal Charter*, with his wife and five young children. They were taking the boys to be educated in the old country and planning to return to Australia a few years later. Their daughter Alice, then fourteen, was being educated in Paris, and on hearing of another possible revolution brewing they advanced their journey and switched boats onto the state-of-the-art 'splendid vessel'. They took with them the portrait of their grandfather Robert Pitt, in the hopes of finding out more about him.

Before travelling Robert apparently had a premonition. He appeared depressed, and he told his cousin William Pitt Faithfull that he thought he would face the same fate as the poor passengers on the shipwrecked *Dunbar*. Then when giving his forwarding address to his brother William he said, *'If I ever get there'*.

Royal Charter was shipwrecked off Anglesea and virtually all the 450 passengers and crew lost their lives, including all seven members of the Jenkins family. Tragically during the storm the captain had ordered everyone to stay below in the saloon, assuring them it would be safer; but then the ship split into pieces and most of the passengers were killed by falling debris. The story was written up by both Matilda Warren Jenkins and, in a book called *The Uncommercial Traveller*, by Charles Dickens.

The loss to the Jenkins family was unspeakable. But it was a loss too to the rest of us, because it is just possible that Robert Jenkins may have been able to unlock the secret of his grandfather Robert Pitt, and discover the answer to the question of why Mary Pitt emigrated to New South Wales.

Afterword

Since I began working on this story my aunt Barbara, the inspiration behind the entire project, died in Sydney in August 2010, aged 99.

She knew I was writing this book but I don't think she ever really appreciated how much I felt I owed her, not just for all the information she gleaned through her years researching the family history – the happiest years of her life, as she described them – but for opening my eyes to my own heritage, and inspiring me to dig beneath the surface of a country I now realise I had only ever known superficially.

Whether or not she would have enjoyed or approved of my endeavours I would like to dedicate them to her, in the hope and expectation that other branches of the family and other generations in the future will keep the family hearth burning and the memory of Mary Pitt alive.

I have created a Pitt family history website at marymatchampitt.wordpress.com, with outline information on the various branches of the first generation of Pitts, including the Faithfulls, Wilshires, Woods, Jenkins and Laycocks. Please feel free to leave (friendly) comments on the site.

I have also started a Pitt family Facebook group at https://www.facebook.com/groups/341776523285974/?ref=bookmarks. Whether or not you are related to the Pitt family I would love to hear from you.

Acknowledgements

Other than my late aunt Barbara I would like to thank my two cousins, Libby White and Frances Oxley-Sidey, for accompanying me on many of our journeys into the family past, in Australia and England respectively.

Thank you to Shelley Weiner for her meticulous and thoughtful editing.

Thanks also and in particular to Michael Burge, for being the first person to read the book and understand what I was aiming at, and for making constructive and perceptive comments without telling me to turn it into a novel. And for designing the updated (2018) cover.

I am grateful to the late Janelle Cust for her invaluable research included in her book *The Family of Mary Pitt;* to Margaret Betts for her hospitality, on many separate occasions, at the old family property called Bronte; and to Olive Hall for sharing her time and her thoughts on May Cottage and 18th century Fiddleford.

Thank you to Rebecca de Saintonge, who bullied and cajoled me all the way; and to Brendon Lunney, whose insight and knowledge of Australian farming was invaluable.

Appendix & Chapter Notes

PROLOGUE: The Loaf of Bread

The scene is my invention, but information on Fiddleford and the miller's family is taken from *Where Elm Trees Grew* by Olive Hall.

CHAPTER 1: Lord Nelson's brother in law

Most of the information on George Matcham, including extracts from his letters, facts concerning the Nelsons and Hamiltons and the social scene in Bath, is taken from *The Nelsons of Burnham Thorpe,* by Mary Eyre Matcham, George's great granddaughter. George and Kitty did meet in Bath but the precise circumstances are invented.

The letters from Nelson to George Matcham are in the National Maritime Museum, Greenwich, London. (Nelson's Personal Papers, MAM 1, photocopies of the originals)

It was George Matcham who organised Reverend Nelson's funeral in 1802. In the same year he lent Horatio Nelson £4000 to buy Merton Place.

George's visit to May Cottage is my invention, as are the characters and appearances of the Pitt girls. There is no evidence Hester had to stop her schooling for financial reasons. The only recorded evidence of poverty in the Pitt family was the fact that they were living rent-free. (And their decision to emigrate of course.)

As for George and Kitty Matcham's views on Nelson and Lady Emma, according to Mary Eyre Matcham:

'*To her dying day Catherine would flush hotly at any criticism of her brother's conduct, but even to the most privileged she only said "He had great excuses" or "She* [his wife, Fanny] *was so very cold"*'. *However 'Neither the influence of the wife, who had been unsympathetic and often ungracious to them, nor that of Lady Hamilton a woman whose unhappy past, though whitewashed, could never be forgotten, with all her gushing attentions, enthusiasm, beauty, and vulgarity could bring estrangement between the Admiral and his family.' (The Nelsons of Burnham Thorpe,* p 183)

CHAPTER 2: 1800: A proposition

The following letters written by George Matcham are evidence of his knowledge and interest in the colony:

To Alex Davison (agent and friend of Horatio Nelson), 21 January 1792:

'The proposals made to free settlers in New South Wales, have induc'd me to request a grant of land on condition of my sending one or more families. A skilful farmer [possibly Thomas Rose] *has offer'd to go there with his family (on my account) by the first ship, and I make no doubt of being able to send more colonists by the other vessels which are going this year. My view is to make a provision in that country for my younger son*, and as I shall send him some years hence with three or four thousand pounds, I wish for such an extent of country as to make it an object of attention to me; ten or twenty thousand acres – two or three hundred acres between Rose Hill and Sydney Cove, or the opposite shore between Rose Hill and the mouth of the harbour (where, I understand, there are no settlers), and the remainder in a direct line towards Broken Bay ... Government will perhaps not think me presumptuous or unworthy their attention on this occasion when they are inform'd that I have inclos'd fourteen hundred acres of waste land in England, which I purpose intirely planting. You will greatly oblige me, sir, if you can procure me a speedy answer, as I wish to prepare the farmer to go by the first ship. I am, etc, G Matcham.'* (Historical Records of New South Wales, hereafter referred to as HRNSW, Vol 1 pt 2, pp 590 & 591)

To Maurice Nelson (Horatio Nelson's older brother, a clerk at the Naval Office), 11 April 1792:

'. . . Whatever settlers go out on my part will be farmers, but as there is a first expence, and an annual expence afterwards, the number must be determin'd by the quantity of land recommend'd to be granted me . . . I hope Mr Dundas [Secretary of State for the Home Department] *will agree with me that twelve thousand acres are the least that can make it an object to me, but as it would be unreasonable to expect all these on the banks of the river leading from Rose Hill to the sea, I only request about two hundred acres on any part of the banks, and the rest in a straight line towards Broken Bay, where we are confident there can at present be no settlers establish'd. If Government think proper I am very ready to purchase the land.*

I mention'd some time since my intention to send out a younger son should the settlement continue to be foster'd by our Government. You thought my scheme visionary, but I augur of my son's future sentiments by my own feelings. I had much rather enjoy the abundance of a country life under a fine sky in a distant part of the British Government than hazard the precarious profession of a merchant in the city . . . I purpose sending my son, well educated, with three or four thousand pounds or more, which in New Holland will enable him to become a considerable and an useful man. I afford him the means, and must, of course, leave him to use them. You see the cause of my earnestness to know whether I can have a grant to answer my expence ... I am, etc, G Matcham.' (HRNSW 1 pt 2, p 615)

The comments about the government's eagerness to encourage settlers to migrate is from the HRNSW and the Historical Records of Australia (hereafter referred to as HRA).

CHAPTER 3: Looking for Mary

Information on May Cottage is from Olive Hall herself, from two books she wrote on local social history, *Where Elm Trees Grew* and *Their Own Dear Days*, and letters she wrote to my aunt Barbara Lamble.

Copies of George Matcham Pitt's letters to his cousin Matilda Warren Jenkins, transcribed by her, are in the Atkinson Family Papers in the Mitchell Library (hereafter referred to as AFP and ML respectively), Sydney.

Letter sent by GM Pitt from Sydney, 31 December 1879:

'My dear Miss Jenkins

... I am sorry I have no portraits of my father, nor of his father. The only one I knew of was the one which you mention was in possession of my Aunt Jenkins [Jemima]. *If my memory serves me right our great ancestor's name was William Pitt* [actually Robert]; *he died when young, and he left a sorrowing wife and four Daughters and one son. I need not say more, only the Daughters were good wives and loving Mothers, and the son (my father) aging, bequeathed to his sons a good name, which unsullied descended to me for my children.'*

There was another Mary Matcham who was born in Dorset in 1755 of Joseph and Martha Matcham, but for a number of reasons Barbara was convinced this is not 'our' Mary.

First, the ages do not tally. On the original mill lease in 1779 Mary was recorded as 'around thirty years old', and her burial certificate in 1815 stated she was 67, both of which indicate she was born in or around 1748. And there was no mention of her being under age on her marriage certificate in 1770, when the 'other' Mary would have been fifteen. Secondly, according to GM Pitt Mary was born in Ireland. Thirdly, there is no indication of the practice of continuous given names within the family: there are no Josephs or Marthas, while there are continuous Thomases and Williams.

The quote about Thomas Macham from George Matcham's obituary is from *The Gentleman's Magazine*, March 1833, p 276.

The full quote from the Sturminster Newton court records, 16 October 1780, reads:

'A gt deal of complaint from Pits wife, of bad behaviour of the old Tapper woman in Fidford House, resolved not to interfere any further – Let par offrs [parish officers] *remove her, if she is a real nuisance or likely to chgable* [chargeable]. *A clamor also about Pew in the Isle.'* (Dorset History Centre, hereafter referred to as DHC, D/PIT/M71.)

Robert Pitt's christening is in the Belchalwell parish records, DHC, MIC/R/1044 RE1/2.

Robert's father William was part of the 'Homage' (a group of tenants who swore allegiance to their lord), and collected money due to the lord. (Barbara

Lamble, *The Pitts of Dorset and Richmond.*)

The definition of a bailiff is from *The Local Historian's Encylopedia,* by John Richardson.

Robert had three siblings: an elder brother Thomas, a younger sister Susanna and younger brother William. His father died at the age of not quite 41, when Robert was fifteen. Thomas, his elder brother, died in 1759, so at the age of twenty-four Robert became head of the family. His mother Rose lived on for another thirty-three years as a widow and died aged 82. (Barbara Lamble)

Robert & Mary's marriage certificate, DHC, MIC/R/472. PE/CHO. (Child Okeford) DHC, RE3/1 p 15.

Robert Pitt's indentures: (in DHC)

i) On 12 May 1766, as a yeoman, for the lease of 'Trout Alehouse' on surrender from his uncle William Belbin, who had held it since 8 May 1759 '. . . *determinable on the lives of the said William Belbin miller and Joseph Belbin his nephew'*. Described as *'All that cottage or dwelling-house commonly called or known by the name of the Trout Alehouse* [aka the 'Fish', later May Cottage] *together with a Garden and Orchard to the same belonging containing in the whole by Estimation One Acre, be the same more or less. All which premises are situate lying and being in Fiddleford aforesaid within the Manor of Belchalwell in the said County of Dorset'*. (DHC, D/PIT/T34)

ii) On 22 September 1779, as a shopkeeper of Child Oakford [sic], between the Right Honourable George Lord Rivers Baron Rivers of Stratfieldsay and Robert Pitt for the lease of the Fiddleford Mills and *'. . . premises hereinafter mentioned for the sum of £5 paid twice yearly . . . '* in consideration of a surrender made by William Belbin. Included in this deed as second and third lives were

'Mary his wife (about thirty years old) and George Pitt his son (about seven years old)'. The condition of the lease was that he *'shall and will put the said Mill and premises in good and tenantable repair and also in consideration of the sum of five shillings of lawful Money'*. Premises included *'All those two water Corn Mills called Fiddleford Mills and all Mill ponds Sluices wears Hatches and appurtenances to the said Mills belonging and also the Cottage or Dwellinghouse now and heretofore used and enjoyed with the said Mills together with one little Close hereto adjoining called the Mill Pleck containing half an acre more or less.'* (DHC, D/PIT/T620)

iii) On the same date (22 September), again as a shopkeeper, with Lord Rivers, in partnership with John Foot, for premises in Child Okeford for the sum of £300 of *'lawful money of Great Britain'*. (DHC, D/PIT/T603)

iv) 18 October 1779: *'Agreed with Robt Pitt to grant one life, after his Uncle and himself, in the old man's tenement, worth £14 per ann. Fine £42.0.0.'* (DHC, D/PIT/M71.)

v) On 18 November 1779 he was granted a loan, or mortgage, by John Harrison of Blandford Forum, gent (of which £129.14.0 plus interest had to be repaid when Robert finally admitted financial failure). (DHC, D/PIT/T620;

Their Own Dear Days, Olive Hall.

vi) On 27 December 1779 between Lord Rivers and Robert Pitt of Child Okeford, shopkeeper, for

'All that mesuage or tenement in Newton within the Manor Sturminster Newton Castle with a garden and Orchard thereunto adjoining containing by Estimation One Acre and One Fardel of Land of the Antient Tenure.'

The house was left in the will of Robert's aunt, Margaret Matcham, nee Belbin (Mary's great aunt), who died childless in 1766. It was written on 28 May 1763 and proved in 1766. It said,

'First I give unto my brother William Belbin and my sister Rose Pitt all my Leasehold Estate lying in Sturminster Newton, during the Life of my said brother William Belbin and after his Decease I leave my said Leasehold Estate unto my two nephews Robert Pitt and William Pitt both sons of my sister Rose Pitt even and equally between them.'

There is no other record or reference to this.

vii) On 17 February 1785 between John Harrison of Blandford Forum, gentleman, John Newman, miller and Robert Pitt of Fiddleford, yeoman. This document reads

'. . . whereas by indenture of mortgage dated 18th November 1779 between the said Robert Pitt . . . and John Harrison did demise . . . whereas the said Mills and Premises being now very Ruinous and out of repair and the said Robert Pitt not being able to repair and keep up the same owing to his distressed circumstances hath agreed absolutely to Sell and assign over the same unto the said John Newman.' (DHC, D/PIT/T620)

Robert Pitt paid back the outstanding mortgage, £129.14.0 plus interest, to John Harrison. John Newman, the new tenant, paid 5/- to John Harrison and £15.15.0 plus 5/- to Robert Pitt. (DHC, D/PIT/T620)

John Newman had the mill up and running in two years and ran it for a further nineteen. He had five children, the youngest of whom was Martha, born in 1793. (Olive Hall, *Where Elm Trees Grew*, p44)

The *Pride & Prejudice* quote is from Chapter 7.

CHAPTER 4: 1800: A decision

The events portrayed in this chapter are imagined.

CHAPTER 5: The worst country in the world

Major Ross's quote is from a letter he wrote to Evan Nepean, Under-Secretary of State in the Home Department (HRNSW 1 pt 2, p 212).

Phillip's remarks on settlers are from letters written to Under-Secretary Nepean, 9 July 1788 (HRNSW 1, pt 2, p 153); and 18 Nov 1791 (HRNSW 1, pt 2, p 557).

CHAPTER 6: 1801: The adventurers

The letter from Horatio Nelson to George Matcham is from Nelson's Personal Papers, MAM 5/6.

Bird's shopping lists, and his register of potential migrants are among the AFP. (MSS 3132, ML)

King's letter of 16 April is from HRNSW 4, p 346.

A copy of Matcham's letter of 5 May is among the AFP.

Commissioner Gambier's full letter, also among the AFP, reads:

'Dear Matcham,

I have the pleasure to acquaint you that I have arranged everything for the embarkation of your good people, agreeably with your wishes. To save time, which runs short with me at present, I enclose (Transport) Commissioner's letter to me on the subject, which pray return to me.

Your friends will therefore proceed to Portsmouth conformably to what I at first wrote you, and on their arrival there make application to Captain Patton, agent for transports in that place. If you think it necessary, I will get a letter to him for them to deliver by way of identifying their persons.

Let me, therefore, know how I am in future to direct you, as you say you are going into Dorsetshire to marshall your adventurers.

Yours very truly SAMUEL GAMBIER (Commissioner of the Navy)'

Bird wrote to Matcham on 8 May 1801: (Original in AFP)

'Sir, I received your three Sunday favors and shall be happy to see you at Sturminster when convenient – In regard as to the people they appears to be all ready as also their Cloathing. Mrs Fish, and Daughter, seems as yet undetermined. As you are not yet certain where they will embark I cannot as yet forward any of their Goods. If they go to Deptford I know of no other Method of sending their Goods but by the Road Waggon from Blandford – they go from there most Days and often take three or four passengers [indecipherable] *some three or four days on the road. There are also Coaches goes through Blandford every Day for London. If they are to embark at Portsmouth a covered Waggon can be procured to carry them and their luggage to Poole being about 24 miles from which place Two hours* [indecipherable] *goes every Tuesday to Portsmouth and are from 6 to 20 Hours running of it.*

I do not recollect of any further information I can give you at present. But shall send to them all tomorrow Morning to hold themselves in Readiness against the Time when I shall have the pleasure of seeing you at Sturminster.

I [indecipherable] *am with due respect to yourself and Mrs Matcham, Your Ob Servt Jos Bird, Sturminster May 8 1801.'*

The description of Portsmouth docks is taken from *The Memoirs of George Suttor.*

CHAPTER 7: Going . . .

The list of *Canada's* cargo is from HRA 3, p 454, 1 Mar 1802.

Mary's original letters are in the AFP.

Lieutenant Braithwaite's original letter to George Matcham.

'Gosport, 29 May 1801

Sir: Although unknown to you I am induced to take the liberty of writing you - as I have just seen a Mrs Pitt who I understand is related to you and is about to embark for Port Jackson in New South Wales – it will be necessary for me Sir to acquaint you that I am just arrived from that Country in His Majesty's ship Buffalo and that I served in that Country near Seven Years. I left this part of the world with Governor Hunter in the Early part of the year 1795 as second Lieutenant of His Majesty's Armed Vessel Supply . . . I am . . . a stranger to Mrs Pitt but I heard by accident she was going to New So Wales I called on her at the request of a person to whom she was known.

I have now sir to acquaint you how former settlers have been treated sent out by the Government. Settlers Sir that are Tradesmen and some that have been bred up in the line of agriculture, on their arrival they have been put on the Store with a ration of Provisions. Women having less than the Men and Children of a certain age having less than the Women, they have been continued in the store for Eighteen Months and allowed two Servants for a family for the same time - when that is expired the Servants are taken from them and theirselves discharged from being any longer an incumbrance on the Government - if after the afore-mentioned expiration of Eighteen Months they can maintain any number of Convicts - they are allowed to do so [and] *have the benefits of their labour but must either find them the Government Rations or pay the Government Twenty pounds pr. annum. I make no doubt Sir that contrary* [sic] *directions to these proceedings have been sent to Governor King with respect to Mrs Pitt – if any further information can be of any Service to Mrs Pitt I shall be happy to give it.*

I have the Honor to be Sir your very honourable Servant, Lieutenant Robert Braithwaite.' (ML, Code Ab 114)

CHAPTER 8: . . . gone

Details of *Canada* and of travel on board convict ships is taken from *The Convict Ships* by Charles Bateson.

Instructions for masters and surgeons of *Canada, Minorca* and *Nile* is from HRNSW Vol 4, p 399. Other information about the voyage from England to New South Wales is taken from *Sydney's First Four Years* by Watkin Tench (for details of Rio), Anna Josepha King's onboard journal of her voyage to NSW on *Speedy*, 1799/80, NSW State Library. (Microfilm - CY 964, frames 1-62: C 185/1), and James Wilshire, Mary's future son in law, who kept an onboard diary of his voyage to NSW on board *Royal Admiral* in 1800. NSW State Library. (Microfilm CY 1389, frames 1-41, ML, MSS 1296)

CHAPTER 9: The authors of our existence

'The authors of our existence' is originally a quote from *Memoirs of My Life and Writings* by Edward Gibbon, c1796. He may have filched it from Aristotle.

The comment about family historians is from *Australia's Birthstain*, by Babette Smith, p4.

CHAPTER 10: Reinvention

The quote about Kingsford Smith is from Vivien North, in *Picturegoer Weekly*, 17 March 1934.

The John Betjeman quote is from the *Evening Standard*, 24 March 1934.

The Aimée Stuart quote is from *Picturegoer Weekly*, Vivien North, 17 March 1934.

The quote about mum's Australian origins is from Coralie Clarke Rees, *Woman's Budget*, 24 January 1934.

CHAPTER 11: Arrival

The description of Sydney town in 1801 is based on *Memoirs of George Suttor*, *A Voyage Round the World 1800-1804* by John Turnbull and *Tales and Sketches of Old Australia* by G B Barton. The Pitt family's introduction to Governor King is speculative, although the procedure that followed the arrival of convict ships is described by King in the following letter:

'On the arrival of ships with convicts they are visited by the Naval Officer and Surgeon, who report whether there is any contagious disease in the ship. If their report is favourable, I go on board and enquire into the behaviour of the prisoners and passengers during the voyage, interrogating them respecting their treatment, if they have received the ration and other comforts allowed by Government, and finally whether they have any cause of complaint against any person in the ship, which is not only enquired into, but satisfaction made if requisite. After my inspection the convicts are removed to the Supply, hulk, where they remain two days, in which time they are well washed and new cloathed, and are then drafted to the different settlements, placing each ships convicts as much as possible by themselves.' (HRNSW 4, p 868, King to Lord Hobart)

Descriptions of Governor King and his wife are based on a conversation with a guide at Government House in June 2010, and from *Reflections in the Colony of NSW* by George Cale and *The Governor's Lady* by Marnie Bassett.

Having been deported for fighting an illegal duel and allegedly spreading subversive rumours about Governor King, Macarthur was neither punished nor disgraced – the British Government decided they didn't have enough evidence. Instead he spent his time in England courting powerful people and arrived back in the colony four years later with a grant of 10,000 acres of land from Lord Camden.

CHAPTER 12: The legend of Margaret Catchpole

The quote regarding female convicts is from *A Few Observations on the Situation of the Female Convicts in New South Wales* by G H Hammersley.

The lack of convict records on *Canada* and *Nile* is from King to Lord Portland, 1 March 1802. (HRNSW 4, p 719)

Margaret Catchpole's letters are in the ML and the National Library of Australia, Canberra.

CHAPTER 13: Settlement

Details of conditions in the Hawkesbury region, the description of the farming methods and tools is from *Reflections on the Colony of NSW*, p 90; *Macquarie Country* by D G Bowd; and *Hawkesbury 1794-1994: the first 200 years* by Jan Barkley and Michelle Nichols.

Information about Hawkesbury grants and grantees is from *Hawkesbury Settlement Revealed* by Jan Barkley-Jack. William Small, James Blackman and Charles Webb had arrived with the Pitts on *Canada*. William Bowman and Richard Rouse travelled in the same fleet on *Nile* (with Margaret Catchpole).

Governor Philips's remark about the Hawkesbury flooding is from HRA Series 1 Vol 1, p 183.

Lt Grose's remark is from HRA 1, 1, p 470.

In 1800 Phillip reported:

'Thrice in four months have they [the Hawkesbury farmers] *been drove from their habitations to save their lives in trees and pieces of floating wood, until the floods subsided, when they found themselves deprived of every comfort, cloathing, or shelter; their wheat that was housed, that in their stacks, and their growing corn totally destroyed; and what is a great publick calamity, their stock of swine nearly all drowned.*

. . . Had not this last flood happened we might have had a sufficiency of grain for the consumption of this year. But this unfortunate accident has deprived us nearly of half the grain there was in the colony.' (HRNSW 1, 3, p10)

The Hawkesbury farmers' petition to Governor King is from HRA 1, 3, p134.

The story of the murder of the Aboriginal boys and the subsequent trial is from HRNSW 4, p2. It was said at the time that twenty-six white men had been killed by Aborigines on the Hawkesbury in the previous four and a half years, but the number of Aborigines killed by white people, which was not recorded, was undoubtedly much higher.

CHAPTER 14: Foundations

James Horse, transported for life from Ireland, arrived in the colony in 1797 and appeared in the 1805 muster working for Thomas. The 1802 muster mentions 'two convicts' but doesn't name them, so I've taken a small liberty in assuming Horse was one of them.

Horse's crime was unstated. He arrived on *Britannia* and since he was known to be a Defender I am assuming this was the reason for his transportation. It's possible he was involved in an incident in Kildare in 1795, when several Defenders were arrested for administering an illegal oath to the people *'to be true to the French'*. (From *Desperate and Diabolical: Defenders and United Irishmen in Early NSW* by Ruán O'Donnell.) http://members.pcug.org.au/~ppmay/defenders.htm

CHAPTER 15: Government men

Thomas Christmas did not actually arrive in the colony until May 1804, on *Coromandel 2*. He appears on the 1805/6 muster working for Thomas Pitt, so I have definitely taken a liberty here.

According to the 1805/6 muster James Horse was given *'72 lashes on backside for taking the Defenders' oath on board ship'*.

Horse's account of his journey on the Britannia is based on 'The Hell-Ship "Britannia"' (pp60-165) from *The Convict Ships 1787-1868*. It was known as the worst in the history of transportation, *with 'one death to every seventeen prisoners embarked'*. Governor Hunter ordered an enquiry after the ship arrived, and though the court unanimously condemned the excessively cruel actions of Captain Dennott and the negligence of the surgeon, Mr Beyer,

'To the everlasting shame of the British authorities, neither Dennott nor Beyer were punished, except that they were not again employed in the convict service. Governor Hunter sent a transcript of the court proceedings to England, but, as in other instances of a similar nature, no prosecutions were instituted'.

Once again Hunter's attempts at justice were frustrated.

Thomas Christmas's alias, Spicer, is from the National Archives, London. (HO11/1 p 352)

Christmas's trial is quoted verbatim from Old Bailey transcripts:

<http://www.oldbaileyonline.org/browse.jsp?id = t18000917-86-defend868 &div =t18000917-86#highlight> (ML ref t18000917-86).

CHAPTER 16: Bronte

Details of the trees Margaret Betts was planting are from 'Out on a Limb: How Margaret Betts reforested an original Hawkesbury Farm' by Michael Burge, *Blue Mountains Magazine*, June/July 2010.

The Reverend Stanley Smith's remark is from *Australia Imagined* by Judith Johnson and Monica Anderson, p 35.

There is a grave on Margaret's property under what's now her garage. We thought it might have belonged to Margaret Catchpole, who died on *Bronte*. Margaret (Betts) does not want it dug up, understandably.

CHAPTER 17: Settlers or invaders?

The 'black armband' to describe one version of Australian history was coined by the historian Geoffrey Blainey.

Sir Joseph Banks's comments and the notion of *terra nullius* are from p 40 of Thomas Keneally's *Australia, Origins to Eureka*. David Collins's quote is on p 405 of the same book.

Governor King's instructions on how settlers should respond to aggression is from HRA 1 4, p 593, 30 Oct 1802.

The following story appeared as part of an online discussion about life in the pioneering days of colonial Australia. I reproduce it here, with the author's permission, as an example of the extraordinary tenacity of some of the early settlers and how they were tested in ways they would never have been in the old country.

'The Mining Accident by Max Bancroft.

The approximate year was 1894. My Great Grandfather Joseph Bancroft was self-employed and occupied himself mining Emeralds and Sapphires in a remote location 27 miles east of Inverell in New South Wales, Australia.

He and his family were living rough in tents and under canvas fly on a creek bank. His Wife Margaret and nine children were in his company. The eldest child, aged nine, was named Thomas Joseph Bancroft. He was my Grandfather. His eight siblings included two sets of twins (boys and girls). The youngest child was a baby only several days old.

Joseph's daily work involved tunnelling into the creek bank by hammering a crow bar until he had created a hole in which he would set off a charge of dynamite. Once the hole had been created in the bank he would place a length of fuse in a brass detonator cap, and crimp it in place to stop it from falling out by gently squeezing the brass casing of the detonator with his teeth. If you were well off financially, special pliers were available to crimp the detonator case. If you were not affluent, you used your teeth. He had done this hundreds of times and did not consider it particularly dangerous. The detonator cap was then pushed into the end of a stick of dynamite and it was inserted into the hole in the bank of the creek with a stick and the fuse was lit. He would then run and take cover. The loose gravel so created was then washed in water slurry in a tin dish, and the precious stones were picked out.

One day he bit down on the brass case to crimp the fuse. The detonator exploded in his mouth, killing him instantly. His Wife, shocked by the accident ran off into the surrounding scrub and was never seen by my Grandfather again.

Tom, being the eldest child (he was only nine years old) organized the children and they buried their father's body by covering it with river stones to keep the dingoes out of the camp. They remained at the campsite for three days waiting for their Mother to return, during which time Tom managed to keep his siblings fed from the store-bought supplies. He fed the baby on milk arrowroot biscuits moistened in his mouth.

On the third day after the accident, they decided that their Mother was not coming back so Tom organised the family to walk 27 miles back to town to raise the alarm. There were no "made roads" through the countryside, just "wallaby tracks" through the scrub. They set off walking and after travelling for some time came upon a family who had taken up land. Tom explained what had happened and asked if they could take care of the Baby.

The remaining members set off for Inverell again and during the trip Tom gave away all of his Sisters and Brothers to total strangers. He arrived in town and sought out the Crown Sergeant who was also the Magistrate.

The Publican told him the Crown Sergeant was away [so] a rider was sent to fetch him. The publican took Tom under his wing, fed him and gave him shelter. The Crown Sergeant/Magistrate arrived some time later and dispatched a party with a horse drawn dray to the campsite, where the body was disinterred and brought back into town for a Post Mortem, Coroners Enquiry and Burial at Bingara Cemetery.

Following this, Tom was found a job sweeping the floors with a Shearing team. He eventually became a "Gun Shearer" and by the age of eighteen had his own shearing team.

In his seventies he said he had never seen any of his siblings since giving them away to strangers. It was his habit to read the morning newspaper and he often joked that he would look for his name in the death notices.

One day he spied his Brother's name and journeyed down to the General Post Office and booked a trunk line call to the Funeral Director mentioned in the newspaper as handling his Brother's Funeral. He identified himself and related the story of his father's death and was told it was definitely his Brother. He went down to Central Railway Station and booked a train ticket to the country town and later attended the funeral, where he met one Brother and one Sister.'

There was more to Mr Bancroft's grandfather's story:

[He] *'...was the second man in Australia to earn his licence to operate steam engines in the shearing sheds.*

In the trade he was known as the 'Expert" and had his own shearing team which included kitchen staff and cook. These days they would call him a contractor.

When he was on a sheep property as the shearing contractor, the squatter deferred to him and was not permitted to enter his own shearing shed.

In order to receive his steam engine drivers license he rode his horse from Moree to Brisbane in driving rain to sit the exam. The journey took six weeks. How he studied for it is a mystery as he was illiterate at the time.

He was not allowed to get any questions wrong. One of the questions asked was, how do you match up two pieces of machinery the surfaces of which are not exactly mating.

His answer was to use brass shims. That answer was correct in NSW but not in Queensland. They called them brass packing pieces.

He failed the exam and had to come back to Brisbane the following year and re sit the exam.

It seems inter state rivalry was strong back then too.'

(<aus-nsw-colonial-history@rootsweb. com>)

Australia as the butt of jokes is from *Australia's Birthstain*, p 205.

'Before long the concept of a convict settlement at Botany Bay became a popular vehicle for political satire and the butt of many English jokes. Having acquired this ridiculous image at the outset, it was some time before the new colony was taken

seriously.' (Jonathan King, *The Other Side of the Coin,* cited in *Australia's Birthstain,* p14)

CHAPTER 18: The house that Thomas built

The construction and the makeup of Thomas's house is based on information in *Architecture In Australia* by J M Freeland, *Reflections on the Colony of NSW* (p 90), *Macquarie Country* and *Hawkesbury 1794-1994: the first 200 years.*

Information about the Pitts on government stores is from King Papers Vol 1, ML A1976, p 108.

David Collins's remark about the indolence of the Hawkesbury settlers is from *HawkesburySettlement Revealed* by Jan Barkley-Jack.

CHAPTER 19: The true proprietors of the soil

The title of the chapter is a quote from Governor King to Bligh in 1807, HRA 1, p65.

Information about the Aboriginal people on the Hawskesbury, including their begging for food from the settlers, is gleaned from a number of sources including *Macquarie Country,* HRA and HRNSW.

The Bible quote is from the Book of Genesis, 1.28.

The questionnaire from the Committee on Land Bill, Notes and Proceedings, Legislative Council is taken from *Squatter's Castle: the life of Edward Ogilvie* by George Farwell.

CHAPTER 20: Shipwreck

John Wood at the Hawkesbury in possession of a sword is from Janelle Cust's book *The Family of Mary Pitt* (Particular of Arms in Possession, SRNSW 4/1719, Reel 6041).

The account of John and Lucy's exploits in the south Pacific and their shipwreck is taken from John Turnbull's book, *A Voyage Around the World in 1800–1804, Volumes 2 & 3.*

Lt Fowler's handwritten letter is in Banks Papers Vol 4, 1801-20 P209, FM4/1747 (ML). <http://www2.sl.nsw.gov.au/ banks/ series_68/68_03.cfm> (State Library, Banks Papers online) Section 13: Series 68 (CY 3009 / 383). Information about John Wood is from *The Family of Mary Pitt,* p33.

CHAPTER 21: William Faithfull

The case of Boston's pig is taken from HRA 1, 1, pp602-643, and a transcript of the subsequent trial on the Macquarie University website: <http://www.law.mq.edu.au/research/colonial_case_law/nsw/cases/case _ index/1795/boston_v_ laycock_ mckellar_faithfull_and_eaddy>

CHAPTER 22: The Palmers

I have no idea how Hester and James Wilshire met but the Palmers were well known socialisers and they did hold grand parties at their magnificent harbourside property.

Information on society and social behaviour in early New South Wales is gleaned from the following:

'Etiquette is, if possible, more studied among our fashionable circles than in those of London itself. If a lady makes a call, she must not attempt a repetition of it until it has been returned, on pain of being voted ignorant of due form. Morning visits, too, are made in the afternoon; afternoon calls near the hour of bed-time ...' (Peter Cunningham, *Two Years in New South Wales*, p 111)

'The truth is that the colony had become an awful parody of England, a parody that was predicated upon convictism . . . the most extreme social niceties were of the utmost importance in keeping one from 'convict pollution'. It was simply not possible, for example, to approach someone in the street and address them, even if you had been introduced in polite society the night before. "Upon my life, I don't know you, sir!" was the bellowed response to such a threatened breakdown of the precarious social order.' (Tim Flannery, *The Birth of Sydney*, Introduction pp 38/39)

'. . . . the state of society here . . . is excellent and the first people are so particular that you cannot get into their circle without first rate introductions and can only keep in it by first rate conduct. The smallest error in a man's conduct here, (which would scarcely be noticed at home) would send him out of the first immediately which is most proper in a country where there are so many different grades.' (Patrick Leslie, letter, 1835, cited in Joanna Gordon, ed., *Advice to a Young Lady in the Colonies*, pp 5 & 6)

The description of Woolloomooloo House is taken from a painting by John Bolger (State Library, Sydney), and from the historian Barry Dyster, quoted in *Hawkesbury Settlement Revealed*, p193.

The quote from Governor King's letter to Nelson is from *The Nelsons of Burnham Thorpe*, p184.

The description of James Wilshire is from John Spurway, ed., Australian Biographical and Genealogical Record Series 1, Society of Australian Genealogists, Sydney 1992, p478 (reproduced in *The Family of Mary Pitt*).

Thomas's three convict workers and 230 acres are listed in the muster of 1805.

CHAPTER 23: Jemima

Robert Jenkins's background is taken from the Australian Dictionary of Biography, Volume 2, (MUP), RFJ Holder, 1967.

The quote is from Jenkins's letter to his mother and sisters. The original (water-stained and incomplete) is among the AFP.

Information about Austin Forrest is from *The Family of Mary Pitt*.

Jemima and Forrest's was the first marriage to be registered at the

Hawkesbury parish church, but it was not St Matthew's, which was not built until some years later. (V1810 1001 3A/1810; SAG 53, St Matthew's, on shelf of ML.)

On 9 and 16 November 1811 the *Sydney Gazette* carried the announcement: '*All claims and Demands against Captain Austin Forrest or Mrs Forrest are to be presented for Payment immediately, they being about to leave the Colony.*' (p 2, col 3)

CHAPTER 24: Robert Jenkins

The description of Jenkins's house in George Street is as he described it in his letter to his mother and sisters.

The description of Jenkins himself is taken from his portrait, in the ML (reproduced in *The Family of Mary Pitt*).

Information about General Holt is from the Australian Dictionary of Biography. The story of the delivery of Jenkins's letter is from Volume 2 of *Memoirs of Joseph Holt, General of the Irish Rebels, in 1798*.

CHAPTER 25: An ideal husband

Elizabeth Macarthur ran her husband John's sheep farms when he was out of the country, which he very often was. He was exiled twice, once by Governor King and later again after the Rum Rebellion. The farms prospered under Mrs Macarthur's supervision and much of the credit for the breeding of the Merino sheep that once formed the backbone of the Australian economy is due to her rather than her husband.

Mary Reibey was transported for stealing a horse but went on to become one of the richest and most successful women in New South Wales when she took over her husband's businesses after his death.

CHAPTER 26: The settler and the convict

Margaret's experiences in the colony with the Palmers and the Rouses etc., including saving lives in the flood, missing parcels and sending her love to John Cook, are all taken from her letters.

CHAPTER 27: The Laycocks

Information on the Laycocks is taken from *Hannah Laycock of King's Grove Farm* by Sheila Tearle, and *A Pioneering Australian Family* by Ken Laycock.

The quotes concerning the Laycock girls is from Wentworth Family Papers, ML A751 pp61, 89, 90 (cited in *The Family of Mary Pitt*).

Hannah, Rebecca and Elizabeth left England for New South Wales in *Canada* on 23 March 1810 and arrived on 8 September the same year. Thomas

Laycock senior had died in the colony in December 1809, just three months before they left England, so there is no way they could have known of his death before they sailed. (Though it is possible news reached them en route.)

According to Ken Laycock, in 1805 Thomas Laycock called his son in public, *' . . . you young bugger, you rascal. What were you doing walking with my housekeeper? But she is no strumpet'*.

In 1805 Thomases senior and junior were arrested for *'using threats and language in the public streets of the most mutinous tendency . . .'* and in November 1806 they were court martialled, found guilty and imprisoned, and Laycock senior was dismissed from the Corps. (*The Vaucluse Estate from 1793-1829*, Journal of the Royal Australian Historical Society)

As stated by Ken Laycock, the full charges against Thomas in his court martial were:

'i. Calling Major Johnston a rascal and other things.

ii. Threatening Johnston and publicly declaring he would call him out and take a shot at him.

iii. Exciting disorder. Publicly advising his son to challenge Capts Abbott and Minchin.

iv. Declaring Abbott and Minchin were a set of damned rascals and calling his son a bugger and a rascal. (Cancelled)

v. Cancelled.

vi. Treating His Majesty's service with contempt by publicly declaring he did not give a damn for his commission.

vii. Drinking in pub with known Irish rebels and prostitutes. (Cancelled.)'

The Castle Hill Rebellion was an attempt by Irish convicts working on the government farm at Castle Hill to take over the colony on 5 March 1804. They were intending to march to Parramatta, stealing weapons from settlers on the way, join up with more rebels and then torch Parramatta before marching back to the Hawkesbury. Unfortunately for them the news leaked to the authorities rather than to their rebel friends in Parramatta.

Martial law was declared, and Major Johnston of the NSW Corps marched with 50 members of the corps overnight from Sydney to Parramatta, where they rested briefly before marching on with Quartermaster Laycock and 50 more armed civilians towards the Hawkesbury in pursuit of the rebels. At Castle Hill, Johnston and his men confronted the 233 rebels and their leader Cunningham, who demanded *'death or liberty'*. Johnston and his trooper managed to trick Cunningham and the other rebel leader Johnston (no relation) to separate from the rest, at which point they put guns to their heads and *' . . . drove them with their swords in their hands to the Quartermaster'* [Laycock], who promptly clouted Cunningham on the head with his sword so hard he virtually killed him. Laycock was then ordered to 'advance and charge the main body of the rebels', which he did, and the fleeing rebels were pursued as far as the Hawkesbury where the survivors were taken prisoner and Cunningham, already half dead, was hanged. (The other rebel leader

Johnston escaped.) In his report to Lt Colonel Paterson Major Johnston said, *'Any encomiums I could pass on Quartermaster Laycock and the detachment I had the honour of command would fall far short of what their merit entitles them to.'* This was the same Major Johnston whom Laycock only one year later tried to challenge to a duel. (From *Death or Liberty*, Major George Johnston's account of the Vinegar Hill Uprising, cited in *The Birth of Sydney*, pp 198-199)

Samuel Laycock being court martialled for playing cards with a private soldier is from *A Pioneering Australian Family*.

Information on Hannah and her sons' grants is from *Kingsgrove: The First Two Hundred Years* by Ron Hill & Brian Madden.

CHAPTER 28: The visit

This scene is based on Governor Macquarie's journals, extracts reproduced below, recording his visit to King's Grove Farm in December 1810, and to Mary and Jemima's properties on the Hawkesbury the week before. Macquarie's comments on the colony as a whole are taken from elsewhere in his Journals.

'At 1 p.m. we set out again from Capt. Townson's for Mrs. Laycock's Farm near Cook's River, and arrived there at half past 2 o'clock. ---We found Mrs. Laycock and her two Daughters at home, in a very neat comfortable well built Farm House and well furnished; the good old Lady's Farm being also in a forward state of improvement in other respects. ---After resting for half an hour at Mrs. Laycock's, we pursued our Journey on to Canterbury.' (Macquarie's Journals, Thursday 13 December 1810)

'. . . I accompanied Mrs. M. in the Carriage this morning to pay Visits, immediately after Breakfast, to Mrs. Cox, Mrs Pitt, Mrs. Evans & Mrs Forrest, all residing in different Parts of the Richmond District.' (Macquarie's Journals, Wednesday 5 December 1810)

The description of the governor is based on various portraits of him painted at the time.

CHAPTER 29: Thomas Pitt and the Rum Rebellion

The story of Bligh being discovered hiding under a bed is from a letter written by Major Johnston to Capt Piper on 2 Feb 1808. (HRNSW 6, p 463) It is said Lance Corporal Marlborough may well have been bending the truth, for propaganda reasons.

The makeup of the criminal courts is from *Voyages Round the World*.

The Michael Duffy *Sydney Morning Herald* quote is dated 28 January 2006.

The 1 January 1808 petition is from HRNSW 6, p 411.

The 30 January petition is from HRNSW 6, pp 458/9.

The description of the post-coup revelling is taken from testimony given by Martin Mason, a Hawkesbury settler, in the subsequent court martial of Major Johnston:

'About 27, 28, 29, 30, 31 January there was a general state of intoxication, riot, and confusion, with the detachment of soldiers at Green Hills, consisted only of about 12, plus sergeant and corporal. The sergeant who commanded was present on the 29th and directed the erection of a gallows within 50 paces of my front door. Soldier Butcher brought wood to make a bonfire, and after dark they burnt the Governor and Mr Gore in effigy, represented by tanned hides, from the gallows.' (*Proceedings of a general court martial of Lt Col George Johnston, 5 May 1811*, transcribed by M Bartrum, p 122. ML 994.4020924/B648.1/1.)

Information also is from *Early Hawkesbury Settlers* by Bobbie Hardy.

Johnston's petition, hastily drawn up the night before the coup by Macarthur and addressed to Governor Bligh, read:

'Sir, I am called upon to execute a painful duty. You are charged by the respectable inhabitants of crimes that render you unfit to exercise the supreme authority another moment in this colony; and in that charge all the officers under my command have joined.

I therefore require you, in His Majesty's sacred name, to resign your authority, and to submit to the arrest which I hereby place you under, by the advice of all my officers, and by the advice of every respectable inhabitant in the town of Sydney.

I am, &c., GEORGE JOHNSTON, Acting Lieu't-Gov. and Major commanding NSW Corps.' (HRNSW 6, p 434)

The scene where Thomas is coerced into signing is based on the following testimony given during the court martial by Martin Mason:

'On 28th Jan one Thomas Hobby, an ex officer of the NSW Corps, Mr Fitz, a deputy commissary, and one Thomas Biggers, who kept a sort of grog shop, met at the house of Andrew Thompson and there drew up an address to Major Johnston, sanctioning what had been done. They had assembled a number of their dependents and adherents; and when they were heated with wine and spirits they sallied out to solicit signatures. I myself was solicited 3 times in that day, and was told by Biggers and others, that if I did not sign it I should be in the body of Sydney gaol within 24 hours . . .'

Fitz and Hobby drew up the address and Hobby swore he would make 500 signatures before night. Martin Mason refused to sign. The names of the people mentioned were on the petition, including Thomas Arndell's. The 'Mason' was in fact William Mason, not Martin – the antagonists were being deliberately misleading here. Both Arndell and Mr Divine, Superintendent of Convicts, later confessed to signing the paper without reading it.

Thomas Arndell's letter is from HRA 1, 6, p 565.

John Brennan's letter is from Banks Papers Vol 22, 1806-1811 p 359.

It is said Wilshire 'became' Deputy Commissary in September 1808, but he already held that position when he testified in court on Palmer's behalf in January of that year. Palmer was accused of fraud by the military regime, stripped of his office and subsequently gaoled. (HRNSW 6, p 435)

A lot has been written since concerning that letter of 30 January. At Johnston's trial a copy only of the letter with transcribed signatures was produced, since it was claimed the original was illegible due to blotting. (The list of signatories – 69 of them, including Thomas's – is reproduced online at <www.image.sl.nsw.gov.au/banks/70466.jpg>. Thomas's is wrongly cited in the HRNSW as 'M Pitt'.) Of the supposed 280 names attached to the original document *'it was alleged that only those of Fitz, Arndell, Hobby and Badgery were originals'*. (HRNSW 6, p 459) So there is a distinct possibility than some if not most of them may have been forged.

The following memorials were sent following the coup by the Hawkesbury settlers and others, but Thomas's name was not on any of them.

To Colonel Paterson on the 30 June 1808, protesting

'. . . against the means adopted to obtain signatures to a paper carried round to sanction what was done on that day [26 January] *threatening individuals with imprisonment; to be sent out of the Colony by the first ship; and that they would be Marked Men who refused to sign it'*. (HRA 1, 6, p 574)

To Major Johnston on 11 April 1808 expressing dismay at the appointment of John Macarthur *('the scourge of this colony')* as Colonial Secretary. (HRA 1, 6, p 574)

To Viscount Castlereagh on 17 February 1809 swearing the

'. . . memorialists had no hand, act, or part in the rebellion that now exists in this colony. That they do abhor and detest the said act . . . and were every way fully satisfied and content under His Excellency's [Bligh's] *administration . . . That nearly whole districts were bought up by a few wealthy individuals, and the most obnoxious convicts placed on them as tenants . . . The officers were interested in impeding agriculture: the more settlers were ruined the cheaper they could purchase estates . . . That when your memorialists applyed for protection they were . . . lyable to be dragged to prison by convicts and locked up without meat, drink, fire, or candle, or even straw to lye on, with the most abandoned thieves. That in one instance one of your mem.'s was locked up in the same cell with three malefactors under sentence of death, tried and fined, and imprisoned without being taken before a magistrate ... The settlers name is John Bowman'*. (HRNSW 7, pp 33-35 and 78-80)

Bowman's 'crime' apparently was to call Nicholas Bayly, the Colonial Secretary (and Elizabeth Laycock's brother in law) *'a rogue'*. This letter was signed among others by William Bowman, Thomas Arndell and Richard Rouse.

George Suttor was summoned to court for refusing to attend a muster ordered by Lt Governor Foveaux and for writing scurrilous articles about the new regime. In court he said, *'. . . the same motives which induced me to decline mustering, induce me to deny the authority of this court. To His Excellency Governor Bligh, my allegiance is due, and to him alone as the lawful and rightful Governor of this territory. My unprotected wife and children I leave to the mercy of God'*. (*Memoirs of George Suttor*)

The court, composed wholly of military officers (among them Thomas Laycock Jnr, who was not a party to Suttor's treatment), sentenced Suttor without taking evidence in his defence *'to be imprisoned for six calendar months and to pay a fine of one shilling'*. His servants were taken from him and his wife and five children, his farm and his stock *'were left to the mercy of the aborigines'*. As it happens his resourceful wife managed quite well without him and managed to increase the stock on their property. (And Suttor eventually ended up a wealthy man.)

John Palmer lost his job as Commissary, had his books, papers and keys seized and was told 'to consider myself under an Arrest'. (Letter from John Palmer to Bligh, <www.adb.online.anu.edu.au /biogs/A020276b.htm>)

The following year he was sentenced by the rebel administration to three months' imprisonment for declaring New South Wales to be in a state of mutiny.

Fitz's 'offer' is from HRA 1, 6, p 272.

CHAPTER 30: Thomas and Elizabeth

William Faithfull received 1000 acres, the Wilshires 570 and Jemima 500, all under the military regime. (*The Family of Mary Pitt*, p 31)

Thomas and Elizabeth's marriage certificate is in the Register of BDMs, code V18131455 3A/1813.

The *Sydney Gazette* announced on 20 February 1913:

'MARRIED. On Monday last at the Church of St. John, Parramatta, by the Reverend Mr Marsden, T M Pitt, of Nelson and Bronte Farm, to the amiable Miss Elizabeth Laycock, daughter of Mrs Laycock, of King's Grove Farm.'

Jemima and Robert Jenkins's marriage certificate is in the parish records of St Phillip's Church, Sydney, on the shelves of the ML. Eber Bunker was the father of Thomas Laycock Jnr's wife Isabella.

CHAPTER 31: Reflections

In the muster of 1805/06 Mary is listed rather confusingly as *'living with wife. Mr Wilshire'*. (Microfilm PRO59, ML.)

May Cottage still flooded occasionally in Olive Hall's time, and when we first visited in 2008 the river Stour had once again burst its banks, though it hadn't quite reached the road or the houses.

The floods at the Hawkesbury were real enough, but there is no record of how or if Mary and Thomas were affected by them.

The two floods of 1806 were described in the *Sydney Gazette* thus:

[By] *'daylight on Saturday morning a scene of horror presented itself in every quarter . . . many farms were then under water; the rain continued without intermission, and a rapid rise was in consequence observable . . . In the course of this dreadful day . . . upwards of 200 wheat stacks were swept into the stream, and carried down the river with incredible velocity: stock of all descriptions were seen floating about and on the tops of the stacks.'* Boats were commandeered to rescue *'the settlers' families from the roofs and ridges of the houses, where many had for whole hours clung despairing of assistance . . . The distress and horror of that evening can neither be described nor imagined . . . torrents of rain pouring with unabating fury . . . in the evening the dismal cries from distant quarters . . .*

Nearly 300 persons, saved from the deluge by the humane perseverance and incredible exertions of their rescuers, were released from the state of actual famine by a supply sent from the Green hill in consequence of His Excellency's [Governor King's] *request to Mr Arndell to afford the sufferers every assistance and relief.'* (*Sydney Gazette*, 27 March 1806)

Margaret Catchpole also described the flood in a letter to Mrs Cobbold dated October 1806:

'Before the stream, some poor creatures riding on their houses, some on their barns crying out for God's sake to be saved, others firing their guns in the greatest distress for a boat. There were many thousands of head of all kind of cattle was lost, and so many bushels of all sorts was lost of grain. So now this place is in great distress for wheat.'

A letter sent from Green Hills (from person unknown) said:

'With regret I inform you of the dreadful scene that at the present moment chills me with excessive horror. The whole of this extensive settlement is one uninterrupted sheet of water. The lower range of houses upon the Green Hills is immersed; and the River has formed a juncture with the South Creek, across the Hills . . . The danger approached with a rapidity never before witnessed; and the cries of the numerous families who were more imminently exposed were rendered still more agonising by the impracticability of affording them immediate relief . . .' (*Sydney Gazette*, 6 August 1809, p 2a).

The description of Richmond is from *Macquarie Country*.

CHAPTER 32: Mr and Mrs Thomas Matcham Pitt

Thomas's signatures on letters from the Hawkesbury settlers to Bligh are in HRNSW 6: August 1806 (p 190); 29 January 1807 (p 237); 25 February 1807 (p 257); 1 January 1808 (p 411).

The welcome letter to Governor Macquarie was dated 1 December 1810. *Hawkesbury 1794-1994, the First 200 Years.*

The dinner to honour Macquarie took place on 16 January 1813 and was attended by:

'. . .nearly 150 persons, among whom were Gentlemen of the first respectability.

. . .At six the Company sat down to an excellent dinner accompanied by the full Band of the 73rd regiment . . . the stewards were seated at equal distances from each other; and the rest of the company placed themselves promiscuously without respect to rank or difference of condition . . .

They toasted "The King, the Prince Regent, the Queen and the rest of the Royal Family, Success to the British Arms, by Sea and Land . . . Governor Macquarie . . . Governor Phillip . . . Mr Wilberforce . . . Religion and Virtue . . . Unanimity . . . Prosperity . . . an Export Trade . . . The intended Library . . . Lt Col O'Connell, and the 73rd regiment; Good Night!"' (*Sydney Gazette*, 30 January 1813)

William Faithfull also served on the jury at the inquest into little George Rouse's death. (Colonial Secretary's Papers, Reel 6021; 4/1819 p611/2.)

Interestingly he signed his name, whereas five years earlier he had marked his marriage certificate with a cross.

Mr Harris's quote is from *Macquarie Country*, p182.

Thomas's convict servants from the 1814 muster were John Weston, life, convicted Kent; Richard Lawson, life, convicted London; Philip Butcher, life, convicted Sussex; Darby Ryan, 14 yrs, convicted Cork.

Thomas testifying on behalf of his convicts is from Colonial Secretary's Papers. Darby Ryan, an employee for three years, in his 50s, *'behaved himself sober and honest'*. (Fiche 3173; 4/1849 p 67, 29 June 1816). John Weston, employee for seven years, *'conducted himself much to my satisfaction'*. (Fiche 3182; 4/1853, p 365, 1 October 1817)

Reference to young James Scott is from Colonial Secretary's papers, Fiche 3307; 4/7208.

Regarding the Scott family: since the first draft of this book I have discovered William, Margaret and James were siblings, and that they were Scottish rather than Irish. Their full story is told in the sequel to this book called *A Country to Be Reckoned With.*

Some time before the coup George Crossley had claimed he had heard Thomas say that he'd heard from another party that Macarthur had *'expressed in his presence certain words relative to the Government of this colony'*, which words Crossley had passed on to Governor Bligh. During the trial Macarthur, cross examining John Palmer, said,

'Did not Mr Pitt contradict the Charges of Crossley and in y'r presence call Crossley a perjured old Villain?' [Palmer replied] *'He did, until Crossley was put on his oath, when Pitt acknowledged in part the charges.'* (HRA 6, pp 280/281, 288, 337/8 & 342.)

Thomas's dispute with Thomas Biggers in 1807 is from *Rough Minutes of Proceedings and Related Case Papers 4 July 1806*, SRNSW, *Sydney Gazette*, 14 Aug 1808, p 2a,b. (Cited in *The Family of Mary Pitt*, p 27) Promissory notes were highly unsatisfactory modes of transaction. Thomas had sold his mare and received a promissory note from Biggers that was supposedly as good as ready money; but when he came to redeem it the original issuer, William Gore, was unable to oblige. The case went against Thomas for not taking the precaution of signing the note when he first received it.

A copy of Thomas's will is in the SAG, Sydney - the original went missing some years ago. His obituary is from the *Sydney Gazette*, 3 February 1821.

CHAPTER 33: Elizabeth

William Scott first appeared on the 1822 census under the Pitt family working as a labourer, no named employer. His precise relationship with George is invented, but the children he had with Elizabeth were very real.

The 'dead sister act', so-called, was one of the laws that was enforced only if someone complained. Jane Austen's brother Charles for instance was allowed to marry his dead wife's sister in 1820, albeit to the disapproval of his family (Claire Tomalin, *Jane Austen*, p 280). It is assumed the complainant in William and Lucy's case was the Reverend Fulton.

Thomas Laycock's will is from *A Pioneering Australian Family*.

Rebecca returning to England is also from *A Pioneering Australian Family*. There have been rumours of Rebecca dying with her husband in the wreck of the *Royal Charter*, which also took the lives of several members of the Jenkins family in 1859. Not knowing her married name this is impossible to check.

Hannah Laycock's will is from *Lives Obscurely Great: Hannah Laycock of King's Grove Farm*, by Sheila Tearle, 1980.

CHAPTER 34: Moving on

Sydney's volcanoes are from *Australia's First Lady: Elizabeth Macarthur* by Lennard Bickel (Sydney: Allen & Unwin, 1991)

Prisoners engineering their transportation to Botany Bay is from *Australia's Birthstain*, pp 107 & p63.

EPILOGUE: Dynasties: the generations that came after

Personal details of George Matcham are taken from his own (unpublished) writings, called *Parental chitchat*, in the British Library.

A copy of George's letter to Thomas, transcribed by Matilda Warren Jenkins, is among the AFP.

Charles H N Matcham's letters are on microfilm in the ML, transcribed by Mary Eyre Matcham at her father's request for Miss M J Warren Jenkins. (CY4729).

Bibliography

PUBLISHED BOOKS

Austen, Jane, *Pride and Prejudice,* London: Penguin, 1988. (Originally published 1813)

Barkley, Jan & Nichols, Michelle, *Hawkesbury 1794-1994: the first 200 years,* Windsor: Hawkesbury City Council, 1994

Barkley-Jack, Jan, *Hawkesbury Settlement Revealed,* Rosenberg Publishing Pty Ltd, 2009

Barton, GB, *Tales & Sketches of Old Australia,* Sydney: Picturesque Atlas Publishing Co, 1886

Barton, GB, *The True Story of Margaret Catchpole,* Sydney: Cornstalk Publishing, 1924

Bassett, Marnie, *The Governor's Lady,* OUP, 1940

Bateson, Charles, *The Convict Ships, 1787-1868,* Brown, Son & Ferguson, 1959

Bickel, Lennard, *Australia's First Lady: Elizabeth Macarthur* (Sydney: Allen & Unwin, 1991)

Bowd, DG, *Macquarie Country,* Library of Australian History, 1979

Brunton, Donald, *The Rose Family of the Bellona,* Thomas and Jane Rose Family Society, 1995

Caley, George, *Reflections on the Colony of NSW,* Sydney: Angus & Robertson, 1967

Cobbold, The Reverend Richard, *The History of Margaret Catchpole,* Ipswich: The Debden Bookshop Ltd, 1971 (facsimile edition). Originally published London: Henry Colburn, 1847

Crowley, Frank, *A Documentary History of Australia Vol.1: Colonial Australia 1788-1840,* Nelson, 1980

Cunningham, Peter, *Two Years in New South Wales,* London: Henry Colburn, 1927

Cust, Janelle, *The Family of Mary Pitt,* 2009

Farwell, George, *Squatter's Castle: the Story of a Pastoral Dynasty,* Melbourne: Landsdowne Press, 1973

Flannery, Tim (ed), *The Birth of Sydney,* Melbourne: Text Publishing Co, 1999

Fletcher, Brian, *Landed Enterprise and Penal Society,* Sydney University Press, 1976

Freeland, J M, *Architecture in Australia*, National Library of Australia, 1967
Gordon, Joanna (ed), *Advice to a Young Lady in the Colonies*, Melbourne: Greenhouse, 1979
Hall, Olive, *Where Elm Trees Grew*, 1988
Hall, Olive, *Their Own Dear Days*, 1992
Hardy, Bobbie, *Early Hawkesbury Settlers*, Kenthurst, NSW: Kangaroo Press, 1985
Hill, Ron & Madden, Brian, *Kingsgrove: The First Two Hundred Years*, Campsie: Canterbury and District Historical Society, 2004
Hughes, Robert, *The Fatal Shore*, London: Pan Books, 1987
Inglis, KS, *The Australian Colonists*, Melbourne: Melbourne University Press, 1974
Johnston, Judith and Anderson, Monica (eds), *Australia Imagined*, Perth: UWA Publishing, 2005
Keneally, Thomas, *A Commonwealth of Thieves*, New York: Random House, 2006
Keneally, Thomas, *Australians: Origins to Eureka, Volume 1*, Sydney: Allen & Unwin, 2009
Laycock, KG, *A Pioneering Australian Family*, Laycock, 2000
Martin, Megan, *Settlers and Convicts of the Bellona, 1793: a biographical dictionary*, Griffin Press, 1992
Matcham, Mary Eyre, *The Nelsons of Burnham Thorpe*, London: John Lane, The Bodley Head, 1911
Norton, Judith & Horace, *Dear William: The Suttors of Brucedale, Sydney*: Suttor Publishing Committee, 1994
Richardson, John, *The Local Historian's Encylopedia*, London: Historical Publications Ltd, 1974
Ross, Val, *A Hawkesbury Story*, Library of Australian History, 1981
Smith, Babette, *Australia's Birthstain*, Sydney: Allen & Unwin, 2008
Suttor, George, *Memoirs of George Suttor 1774-1859*, Dubbo, NSW: Review Publications, 1977
Tearle, Sheila, *Hannah Laycock of King's Grove Farm*, Sydney: Hurstville Historical Society, 1972
Tench, Watkin, *Sydney's First Four Years*, Library of Australian History, 1983. (Originally published by Debrett, 1788)
Turnbull, John, *A Voyage Round the World in 1800-1804, Volume 2*, London: Richard Phillips, 1805

UNPUBLISHED BOOK

Lamble, Barbara, *The Pitts of Dorset and Richmond*

DORSET HISTORY CENTRE

Belchalwell parish records, Robert Pitt's christening: MIC/R/1044 RE1/2

Child Okeford parish records, Robert & Mary's marriage certificate, p15, DRO MIC/R/472; PE/CHO. RE3/1

Robert Pitt indentures:

12 May 1766 for the lease of 'Trout Alehouse', D/PIT/T34

22 September 1779 for lease of Fiddleford Mill, D/PIT/T620

22 September 1779 for lease of premises in Child Okeford, D/PIT/T603

18 November 1779 for loan by John Harrison, D/PIT/T620

17 February 1785, surrender of lease of Fiddleford Mill and repayment of loan to John Harrison, D/PIT/T620

Sturminster Newton Court Records, 16 October 1780, quote re Mary Pitt: DRO.D/PIT/M71

MUSEUMS & HISTORICAL SOCIETIES (England)

The National Maritime Museum, Greenwich (letters from Nelson to George Matcham, (Nelson's personal papers, MAM1)

Sturminster Newton Museum, Dorset

THE BRITISH LIBRARY (London)

Matcham, George Jnr., *Notes and observations on the character of Admiral Lord Nelson*, (extracts under George M.)

Matcham, George, *Parental chitchat*, personal papers

MITCHELL LIBRARY (Sydney)

The Atkinson papers, MSS 3132: Original handwritten letters by Mary Pitt, Joseph Bird, Samuel Gambier, Robert Jenkins

Bartrum, M, pp122- 126. *Proceedings of a General Court Martial of Lt Col George Johnston*, 7.5.1811

Bertie, C H, Pioneer Families of Australia, "The Faithfulls", *Home* (Sydney) 2 Nov 1931

Bonwick Transcripts Box 88

Braithwaite, Lt Robert, original letter to George Matcham, Code Ab 114

Catchpole, Margaret, letters

Colonial Secretary's papers Fiche 3268

Hammersley, G H, *A Few Observations on the Situation of the Female Convicts in New South Wales* (papers A 657)

Hawkesbury Parish Church records, V1810 1001 3A/1810; SAG 53, St Matthew's

Historical Records of New South Wales (HRNSW),Vol 1 pt 2, Vols 2, 3, 4, 5, 6

Historical Records of Australia (HRA), Vols 1, 3, 4, 7, 8, 10

Jenkins, Matilda Warren, *Narrative of the wreck of SS 'Royal Charter'*, 1884

King, Anna, journal of her voyage to NSW (CY 964, frames 1-62. C 185/1)

King Papers Vol 1 p108

Macquarie, Lachlan, Vol 8: Journal of Governor Macquarie's inspection of the Interior of the Colony commencing Tuesday 6th Novr. 1810

Matcham, Charles Horatio, letters, CY4729
Meredith, Louisa Ann, *Notes and Sketches of NSW 1839-1844*
Rubenstein, William D, All-Time Australian 200 Rich List 1788-1849
Suttor family papers 1774-1929
Wentworth Papers 1801 - 1808
Wilshire, James, onboard journal of his voyage to NSW, Microfilm CY 1389, frames 1-41, MLMSS 1296

STATE LIBRARY OF NEW SOUTH WALES

Pitt, George Matcham, Evening News, 5 December 1890 <www.sl.nsw.gov.uk> (Electronic records / family history)
Letter from Bligh to Major Johnston <www2.sl.nsw.gov.au/banks> 17 Feb 1809 Address to Bligh from Hawkesbury settlers

NEWSPAPERS & PUBLICATIONS (England)

Betjeman, John, *Evening Standard*, 24 March 1934
Brown, Ivor, *Observer*, 30 November 1033
Matcham, George, obituary: *The Gentleman's Magazine*, March 1833, p276 <books.google.com/books>
North, Vivien, *Picturegoer Weekly*, 17 March 1934
Rees, Coralie Clarke, *Woman's Budget*, 24 January 1934

NEWSPAPERS & PUBLICATIONS (Australia)

Burge, Michael, 'Grit and Gentility', *Blue Mountains Life Magazine*, March/April 2010, Vintage Press, Australia
Burge, Michael, 'Out on a Limb', *Blue Mountains Magazine*, June/ July 2010, Vintage Press
Duffy, Michael, *Sydney Morning Herald*, 28 Jan 2006
Sydney Gazette:
30 Oct 1803: John Wood's accident
27 March 1806, Hawkesbury flood
6 August 1809, Hawkesbury flood
16 November 1811 & 11 January 1812, trouble between Aborigines and settlers
30 Jan 1813, Anniversary Day commemoration dinner
1 February 1817, Anniversary Day celebrations
30 January 1819, Windsor Benevolent Society
3 February1821, Thomas Pitt death notice

JRAHS

Biographical sketch of Robert Jenkins, Vol 8 (1922) *Illawarra Mercury* 23, 27 November 1901

Fletcher, Brian, *The Rum Rebellion*, Sept 1968. Refs p235/236
Was John Boston's pig a political martyr? 1985, No 71 part 3

SOCIETY OF AUSTRALIAN GENEALOGY (SAG)

Library: electronic resources; pioneer index

WEBSITES

<www.sog.org.uk> (Society of Genealogists)
<www.nationalarchives.gov.uk>
<www.oldbaileyonline.org>
<www.hawkesburyhistory.org.au>
<http://www.sydneyolympicpark.com.au/education_and_learning/history/colonial_history> (Thomas Laycock's grant)
<http://webspace.webring.com/people/ic/chrisdaley/Grand-Children-of-Thomas-Laycock-and-Hannah-Pearson> (Elizabeth Pitt & William Scott's children)
<http://members.pcug.org.au/~ppmay/defenders.htm> (The Defenders' oath)
<www.law.mq.edu.au> (Transcript of Boston pig incident)

AUSTRALIAN DICTIONARY OF BIOGRAPHY

Holt, General. <http://adbonline.anu.edu.au/biogs/A010509b.htm>
Jenkins, Robert, Volume 2, (MUP), RFJ Holder, 1967
<http://adb.anu.edu.au/biography/jenkins-robert-2274>
Palmer, John, letter to Bligh
<www.adb.online.anu.edu.au/biogs/A020276b .htm>

OTHER

Bancroft, Max, *The Mining Accident* (posted on <aus-nsw-colonial-history @rootsweb. com>)

Index

Author biography

Patsy Trench is a bilingual Anglo-Aussie, born and bred in England to an Australian mother and Anglo-Irish father. She began her working life as an actress, in the UK and in Australia, where the highlights were working alongside the legendary Chips Rafferty and Skippy the bush kangaroo. She has been a scriptwriter, script editor, playscout and lyricist and co-founder of The Children's Musical Theatre of London.

She is the mother of two adult children and lives in London with a Freedom Pass. When not writing books she organizes theatre tours and teaches theatre part-time at Kingston University to visiting students from overseas.

Also by Patsy Trench:

A Country To Be Reckoned With (2018), the story of Mary Pitt's grandson GM Pitt, pioneer farmer and founder of the stock and station agent Pitt,, Son & Badgery.

The Awakening of Claudia Faraday (2019): a novel set in 1920s England about a society woman behaving badly.

The Purpose of Prudence de Vere (2019): The remarkable memoir of Claudia's best friend, good-time girl and free spirit.

www.patsytrench.com

www.ingramcontent.com/pod-product-compliance
Lightning Source LLC
Chambersburg PA
CBHW021119300426
44113CB00006B/214

* 9 7 8 0 9 9 3 4 5 3 7 1 7 *